17 30

Money, Financial Flows, and Credit in the Soviet Union

NATIONAL BUREAU OF ECONOMIC RESEARCH

Studies in International Economic Relations

Money, Financial Flows, and Credit in the Soviet Union

GEORGE GARVY

VICE PRESIDENT AND SENIOR ADVISER (RETIRED)

FEDERAL RESERVE BANK OF NEW YORK

PUBLISHED FOR THE

NATIONAL BUREAU OF ECONOMIC RESEARCH, INC.

BY

BALLINGER PUBLISHING COMPANY

Copyright © 1977 by the National Bureau of Economic Research, Inc.
All rights reserved.
Printed in the United States of America.

Library of Congress Cataloging in Publication Data

Garvy, George.
Money, financial flows, and credit in the Soviet Union.

    (Studies in international economic relations: 7)
    Bibliography: p. 204
    Includes index.
    1. Finance—Russia. 2. Money—Russia. 3. Banks and banking—
Russia. 4. Credit—Russia.

I. Title.   II. Series.
HG186.R8G37   332'.0947   76-58491
ISBN 0-87014-518-5

V

Relation of the Directors to the Work and Publications of the National Bureau of Economic Research

1. The object of the National Bureau of Economic Research is to ascertain and to present to the public important economic facts and their interpretation in a scientific and impartial manner. The Board of Directors is charged with the responsibility of ensuring that the work of the National Bureau is carried on in strict conformity with this object.

2. The President of the National Bureau shall submit to the Board of Directors, or to its Executive Committee, for their formal adoption all specific proposals for research to be instituted.

3. No research report shall be published by the National Bureau until the President has sent each member of the Board a notice that a manuscript is recommended for publication and that in the President's opinion it is suitable for publication in accordance with the principles of the National Bureau. Such notification will include an abstract or summary of the manuscript's content and a response form for use by those Directors who desire a copy of the manuscript for review. Each manuscript shall contain a summary drawing attention to the nature and treatment of the problem studied, the character of the data and their utilization in the report, and the main conclusions reached.

4. For each manuscript so submitted, a special committee of the Directors (including Directors Emeriti) shall be appointed by majority agreement of the President and Vice Presidents (or by the Executive Committee in case of inability to decide on the part of the President and Vice Presidents), consisting of three Directors selected as nearly as may be one from each general division of the Board. The names of the special manuscript committee shall be stated to each Director when notice of the proposed publication is submitted to him. It shall be the duty of each member of the special manuscript committee to read the manuscript. If each member of the manuscript committee signifies his approval within thirty days of the transmittal of the manuscript, the report may be published. If at the end of that period any member of the manuscript committee withholds his approval, the President shall then notify each member of the Board, requesting approval or disapproval of publication, and thirty days additional shall be granted for this purpose. The manuscript shall then not be published unless at least a majority of the entire Board who shall have voted on the proposal within the time fixed for the receipt of votes shall have approved.

5. No manuscript may be published, though approved by each member of the special manuscript committee, until forty-five days have elapsed from the transmittal of the report in manuscript form. The interval is allowed for the receipt of any memorandum of dissent or reservation, together with a brief statement of his reasons, that any member may wish to express; and such memorandum of dissent or reservation shall be published with the manuscript if he so desires. Publication does not, however, imply that each member of the Board has read the manuscript, or that either members of the Board in general or the special committee have passed on its validity in every detail.

6. Publications of the National Bureau issued for informational purposes concerning the work of the Bureau and its staff, or issued to inform the public of activities of Bureau staff, and volumes issued as a result of various conferences involving the National Bureau shall contain a specific disclaimer noting that such publication has not passed through the normal review procedures required in this resolution. The Executive Committee of the Board is charged with review of all such publications from time to time to ensure that they do not take on the character of formal research reports of the National Bureau, requiring formal Board approval.

7. Unless otherwise determined by the Board or exempted by the terms of paragraph 6, a copy of this resolution shall be printed in each National Bureau publication.

(Resolution adopted October 25, 1926, as revised through September 30, 1974)

Contents

Tables

ix

Figures

Preface

THIS study carries forward earlier endeavors of the author to describe the credit and banking system of the Soviet Union in terms familiar in nonsocialist countries while emphasizing its organic links with the centrally directed planned economy. This study was suggested by the late Harry Scherman, a former President of the National Bureau of Economic Research, and financed by a grant from the Harry Scherman Foundation.

A Reading Committee, consisting of Phillip Cagan and Raymond W. Goldsmith of the National Bureau's staff and Professors Gregory Grossman of the University of California, Berkeley and John M. Montias of Yale University read an earlier and more detailed version of the manuscript and made valuable and constructive suggestions. Its present form owes much to the advice of Hal B. Lary on focus and organization.

Dealing with only one aspect of a complex economic system imposes serious limitations. The temptation had to be resisted to broaden the subject and to sketch out, at least in a broad outline, the essential characteristics and mechanisms of the Soviet economy: this would have increased the scope of the project beyond the resources available. I have assumed that the reader is familiar with the basic characteristics of the Soviet economy, on which a number of monographs are available. I have made reference to the underlying real processes and administrative arrangements only to the degree necessary to elucidate how the financial processes and policies related to them. I have furthermore assumed that the reader is familiar with the role of money, credit, and financial processes in the United States and that there is no need to make comparisons in order to emphasize contrasts.

I have avoided semantic discussions about the nature of the Soviet economic system which is variously described as a "centrally-directed," "command," "socialist," or "communist" economy. Applying the word "socialist" to an economic—and political—system which has reduced freedom and choice to a minimum will be, no doubt, repugnant to some readers. I am using "socialist" merely because it is now more widely used than any of the alternative terms.

When a comparison is made with institutional arrangements in the "nonsocialist" world, the U.S. is the obvious point of reference, even though arrangements prevailing in the United States are not necessarily typical for the "free world" nor are adequately identified as a "free enterprise" system. The reader familiar with banking in France or with financing of capital formation in Italy will readily recognize that contrasts can be easily overdrawn, since the U.S. and the Soviet Union represent extreme cases in their respective spheres.

This study is based almost exclusively on Soviet sources. Use of Soviet statistics always requires lengthy discussion of their makeup, limitations, and meaning, so therefore statistical material is included mainly for illustrative rather than analytical purposes. The data shown in the tables serve mainly to establish the order of magnitude and broad trends—hence the use of selected years rather than presentation of continuous time series. Throughout, in the tables as well as in the text, except where specific statements to the contrary are made, the new (1961) ruble is used, into which all data for earlier years are converted.

Money, Financial Flows, and Credit in the Soviet Union

1

Introduction

Background and Summary of the Study

UNTIL quite recently, money and banking ranked fairly low among the features of socialist economies investigated by Western analysts, who generally tended to assign money and credit a subordinate role in achieving policy objectives in socialist countries. Many studies of the Soviet economy almost ignore money and credit and accord only tangential importance, if any, to the banking system and the monetary plans it implements. Other students of the Soviet scene, observing the impressive degree of price stability since the middle fifties, have concluded that the successful management of money must have contributed to maintaining stability and growth, and, in particular, to avoiding the surges in speculative consumer buying that have plagued some other socialist countries. In the latter view, the contribution of monetary management surely goes beyond servicing the credit needs of the economy's socialist sector and adjusting the volume of currency in circulation to the growth in disposable consumer income.

These two views are not altogether contradictory. Even official disclaimers to the effect that monetary management pursues no objectives other than implementation of the plan are compatible with the conclusion that—at least since World War II—it has played an important, if subordinate, part in an overall economic policy aimed at price stability and maximization of financial resources available to support economic growth. The Soviet authorities have been much more successful in controlling the quantity and distribution of money to prevent undesired accumulation of purchasing power than in developing a credit policy to

1

strengthen incentives and generally improve the performance of the economic system.

Evaluating the contribution of money and of monetary and credit planning to the overall performance of the Soviet economy is a complex problem. Trying to answer this broad question would involve assessing such aspects of economic performance as optimal investment patterns, distribution of income, social mobility, the loss resulting from inadequate use of pecuniary awards, and the stifling influence of bureaucracy, as well as the cost of various disutilities (such as pollution) associated with the growth over time of selected output and income indicators. The result of any such assessment, in terms of intertemporal or intersystem comparisons, will depend to a certain extent on the scope of the performance indicators chosen. These need not be confined to GNP, industrial production, the rate of increase in investment or personal consumption, or any combination of these. Price stability would rank high among the indicators likely to be included in any such overall assessment. The specific role of money and other financial variables in such an evaluation will depend on the significance attached to the contribution of each of these variables toward achieving the end results under review.

This monograph does not attempt to assess the contribution of the Soviet Union's financial structure and policy to the growth of its economy. My more limited objective here is to identify the role of money, credit, and financial flows in the Soviet economy and to bring out differences in techniques, as well as similarities in functions, between its monetary and financial arrangements and those in the United States and many other Western countries. Since the Soviet Union has served as a prototype for all centrally directed economies, in Eastern Europe as well as in Asia, the discussion has a broad application.

The monetary and banking system which has emerged after the credit reforms of 1930–1932 remains basic to the economic structure of the Soviet Union. The monobank-monobudget system created in the early thirties was a pioneering move by the first socialist country to provide an optimal financial structure for stimulating planned economic growth. I have referred to this system in other publications as the "standard system."[1] Although

[1] [117] and [232].

it evolved through the largely politically-determined experimentation which was characteristic of the first decade of the Soviet system, some of its distinctive features can be traced back to the Tsarist regime. There are interesting parallels between the role the centrally directed economy assigns to the "monobank"—the all-encompassing bank that is one of the present system's essential features—and the role of Tsarist Russia's State Bank and commercial banking system. Chapter 2, which considers the historical background of the present system, reviews the deep involvement of the Tsarist government with the creation and the day-to-day operations of the Russian banking system, which it considered an important tool of economic development.

Interestingly enough, some of the principles embodied in the Soviet financial and banking system were advocated by a group of vociferous non-Marxist Russian economists and publicists of marginal influence during the last decade preceding the revolution of 1917. Their proposals were of note similar to the banking arrangements that emerged in the Soviet state. Chapter 2 discusses these views and probes into Lenin's views on the role of banks in the socialist transformation of society, which resulted in the nationalization and unification of banking immediately after the October Revolution. The chapter concludes with a review of the Soviet monetary experience and the checkered history of Soviet banking between the collapse of the Tsarist regime and the establishment of the "standard system" with the credit reforms of 1930–1932 and of those features of the economic reform of 1965 which affect financial firms.

The balance of the monograph is devoted to a discussion of the standard financial system with its twin pillars—the monobank and the unified budget.[2]

Chapter 3 considers the role of money in a centrally planned economy, beginning with a review of Soviet monetary theory. It goes on to describe the integration of monetary control with the planning process.

Monetary management in the Soviet Union must be viewed as part of an integrated financial policy in which concern with the

[2]Among the various changes in credit and banking arrangements in the intervening period, only those that have broad significance or have survived up to now will be mentioned. References are provided, however, whenever possible, to original sources in which changes superseded by subsequent developments are described in greater detail.

real outcome of the economic process requires decisions of options, relating to levels and structure of prices and taxation or forced versus voluntary savings, for instance, that may involve money and credit only in an implementary way. In the context of Soviet economic policy, monetary management replaces monetary policy. Management of money is part of an overall financial strategy. It involves direct determination (referred to in the Soviet Union as "planning" and "control") rather than indirect regulation of the quantity and use of money and credit.

However, the crucial difference between the Soviet Union and nonsocialist countries is not the absence of mechanisms linking extension of credit and thus the creation of money to liquidity of banks or the use of interest rates as a means of controlling the volume and the use of credit, but, rather, the basically different role assigned to money and credit for achieving economic goals. The implementary role of credit and the derivative nature of money flows are inherent in a system in which production objectives are stipulated in physical terms, and money and credit are supplied in quantities and through channels designed to achieve output patterns and uses determined by planners. Money is needed as the universal accounting equivalent and as a medium for achieving planners' objectives with greater flexibility than direct barter would permit. At the same time, in the socialized sector, money cannot be permitted to interfere with planners' intentions. It can become effective only jointly with goods orders (vouchers) issued to implement plan objectives. Conversely, planners determine the level of cash balances appropriate for each individual enterprise and adjust these balances through loans, grants, and subsidies, as well as through transfers from or to other units.

During the last decade, Soviet monetary theoreticians have gradually recognized that writings by Marx could not serve as ready-made guides for a socialist economy, since their point of reference was a very early stage in the development of the capitalist credit and financial system. They are still far from having developed a monetary theory for a socialist society.[3]

---

[3]On the difference between the Soviet and the Western approach to monetary analysis, see Hodgman in Holzman [122], pp. 105–106. The following remark by Gekker is also relevant: "The paucity of data in the field of price and monetary statistics invited speculation on the why rather than on the what or the how of any numbers that now exist, and

Many of the changes introduced by the 1965 Reform[4] grew out of dissatisfaction with the way credit and financial processes functioned under the standard system. Chapter 3 concludes with a discussion of the developments leading to the Reform and the modifications to the credit system it introduced.

Chapter 4 is devoted to a description of the banking system. The monobank system centered on the State Bank (Gosudarstvennyi Bank, usually abbreviated as Gosbank) now also incorporates the savings bank system.[5] While the State Bank as such deals with virtually all parts of the economy (*kolkhozes*—collective farms—as well as state enterprises) and the various government units, savings bank offices, which have been an integral part of the State Bank for more than a decade, serve primarily the needs of households. This chapter also discusses the activities of the Investment Bank which have been much curtailed by the Reform. But even prior to the Reform this institution had few functions other than serving as the Treasury's disbursing and supervisory agent for all nonreturnable grants, which were the only outside source for financing fixed investment. So far, the reforms launched in 1965 have not materially affected banking structure, although they have increased, actually and potentially, the role of the banking system in channeling outside investment funds—reserved to the budget since the creation of the Soviet state.

The interaction of the financial system with the major sectors of the Soviet economy: governmental, state enterprise, household, agricultural, and foreign, is treated in Chapters 5, 6, and 7.

The physical as well as functional separation of enterprise money from household money is one of the basic aspects of finance in the Soviet economy. Much of the activity of the State Bank is focused on preventing spillovers from one kind of money into another. The monetization of economic relations between the state and the *kolkhozes* in the middle 1950s has generalized the use of money without significantly undermining "control by the

---

which we use for measuring and judging the performance of the Soviet economy" [161]. Some of the limitations of monetary data are discussed in Appendix B. All numbers refer to the bibliography.

[4]Throughout this monograph, whenever the first letter of "Reform" is capitalized, reference is made to the sum total of the reform measures.

[5]The State Bank's internal structure is described in greater detail in Appendix A.

ruble,'' which is one of the basic means through which the performance of the Soviet economy is monitored.

In the Soviet Union, the choice between money and near-money is not open to enterprises and exceedingly limited for households. Liquidity is not a major consideration entering enterprise decisions. The significance of money in the accounts of socialist enterprises is fundamentally different from that of cash balances in firms in nonsocialist countries. Administrative transfers of cash balances between enterprises diminish an enterprise's interest in using them more efficiently and in releasing cash by minimizing inventories and other nonfinancial forms of working capital.

The money and credit system which took shape in the early thirties, and underwent only marginal changes in the following forty years, has proven to be a workable technical solution for an economy in which achievement of optimal resource allocation and maximum productivity are sought through administrative decisions rather than market-oriented processes. Within this system, various organizational alternatives are available. These alternatives are limited, however, because the concepts of money as an absolute carrier of options and the discretionary extension of credit are incompatible with a centrally planned and administratively directed economy. Money as an absolute claim on resources would conflict with all-encompassing planning in physical terms. In the household sector, however, with the fairly rapid increase in real incomes after the initial period of post-World War II reconstruction, money savings of households did emerge as a new factor, severing the previously rigid link between receipts and disbursements of income. Expanding domestic travel and internal migration also required more sophisticated planning of the availability of goods and services in the areas where incomes were spent but not earned. But so far neither the accumulation of household purchasing power ''on the wing'' nor the use of redundant enterprise balances in ways that might conflict with planners' intentions have presented serious problems.

Chapter 5 describes the institutional arrangements that assure the separation of the two money circuits and briefly touches upon the role of financial planning in adjusting the level of both flows to the requirements of a growing and changing economy. It also reviews the role of the unified budget in the centralization of financial resources for economic purposes while at the same time providing for ordinary administrative and other budgetary expenditures typical for the various levels of government in nonsocialist countries.

The credit system that emerged from the reforms undertaken in 1930–1932 is dealt with in Chapter 6. Since then it has undergone only relatively small changes, mostly of a purely organizational and procedural nature and not affecting the original role assigned to credit.

In the Soviet economy, extension of credit is denied a macroeconomic function and is, in the main, related to the attainment of microeconomic goals. Credit has been mainly a means of providing enterprises with the financial resources necessary to carry planned inventories and to finance the collection gap.

Foreign financial relations of the Soviet Union are considered in Chapter 7. Although foreign trade is not among the most important aspects of the Soviet economy, recent developments in East-West trade have focused a great deal of attention on this area.

The same central direction of production that isolates the enterprise sector from the direct influence of market forces removes the domestic economy from international pressures. Export and import prices, for example, bear little relation to relative domestic prices. The difference between the ways in which trade with the West and with other socialist countries is conducted is discussed in Chapter 7, as are the international financial institutions of the COMECON.

In Chapter 8 the focus shifts to the macroeconomic aspects. Here, the ability of the Soviet monetary system to maintain aggregate equilibrium and minimize inflationary pressures is considered. While the problems are broadly similar to those confronting monetary authorities in the West, Soviet monetary policy and performance cannot be analyzed on the same basis as in market economies.

For one thing, the Soviet monetary performance cannot be subjected to the kind of quantitative macroanalysis usually applied to nonsocialist economies,[6] where monetary actions

---

[6] Thus, for instance, Soviet inventory data are estimated largely from bank loans (see Moorsteen and Powell [134]); therefore, correlating inventories with loans would be based on basically identical data. It is worth noting that for China, where loan data are not

affect spending units through changes in liquidity and the cost and availability of credit as well as through the consequent changes in expectations generated. In such economies, the demand for money is related to yields on near-money and other financial assets. Whether their monetary authorities pursue a passive or an active policy, its results are reflected in changes in the quantity of money and interest rates. Even when a country's policy target is the money supply (however defined), changes in the supply of money in relation to changes in the demand for it—together with the related changes in the expectations engendered—will be reflected in the level and structure of interest rates.

In the Soviet Union, because of the separation of the payment streams into two compartments and the considerable differences between the functions of money in these two circuits, the concept of total money supply has only limited analytical significance. Manipulation of the total quantity of money (as contrasted with currency in circulation) is not a policy objective. Standard Western analytical models for testing monetary aspects of economic processes are not applicable to the Soviet reality, both because of the basic differences in the role of motivation in the behavior of enterprises and the lack of the necessary data.

Furthermore, in the Soviet Union the basic problem of a rapidly growing economy—inflationary pressures—is not dealt with primarily through monetary policy. Instead, administrative controls are applied in combination with credit, budgetary, and income policies, which tends to mask the basic macroeconomic objective: to regulate monetary demand in the household sector in relation to the projected increase in the availability of consumer goods and services.

While the lack of relevant statistical data and the complications arising from the simultaneous existence of several consumer markets with different price levels preclude detailed analysis, a broad review of Soviet monetary experience is presented. The period of

---

available, K. H. Hsiao [123] used the reverse procedure, estimating bank loans from inventory data. By contrast, in some socialist countries, including China, relevant data on the money supply and its composition and ownership are available for at least some limited periods. This permits some quantitative explorations, including the construction and testing of models of inflationary processes originating in wage drift, activation of household balances, excessive accumulation of inventories, or other developments not foreseen in plans.

upheaval between the Revolution and the stabilization of the Soviet currency in 1924 and the following period ending with the credit reforms of 1930–1932 are discussed in Chapter 2, while Chapter 8 describes the three more recent periods. Of these five periods the first four, ending with the currency conversion of 1947, were characterized by almost continuous inflation at varying rates. The inability of the State Bank, even after the credit reforms of 1930–1932, to prevent overspending of funds earmarked for wage disbursements contributed significantly to inflationary pressures which could not be offset by other policies. In contrast, after the currency conversion of 1947 designed to eliminate the war-generated overhang of liquidity, prices declined in markets alimented by the freely disposable food surpluses of *kolkhoz* farmers and as a result of administrative cuts in state stores as well. A period of declining consumer prices was followed by virtual stability beginning with 1954, resulting in part from a selective reduction of turnover taxes.

Concluding Observations

Despite the apparent success of the Soviet financial system in keeping inflationary pressures in the postwar period within bounds and official retail price indexes stable or declining, the system's inability to allocate resources efficiently, to provide incentives to increase productivity, and to respond to developments not anticipated in plans has been recognized. The Reform of 1965 was in part due to this recognition. The modifications announced at this time were limited in scope, however, and those actually implemented, almost a decade later, still made only modest advances. Indeed, there is evidence of backtracking on some of the initial changes. Chapter 9 offers some explanations for the failure of the Reform to modify the system significantly and suggests some implications of this failure.

The example of most of the smaller socialist countries shows that there is considerable room for developing a constructive socialist monetary policy, even within the framework of a centrally directed economy, and the failure of the Soviet Union to do so no doubt accounts for the disappointing results of its economic reforms. In some of the countries of Eastern Europe, the basic characteristics of the Soviet monetary system—such as separation of the monetary circuits and the foreign exchange monopoly—have been retained, but negotiated credit extension has been at least partly substituted for direct administrative guidance. The emphasis in ranking has been shifted from accounting control of plan fulfillment to the evaluation of efficient use of credit by individual enterprises. In this process, banking has achieved a considerable degree of independence in developing credit standards, as well as in determining the amount of credit to be extended in each case and in negotiating and enforcing specific lending terms within the narrow range of alternatives available. Much of the microeconomic control inherent in a centrally planned economy has been shifted from ministerial bureaucracy to bank offices, even though the basic structure of a monobank is retained, and banks continue to operate within the limits of centrally determined overall credit ceilings and an interest rate structure that remains quite rigid.

In the Soviet Union, no such evolution has taken place as a result of the Reform. In contrast to reforms introduced in Hungary and, on a less ambitious scale, Poland, and attempted in Czechoslovakia—all of which followed the earlier path-breaking example of Yugoslavia—their goal has been merely to improve some operational aspects of the centrally directed economy.

The greater flexibility toward which banking has evolved in some of the socialist countries is part of their general effort to introduce at least some of the elements of the market into a centrally directed economy. They endeavor to find a workable combination of essentially indicative planning with mechanisms and processes that use the market place, its information potential, and the feedbacks generated by consumer choice (and in some instances, by producers' choice as well). The Soviet Union has persisted in rejecting the possibility of replacing administrative centralization with a socialist market. This rejection has limited the objectives and scope of the reforms introduced in 1965. It explains the retention of all those features which, since the credit reforms of 1930–1932, have made the State Bank an integral part of a complex administrative apparatus designed to implement planners' objectives. The 1965 Reform reduced the range and details of planning indicators, introduced limited feedbacks from the market for consumer goods, placed greater emphasis on financial incentives at the microeconomic level, and restructured the costs entering into the administrative determination of prices. One of the Reform's main features involved diverting at least part of the financial flows away from nonreturnable grants, thus increasing the role of credit in capital formation. It was expected that increased and generalized use of financial incentives would increase efficiency of investment, reduce wasteful use of resources, and stimulate the labor force (above all, managerial and technical staffs) to greater effort. Other aspects of the Soviet financial system have been hardly touched by the Reform (although some marginal changes had been taking place even prior to its launching).

The reform of "economic steering," the official term designating the reforms of 1965, has put into relief the various limitations of money and credit in a centrally directed economy that retains central allocation of real resources. While it has shown that the Soviet financial system can accommodate a restructuring of financial flows, it has, at the same time, demonstrated the limitations of the role of money in a system in which administrative decisions substitute for market processes and feedbacks are minimal.

Bank officials remain administrators of policies determined by the central authorities and uniformly applied through the entire system of the monobank. The reliance on the banking system for monitoring the performance of the entire socialized economy has not diminished; if anything, it has increased with the monetization of the relationship between collective farms and the state that began in the mid-fifties. While control by the *forint* in Hungary or by the *zloty* in Poland has turned more and more into control through the terms of credit extension, in the Soviet Union it is still the flow of accounting data produced by the monobank that gives the measure of its contribution to keeping the economy on the beam, rather than the quality of decisions made by bank officials on the firing line. In fact, there is no firing line; for the issuance of credit, rather than having become a matter of negotiation between bank and borrower, retains its strictly implementary and semiautomatic character. The current generation of Soviet bank officials differs from its predecessors of fifty years ago mainly in the quality of their training, not in the scope of their jobs.

The failure of overall economic performance to improve under the Reform provides no strong incentives for further experimentation along the lines laid down in 1965. At the same time, it has provided ammunition for those who have been opposing the Reform from the very beginning, and has stiffened the bureaucratic resistance to any change inherent in centralized, administratively controlled economies.

The future development of Soviet banking and credit depends on whether the Reform will remain a disappointing attempt to increase the use of financial processes and pecuniary incentives within the traditional framework of a centrally planned economy, or whether challenges to economic performance in the years to come will lead to efforts to combine central setting of overall goals with their implementation through a socialist market.

2

The Origins and Evolution of the Soviet Banking System: An Historical Perspective

THE banking system that emerged after the October Revolution and, more specifically, after the credit reforms of 1930–1932 is unique in many respects. To be sure, examples of banking institutions combining central banking and commercial banking may be found in some nonsocialist countries. In the less developed countries, central banks have frequently assumed a leading role in implementing development programs by providing the necessary financial institutions, instruments, and markets. Even in some leading industrial countries such as France and Italy large commercial banks are owned by the government. The uniqueness of the Soviet banking system lies, rather, in the complete integration of monetary processes within the system of central planning, and in the credit and foreign exchange monopoly of the State Bank, which has broad powers of control over the performance of the entire state-owned segment of the economy.

In historical perspective, the position of the State Bank of the U.S.S.R. (Gosbank) today may be viewed as the ultimate expression of a relationship between government and banking that has its roots in Tsarist Russia. Making active use of official guidance, support, and stimulation to push the backward country toward modernization, the Tsarist government was one of the first anywhere to press banking into the service of economic progress. A

13

brief look at the past, therefore, may be useful in throwing light on this development.

The State and Banking Prior to the Bolshevik Revolution

Several aspects of the banking arrangements after War Communism actually had close antecedents in the institutions of Tsarist Russia. Prior to 1917, government initiative frequently substituted for private initiative when it came to achieving specific objectives of economic policy and creating the financial institutions required to stimulate capital formation and economic growth.[1] Throughout the eighteenth and most of the nineteenth centuries, the state provided capital and credit (first through official banks and later through control of the privately owned banks) for significant segments of the manufacturing and mining industries, railroads, and utilities.

All of Europe's central banks, which, except for that of Sweden, were privately owned prior to World War I, made important contributions to the development of their countries' economic potential through direct lending to the private sector as well as through discount operations. In numerous cases they facilitated the financing of factories, railroads, and other facilities built in the national interest, frequently with a view to their military value. But only Tsarist Russia's State Bank, which had maintained its position as the leading source of commercial credit even after becoming the bank of issue, consistently undertook credit operations in the interest of economic development and in this connection frequently took credit risks incompatible with normal business practice. It made loans under conditions that, in some cases, were equivalent to subsidies, and occasionally waived repayment, effectively transforming loans into grants, in order to nurse through enterprises judged essential from the national standpoint. It even supplied capital indirectly to industry through loans collateralized by new securities, and provided part of the initial capital for some new banks.

The history of Russian banking is a striking example of the complete dependence of a central bank on the Ministry of

[1] For Saint-Simonist influence on several ministers of finance, see Normano [136], Ch. 1.

Finance, and of the use of the banking system (both government and privately owned) as a tool for implementing official policy. In no other country prior to World War I was the central bank so clearly a tool of government, so openly controlled by the Ministry of Finance,[2] and so heavily involved in private credit operations designed to stimulate industrial development and to serve the national interest.

The history of banking in Russia prior to the revolution of 1917 unfolds as a succession of government efforts to provide the country with a minimum of modern banking facilities—originally, to carry on trade with foreign countries; later, to support the landed gentry, the backbone of the nation's social and political structure; and ultimately, to develop a modern industry and the requisite network of railroads and other transportation and communication facilities.

The first part of Russian banking history, covering more than two centuries before the establishment of the first privately owned commercial bank in 1866, can be written in terms of the vicissitudes of not more than a dozen state-owned institutions.[3] These were operated by state officials (or former officials), pursuing objectives defined by the Ministry of Finance (or its predecessors), directed by the department of Credit Administration within the Ministry, and supervised by a high-level board whose members normally included officials of ministerial rank and, at times, close relatives of the Tsar.

Credit institutions other than commercial banks originating before the 1860's were also sponsored either by the central government (widows' and orphans' provident banks, for example, which antedated the first state commercial banks and later evolved into savings bank-type institutions), or by provincial and local

---

[2]In prerevolutionary Russia, the Ministry of Finance was in full charge of maintaining the external value of the ruble and the country's foreign credit. By active intervention in foreign exchange markets, it succeeded in maintaining a strong foreign exchange position for the ruble. In particular, it used part of the proceeds of its heavy foreign borrowings to build up large official holdings of gold, a significant part of which was held abroad. These holdings were used, when necessary, to buy up notes, trade bills, and other ruble claims clandestinely in order to maintain the strength of the ruble in foreign exchange markets. Tsarist Russia also engaged in secret support operations on European stock exchanges where shares of Russian corporations and Russian bonds (government, government-guaranteed, and private) were traded.

[3]For a more detailed discussion, see Garvy [233] and Gindin [32], [33] and [34]. See also Borovoy [17].

governments (noblemen's land banks and savings banks, respectively) as part of a program formulated by the central government.

From the beginning, credit from these government supported financial institutions played a crucial role in investment funding, given the scarcity of alternative sources of funds for opening mines or starting the first industries. Some of these institutions were patterned after foreign models (the discount offices, for example), while others, such as the "copper banks" designed to monetize copper (see footnote 3), grew out of conditions peculiar to the empire of the Tsars.

Since one's standing at court was frequently a more important factor in obtaining loans than either the creditworthiness of the borrowing firm or the prospective profitability of the projects to be financed, many government banks soon found their assets frozen. In some instances, existing institutions had to be liquidated, only to be replaced by others with similar purposes and sources of funds. This situation was characteristic of the period before 1861, when banking resources consisted almost exclusively of initial capital received from the State Treasury and replenished by it at various intervals in subsequent years. The fragmentary statistical data available for that period suggest that, despite administrative ingenuity in creating a variety of distinct credit institutions, the banks' total resources derived from both budgetary appropriations and deposits were relatively small.

Modern banking came to Russia at the time of the liberation of the serfs in 1861, just a few years earlier than the creation of the national banking system in the United States. The restructuring of the Russian banking system followed the financial crisis of 1857–1859 and resulted in the liquidation of practically all state credit and savings institutions. Commercial banking, which developed rapidly in the last fifty years before the 1917 revolution, was to a considerable extent subject to official tutelage, even though foreign participation in private banking capital was significant. It was highly centralized; in the last few decades preceding the revolution, fewer banks were in operation than in either the United Kingdom or Germany. On the eve of World War I, twelve institutions accounted for 79 percent of the assets of all commercial banks. P. P. Migulin, the author of one of the few existing monographs on the history of Russian banking prior to 1917, concluded that "from the very beginning in this field we had no private initiative, and the government was forced to assume it." His prescription for the reorganization of the Russian banking system included important elements of the Soviet credit system as it existed prior to the abolition of the specialized banks, as well as the creation of central agricultural, industrial, and mortgage banks under joint state-private ownership. He envisaged survival of privately and mutually owned commercial banks only if they were subject to strict government control.[4] However, official banks continued to play an important role, acting as conduits for direct and indirect government subsidies.[5]

After about 1875, the big banks which began as deposit and discount banks became mixed banks ("banques d'affaires") by engaging in securities underwriting. They held a relatively large part of their assets in equity securities, many of which were issued by government-sponsored or government-favored corporations, or by firms heavily dependent on government orders. Banks became increasingly aggressive, and for the largest among them underwriting and investment activities became very important. They provided entrepreneurship to industry, but were often misused by promoters and speculators.

Mixed banking played a considerable role in the industrial upsurge of the 1890's. The banks controlled a significant number of businesses, including many of the largest firms with the most advanced technology, and actively promoted mergers and monopolies.[6] A. Gerschenkron's thesis that, in the last decade of the nineteenth century, the mixed banking system of Russia was able to assume a leading role in the process of industrialization, is a familiar one.

A third period of Russian banking opened with the resumption of rapid growth after the depressing effects of the Russo-Japanese War were overcome. Mixed banks became a key element in the process of industrialization in their role as channelers of private capital into the new and more dynamic branches of industry and as vehicles for government subsidies and other forms of official

[4]See [62], pp. 437–439.
[5]The savings bank system was operated by the government through the State Bank. It was quite extensive (8,553 offices in 1914), but highly centralized.
[6]See Gindin [32], and Crisp, in [105].

support. Their activities in the decade preceding World War I were of a nature to support the view, widely held among Western European (particularly German) socialists, that banks had become the masters of industry. This view, as we shall see in the following section, became the basis of Lenin's characterization of the banking system as the "ready-made tool" for establishing a socialist economy and for administrating it.[7]

The state remained an important source of financing for industrial entrepreneurs through the intermediation of the State Bank, where budgetary surpluses were accumulated, while foreign loans to industrial corporations and railroads were supported by state guarantees. A foreign observer concluded that the St. Petersburg banks were "Russian in appearance, foreign with regard to their resources, and ministerial as to risk bearing."[8]

On the whole, the financial structure of Russia remained underdeveloped until the Revolution. As a result of the country's economic and social backwardness, commercial banking offices and financial institutions other than banks were concentrated in the larger cities, and financial markets and instruments were limited.

Toward the Concept of a Monobank

The idea that the banking system could make an important contribution to the economic transformation of Russia can be traced to the writings of Russian statesmen and economists, some of whom were ardent slavophiles, going back to more than a century before the revolution of 1917.[9] The first illegal Marxist group was yet to be formed when, before the turn of the century, some writers already advocated economic development via the state; a fiat currency managed by the state with the goals of domestic price stability; isolation of the ruble's international value from market forces; and a credit system that would help industrialize Russia under state guidance.

During the controversy surrounding the introduction of the gold

[7]See Garvy [232].
[8]Aghad [97], pp. 136–137.
[9]For details, see Garvy [233].

standard in 1897, views were expressed in favor of a banking and credit system very similar to the one that emerged following the Bolshevik Revolution and which assumed its present form with the credit reforms of 1930–1932. For instance, S. Sharapov, one of the leading opponents of the gold standard, advocated the use of "absolute money," completely divorced from precious metals and merely a conventional unit of account. He claimed that, in the last analysis, the domestic value of money depended on the faith of the population in the strength of its autocratic government. To support his view, Sharapov referred to long periods of Russian history when fiat money, such as leather money or paper assignats,[10] had been widely used. Sharapov held that "a country capable of an autarkic development, such as Russia, can achieve through the use of absolute money tremendous economic development, without depriving anybody of his livelihood and without risking any economic crises." He believed that the only meaningful limit to the expansion of credit was full employment, and that the only rational means of putting finance in the service of economic development was the creation of a "universal bank." Its operations in issuing credit and controlling the money supply would be governed by the needs of the economy and would not be restricted by any "prejudices" and irrelevant limitations, such as the size of the reserves of precious metals. Sharapov favored an expansion of credit and a fiduciary issue of paper money to the point where all productive resources of the society would be fully utilized.

In advocating creation of a universal bank, Sharapov anticipated the monobank. His plan provided for the merging of the State Bank into a "Great Treasury" which would absorb the network of local Treasury offices and perform all fiscal functions in close cooperation with the State Treasury, which would continue to function as an agency of the Ministry of Finance. The "Great Treasury" would, in effect, have a virtual credit monopoly.

Sharapov favored a stable domestic price level and varying the external value of domestic paper currency in relation to gold. In order to avoid business fluctuations, the State Bank should regu-

---

[10]Paper assignats were issued in Russia a decade before the French Revolution, although their invention is generally credited to the later event.

late the quantity of money independently of the amount of gold and foreign exchange reserves. To facilitate regulating the external value of the ruble, he logically advocated a state monopoly for all foreign exchange transactions. "The very question of [managing of exchange rates by an agency of the state] is being raised here for the first time, and it is quite impossible to say how soon the Russian state will accomplish this task." We know the answer now: it took less than a generation. Incidentally, Sharapov preferred, as Soviet planners do, using historical average prices rather than current market prices as a guide to foreign trade policy.[11]

Lenin's Views on the Role of Banking

There is no evidence to indicate that Lenin's views on the role of the banking system in the period of transition to a socialist economy, formed in the years immediately preceding the revolution of 1917, were influenced by the banking and monetary reforms advocated by Sharapov and other contemporary writers.[12] Nevertheless, Lenin envisioned a single state bank, supported by a state foreign exchange monopoly, as the "skeleton of a socialist society"[13] and the core of a socialist administrative apparatus controlling the economy.

All of the elements of Lenin's much-quoted passage on the role of banks in building socialism (see page 21) can be traced to the beginning and the middle of the nineteenth century, to Saint-Simon and Marx. But it is likely that his advocacy in 1917 of using the banking system as a tool for the socialist transformation of society was more directly related to the discussion in the pre-World War I social-democratic literature concerning the role of banks in forging powerful industrial combines and their control over industry. Lenin's specific prescription for using banks as an administrative as well as an economic tool was derived from the contemporary theories of some radical and socialist writers of

[11][73], p. 88. For an interesting discussion of monetary theory in prerevolutionary Russia, see Vlasenko [90].

[12]For a fuller discussion, see Garvy [233].

[13]See footnote 15 below.

Western Europe, including Hobson (1902), Helphand, better known as "Parvus" (1910), and Hilferding (1910), with whose works he became familiar during his long years of exile. He used their analyses of the role of banks in advanced industrial countries, expanded by studies of more recent developments, in his book on imperialism, and made the concepts of "financial capital," "monopoly capitalism," and "economic imperialism" his own. Thus, in 1907 he wrote:

> Scattered capitalists are transformed into a single collective capitalist. When carrying the current accounts of a few capitalists, the banks, as it were, transact a purely technical and exclusively auxiliary operation. When, however, these operations grow to enormous dimensions we find that a handful of monopolists control all the operations, both commercial and industrial, of capitalist society. They can, by means of their banking connections, by running current accounts and transacting other financial operations, first *ascertain exactly* the position of the various capitalists, then *control* them, influence them by restricting or enlarging, facilitating or hindering their credits, and finally they can *entirely determine* their fate, determine their income, deprive them of capital, or, on the other hand, permit them to increase their capital rapidly and to enormous proportions, etc. [Italics in the original.][14]

Lenin advocated the creation of a single government bank as a means of assuring control over industry, but also because he believed that a nationalized banking system could be easily reshaped into the core of the socialist state's administrative apparatus. In a passage much quoted by Soviet authors, he wrote a few days before the October Revolution:

> *Without big banks, socialism would be impossible.* The big banks *are* the "state apparatus" which we *need* to bring about socialism, and which we *take ready-made* from capitalism. . . . A single State Bank, the biggest of the big, with branches in every rural district, in every factory, will constitute as much as nine-tenths of the socialist apparatus. There will be country-wide bookkeeping, country-wide accounting of the production and distribution of goods; this will be, so to speak, something in the nature of the *skeleton* of socialist society. [Italics in the original.][15]

[14]See "Imperialism," Petrograd, 1917, in [129].
[15]See [129], vol. 26, p. 106.

An identical view was expressed by Lenin after the October Revolution. "Banking policy must not stop with the nationalization of banks, but must work slowly but decisively toward the transformation of banks into a single accounting apparatus for the regulation of the organized socialist economic life of the country as a whole."[16]

Lenin's notion of the role of banks in building socialism and in directing the economy during the transitional period hardly goes beyond the theme developed by Saint-Simon, Marx, Hobson, Hilferding, and Parvus. Interestingly enough, all discussed the potential use of the commercial banking system, rather than of the central bank, in building socialism. Similarly, Lenin noted that the control which commercial banks had achieved over individual industrial firms resulted in concentration of production in large operating units. He ascribed the banks' ability to exercise this control largely to industry's dependence on them for obtaining additional equity capital as well as credit. Lenin saw their potential for central control and direction of dispersed industries in a country where regional and local units of the government's administrative apparatus were inadequate to deal with economic problems. He was impressed with the technical functions performed by the extensive branch networks dominating the scene in Germany, the United Kingdom, France, and indeed, Russia itself, rather than with the possibility of using monetary and credit policy as a tool for restructuring the economy and achieving adequate growth and stability.

As events turned out after the Bolshevik seizure of power, the monetary and banking system disintegrated under the impact of the civil war and the accompanying inflation. A state bank as envisaged by Lenin, complete with credit monopoly and complex control functions, did not materialize until almost fifteen years later, with the first Five-Year Plan well under way. When it did, the heritage from another epoch was unmistakable—an epoch when enlightened bureaucrats under an authoritarian regime had tried to use state-directed credit and Treasury resources to lift

---

[16][129], vol. 36, p. 220.

Lenin anticipated the development of comprehensive flow-of-funds accounts (still not developed in the Soviet Union today) when he wrote: " . . . once the banks are nationalized it will be possible to achieve a state of affairs when the government knows from where and when millions and billions of ruble payments flow." (Ibid., vol. 34, p. 163.)

Russia from centuries of economic backwardness. Sharapov would have easily recognized his "universal bank."

Soviet Banking Before the Credit Reforms of 1930–1932

On the first day of the Bolshevik coup, October 25, 1917 (old calendar), an armed detachment of workers and soldiers, under direct orders from Lenin, occupied the main office of the State Bank in Petrograd. The Bolsheviks were determined not to repeat the mistakes of the Paris Commune, which had respected the Banque de France and left its gold stock and supply of unissued notes inviolate. (At that time, the privately owned Banque de France functioned also as a bank of issue.) The Bolsheviks encountered resistance and sabotage, not only from State Bank officials but also from employees who refused to cooperate with the new officials appointed by Lenin's government.

On the day following the Bolshevik seizure of power all commercial banks closed down.[17] Their staffs received salaries for three months in advance, with the understanding that they would abstain from performing their duties as long as a Soviet government was in power, joining the concerted action of the employees of the State Bank and all other government financial institutions and ministries in refusing to serve the new regime. This boycott was fully effective. The few operations that commercial banks did undertake in the weeks following the October Revolution were directed solely toward protecting their assets while contributing to the general paralysis of economic life that, Lenin's opponents hoped, would bring down the new regime.

The new authorities were slow in making full use of the central bank. This was due partly to their lack of knowledge and experience, and partly to the fact that their immediate objective was merely to obtain currency from its vaults to meet the most

---

[17]On the seizure of banks and the ensuing difficulties, see Gindin [31], Atlas [6] and the articles by Azarch, Atlas, and Solovei in *D. K.*, March and August 1967. The standard source in English on the nationalization of banks and the first years of Soviet banking and fiscal policy is Arnold [100], but the detailed and illuminating account of Carr [107], vol. 1, Ch. 8, and vol. 2, sections (e) in chapters 16, 17, and 18 is superior. For a detailed account of the nationalization by the former vice president of the Central Committee of Russian Banks, see Epstein [114]. A comprehensive description of Soviet banking in the early fifties may be found in Grossman's chapter in [102].

pressing needs. Manifestly, the effective boycott by the bulk of bank employees made the use of the banking system as "the skeleton of socialist society" a practical impossibility.[18] However, during the months that followed, the total disorganization of all banking operations was gradually overcome and by the end of 1917 the cash department of the State Bank was functioning again and some discount and lending operations were taking place. In the middle of December 1917, the State Bank, as an agency of the new political power structure, was given control over commercial banks, simultaneously with the establishment of "workers' and peasants' control" over all private firms, the precise scope of which was to be determined later by agreements with individual banking institutions.

Within a few weeks, however, armed detachments led by representatives of the Bolshevik-controlled local Soviet occupied the head offices of the commercial banks in Petrograd. On December 27, 1917 (supplemented by a decree issued on January 26, 1918), the Soviet government nationalized all commercial banks without compensation of domestic or foreign stockholders by canceling all their shares. The commercial banks were merged into the State Bank, whose name was changed to People's Bank (Norodny Bank) of the Russian Socialist Republic. The nationalization of mortgage banks had preceded that of commercial banks. This earlier act was the logical consequence of the nationalization of all land, with mortgaging of land declared illegal.

The central bank of cooperatives, the Moscow Narodny Bank, was originally spared from the wholesale nationalization of banks. Organized in 1912 by the cooperative movement, which by that time had attained considerable importance, it had thousands of farm cooperatives as shareowners. For this reason, even though the bank as well as the cooperative movement were controlled by socialist parties other than the Bolsheviks, Lenin delayed nationalization for over a year, seeking a compromise. Only when the government failed to achieve control through suasion was the bank nationalized and merged with the People's Bank, the prede-

---

[18]Writing about this period, Z. Atlas, dean of the Soviet historians of banking and credit, commented: "However, the credit and monetary system of Russia, which was in a state of complete disorganization, could not fulfill the role of a powerful fulcrum during the time of transition from capitalism to socialism as predicted by Marx." [165], p. 11.

cessor of the State Bank. At the same time farm credit cooperatives were placed under government control.[19]

In 1918, following unification of all public budgets into a single
national ("unified") budget, the People's Bank became the sole
depository of government funds and was put in charge of all fiscal
operations. Deposit transfers, through advice, draft, or check,
became obligatory for the socialized and cooperative sectors of
the economy. These two measures laid the foundations for the
subsequent separation of payments circuits discussed in Chapter
5. Thus, some of the basic features of the present credit system
emerged within a year of the October Revolution.

Soviet monetary and banking experience between the October
Revolution and the credit reforms of 1930–1932 may be divided
into the two periods 1917 to 1924 and 1924 to 1932. The first
period saw the rapid disintegration of the old monetary and
banking system and the subsequent long but successful struggle to
introduce a stable Soviet currency. These years were characterized by unprecedented hyper-inflation fueled not only by a flood
of currency issued by the Treasury but also by the chaotic state of
public finances, the breakdown of the economy, the virtual cessa-
tion of foreign trade, and the fragmentation of the country as a
result of the civil war. Much of the trade, particularly between
farmers and the urban population, took place on a barter basis.
Business transactions were typically based on valuation other
than the face value of the circulating medium. Considerable quantities of goods were requisitioned by the armies and other military
groups fighting in the civil war and by the related civilian authorities (or paid for in currency issued by them, or in old Tsarist
rubles). At the end of the period (1924), industrial production was
still less than half, and agricultural output, not much more than
two-thirds, of the prewar (1913) level.

Various types of direct controls were applied to cope with the
pervasive scarcities that arose with the destruction of the market
mechanism during the civil war and the superinflation that
deprived money of all its standard functions. During the period
known as War Communism, an overall scarcity of consumer
goods led to demonetization of the economy, and financial rela-

[19]See Fein [175].

tions with foreign countries ceased. The subsequent reintegration of the national territory required central direction in setting priorities and in allocating material resources under conditions of overall scarcities and a chronic shortage of foreign exchange.

Lenin's earlier view that banks should become the backbone of the socialist administration underwent a number of drastic changes not unrelated to the gradual disintegration of the economy. The focus of what consituted top priority for building socialism shifted from a centralized system of accounting and control— which the single bank could have easily provided—to the complex problem of rebuilding the Russian economy on the principles of directive planning.[20] The Supreme Council of the National Economy, the trade unions, and the soviets were successively identified as the carriers of economic transformation responsible for assuring that the decisions reached at the center of government be implemented throughout the whole country, down to the remotest corner. This reversal in policy was complete at the time of the introduction of the New Economic Policy (NEP) in 1921. By this time, a unified monetary system had ceased to exist and the country was in the grip of a wild inflation.[21]

In January of 1920—against a background of civil war, with the area controlled by the central government considerably reduced and transportation and communications almost completely disrupted—the People's (Narodny) Bank, the only banking institution still in existence, was liquidated. Its main functions were transferred to a department of the People's Commissariat (Ministry) of Finance. The economic collapse caused by the civil war was only partly responsible for the demise of the People's Bank. Equally important was the belief in the imminence of a socialist society, reflecting the influence of the extreme left both inside and outside the Communist Party. The People's Commissar of Finance, C. S. Sokolnikov, was quoted as saying that "finance should not exist in a socialist community."[22] Indeed, Marx him-

---

[20]In 1921, Lenin remarked: "Quite a lot was written about the State Bank at the end of 1917 but . . . it all remained largely a dead letter." [129], vol. 33, p. 91.

[21]Chachulin [21] lists 2,181 different local and regional issues of money surrogates that were circulating in the Soviet Union at one time or another.

[22]Katzenellenbaum [126], p. 98. On the intellectual origins of a moneyless command economy, see Wiles [254], particularly pp. 12 ff. "In 1928 [at the start of the first Five-Year Plan] they returned to centralized command, retaining, however, money within the command sector, in a passive accounting role" (p. 16).

self seems to have believed that a socialist society could dispense with money (little, if anything was said about credit), and that vouchers or tokens evidencing the amount of socially useful labor performed were all that the toiling population would require to obtain consumption goods. However, it soon became evident that a new economy could not be built and that the government could not function without a stable monetary unit and credit system.

A return to more conventional banking and credit practices was signaled by the creation, in October 1921, of a new State Bank of the Russian Socialist Republic, placed under the Commissariat of Finance. By the end of the year, the State Bank had begun operations in several of the main cities and its network of branches rapidly expanded in the following years.

The monetary policy that gradually emerged toward the end of this period aimed at creating a stable currency to replace the Treasury Notes (*Sovznak*—Soviet tokens). Issue of the latter increased by 11 to 15 percent per month in the first half of 1921 and by 50 to 70 percent a month in the corresponding period of 1922, the high point of the hyperinflation.[23] The monetary reform of early 1924 that resulted in the creation of a new currency system began with the introduction of the new *chervonets* currency in October 1922, with a statutory cover of 28 percent in precious metals.[24] For a time it produced a "bi-paper standard" until the old currency was completely retired. The complexities of the previous practice of linking business and some other payments to a variety of indexes and the wide use of a computed "commodity ruble" were only gradually overcome.

The gold-backed currency ultimately became the new money of the Soviet state when the currency reform was completed. While its real purchasing power declined in subsequent years, no further currency reforms were undertaken until the end of World War II.

---

[23]See Arnold [100], Table 19, pp. 128–129.

[24]Equivalent to 10 rubles; these were subsequently replaced by notes denominated in rubles.

The similarity of this reform with that of A. Witte which introduced the gold standard in 1897 was noted by Yurovskiy who was closely associated with the currency reform of 1924: "However great the economic upheavals through which Russia and the Soviet Union have passed since 1914, however radical the revolutionary measur s which have severed the link with the past, elements of the past continue to exist in the present, and the laws passed during the recent years are in some part related to the monetary system created decades ago by Witte's reforms." [92], p. 9. See also Atlas [166].

The monetary reform of 1924 was accomplished by an effort to balance the unified budget (for the fiscal year 1924–1925); it made possible the reestablishment of a banking and credit system.

While the monetary reform terminated hyperinflation by the introduction of a "stable ruble," it did not remove the basic causes of inflationary pressures. Prices remained, however, fairly stable between 1924 and 1928, even though currency in circulation almost tripled; the improvement in the availability of consumer goods was apparently great enough to offset this increase. But between October 1, 1928 and June 1, 1932, the volume of currency in circulation almost tripled again, and consumer prices rose sharply.[25] Inflationary forces received renewed impetus from the drive toward forced industrialization, shortages in consumer goods production, and excessive issuance of credit. Rationing of food, introduced in 1928 for the urban population, was made more comprehensive in 1931; it was not abolished until 1936.

The share of private stores in total retail trade, which at the time of the monetary reform still exceeded that of State and cooperative stores combined (57.7 percent in 1923–1924), declined, but was still 5.6 percent in 1930.[26] For a variety of reasons, the official retail price index became less and less representative and, indeed, its publication was discontinued at the beginning of 1931, not to be resumed until 1956.[27]

The creation of a stable gold-backed parallel currency in 1922 permitted the organization, in the same year, of the first state commercial bank for granting long-term investment loans as well as short-term credit—the Russian Trade and Industrial Bank, known as Prombank. A new bank to service consumer cooperatives had been created already at the end of 1921 (the Pokobank) which was later (November 1922) enlarged (under the name of Vsekobank) to serve all types of cooperative organizations, including farm cooperatives.

1922 also saw the introduction of a free market for consumer

[25]R. Powell, "Recent Developments in Soviet Monetary Policy" in [122].

[26]Malafeev [57], table on p. 134.

[27]Numerous price indexes were constructed by various Western scholars, not so much because of the demonstrated defects of Soviet indexes but because few, if any, price indexes were published in the Soviet Union for a long period. After their publication was resumed, Chapman wrote: "I would not hesitate to rely more heavily on the Soviet than on my own retail price index numbers for purposes of comparing the postwar years with 1940." [108], p. 159.

goods and services under the New Economic Policy (NEP). It demonstrated that financial incentives could increase output, but also signaled potential political dangers to the regime. Related developments in the financial field involved an attempt to reintroduce a multichannel system for the extension of credit while maintaining a tight overall control by the resuscitated State Bank.

During the NEP period, L. Kamenev, at that time head of the government (Council of People's Commissars), assigned to credit the role that Lenin had hoped banks would play in the transition period. He described "centralized credit" as "this commanding high which we have created practically out of nothing" and as "the decisive factor in the regulation of the economy, the factor which [introduces decisive corrections and] is capable both of causing and preventing crises."[28]

In 1923, after the creation of the Federation following the end of the civil war, the State Bank of the Russian Republic was renamed "State Bank of the USSR" (Gosudarstvennyi Bank, abbreviated as Gosbank) and became the bank of issue. By 1925, it had retired almost all other currencies previously in circulation, including regional and prerevolutionary issues.

During this second period of Soviet monetary experience, from 1924 up to the credit reforms of 1930–1932, a system of specialized banks was created. The State Bank, however, was not able to control their credit activities, and a good deal of competition between its own lending and that of the other banks developed.

The competing commercial and special-purpose banks were created by the government in the legal form of joint-stock companies. A Bank for Foreign Trade and two banks for agriculture were also organized, and some elements of the prerevolutionary credit system were revitalized, including the savings bank system, credit unions, municipal (communal) banks, and various types of cooperative banks for agriculture, craftsmen, and small entrepreneurs. Several additional institutions to provide credit for producers' and consumers' cooperatives were created during the twenties, but all were liquidated by 1930, at the time of the farm collectivization drive. No cooperative credit organizations have survived.

Before it emerged as the single banking institution of the coun-

[28]*Planovoye Khozyaistvo*, January 1925. See also Atlas [165].

try, the State Bank had begun to perform certain bank functions vis-á-vis other banks. In particular, it was assigned the role of controlling credit policies of all other banking institutions. This control was achieved mainly through administrative means rather than the monetary policy measures employed by central banks in nonsocialist countries.

Credit planning became the main instrument of pursuing overall credit objectives. As early as 1923, the State Bank had begun to elaborate overall credit plans. The first plan to receive the formal sanction of the government covered the initial quarter of 1925. Collection of all government revenue and its disbursement were transferred to the State Bank in 1925, when the network of local offices of the Ministry of Finance was abolished, thus completing a process initated in 1918. In the same year the accounts of all local governments were also transferred to the State Bank.

The central role of the State Bank was enhanced by the issuance of new laws in the middle of 1927, which delineated the activities of various banks and assigned all short-term lending to the State Bank. Their main purpose was to delineate the type of short- and long-term credit each banking institution was to extend (so that an enterprise would not borrow from more than one bank), and to centralize resources, reporting, and control.

The Credit Reform of 1930–1932

Abolition of inter-enterprise credit in 1930 was a final step toward complete control by the planning authorities over allocation of the means of production and inventories and toward the reduction of credit to a purely implementary role. Prohibition of inter-enterprise lending left the State Bank as the only source of short-term credit, except for construction and foreign trade.

The various measures initiated in 1927 laid the groundwork for a series of sweeping changes which began with a Credit Reform (decree of January 30, 1930) and was essentially completed by a reorganization of the State Bank on the basis of a decree issued on May 25, 1932.[29] Also, in 1932, various banks engaged in long-term financing were reorganized into four such banks with well deline-

[29]For details, see Arnold [100].

ated areas of activity and deprived of the remaining responsibilities in the area of short-term credit.

These various changes and the reconstruction of the balance sheet of the State Bank in 1932 are referred to in the Soviet Union collectively as the Credit Reform of 1930–1932. Although these reforms required a significant reorganization of the banking system to be effective, the structural changes that were made subsequently dealt mainly with delineating the spheres of activity of the specialized banks, particularly those which acted as conduits for long-term investment funds. Other subsequent changes were mostly of a procedural and organizational nature. They involved, among other things, merging the specialized banks for long-term financing into a single Investment Bank in 1959 and incorporating the savings bank system into the State Bank in 1961. Otherwise, the banking structure remained unchanged, with the State Bank (Gosbank) occupying the key position, and the Investment Bank (Stroibank) and the Bank for Foreign Trade (Vneshtorgbank) fulfilling specialized, far narrower functions. Various changes in payments instruments, in the details of the deposit transfer mechanism, and in credit procedures were also made after 1932, but the main features of the Soviet banking and credit system have remained basically unchanged to the present day. This standard system has been adopted by other "people's democracies" in Eastern Europe and other areas where communist regimes have become established since the end of the Second World War.

The Economic Reform of 1965

The economic reforms initiated in September 1965 by a resolution adopted by the highest body of the Communist Party (Plenum of the Central Committee) can be characterized as a half-hearted attempt to deal with some of the most obvious shortcomings of the command economy without changing its basic character.[30]

---

[30]This resolution on measures to "improve the management of industry, to perfect planning, and to reinforce economic stimulation" was followed by similar resolutions of the Central Committee and the Council of Ministers on October 4, 1965.

A description of the Reform by leading Soviet economists is available in English in a variety of sources, including a series of articles which appeared beginning in 1965 in *Soviet*

They were conceived as a set of interrelated measures to improve the performance of the "economic steering mechanism" rather than as a basic revision of the Soviet system of resource allocation and the whole economic organization that implements it. From the inception of the Reform, Soviet authorities have tended to minimize the significance of the departures from the old methods. Indeed, they have constantly stressed that their purpose is to improve planning, not to work toward introducing a socialist market economy—the goal pursued in Yugoslavia and later, in a more limited way, in Hungary. Still, the 1965 Reform does represent the first change of any significance in the management of the Soviet economy since the launching of the first Five-Year Plan in 1928. It enlarged the activities of the State Bank by shifting part of long-term financing of industry to credit and by enlarging the use of credit in capital formation by kolkhozes. Otherwise, it left the structure and basic mechanism of the banking and credit system as they had evolved as a result of the changes introduced in 1930–1932.

Prior to the government's action, there had been considerable public discussion by Soviet academicians, administrators, and enterprise managers of ways to improve the operations of the economy. Proposals by Professor Liberman and other economists in the early sixties regarding the improvement of key mechanisms in the Soviet economy had produced an impressive array of arguments in favor of changes that would open, to a limited extent, the centrally directed economy to market forces.

The various steps gradually taken since the fall of 1965 were originally presented as a sweeping reform "to improve management of industry, to perfect planning, and to reinforce economic

---

Life (a Soviet monthly journal published in the United States) including Birman's [218]. The collection of articles prepared for the J.E.C. [153] and proceedings of a conference held in Moscow in June 1965 (Tsagolov, [85]) contain valuable material for the period just prior to the Reform. Various aspects of the Reform are discussed in "Soviet Economic Reforms" and "A Summary Look at Reforms" in Feiwel [115]; and Borstein and Fusfeld [104]. Part 4 includes important articles on the Reform. See also Campbell [224], Grossman [237], Bratus and Ioffe, "Legal Aspects of the Economic Reform in the Soviet Union" in [113], Seidenstrecher [144], and Schroeder [250], and [251]; see also Garvy [234].

Among the voluminous Soviet literature on the significance of the reform for credit and banking, see Rumyantsev and Banich [71], Bachurin [8] and Dzhavadov [25]. For the impact on credit of reforms initiated simultaneously in other socialist countries, see Atlas [7]. References on the early Soviet articles on the Reform, same source, Ch. 6.

stimulation." Its aim was to improve the performance of the economy by reducing the range of detailed instructions from the center—without, however, giving the enterprise manager enough authority to operate the enterprise as an independent, profit-maximizing unit. To a certain extent, the Reform shifted the responsibility for short-run profit maximization from the central planner to the enterprise manager ("director"). It replaced the excessive number of plan targets to be achieved or surpassed by a mere nine success ("directive") indicators, among which total sales, profits, and the profitability ratio occupy a predominant position. The physical output of the principal product, the wage fund, payments into the budget, the value of centrally planned investments, new capacity to be added and goals for the introduction of new techniques, processes and products are the remaining planning indicators of the enterprise plan. Under the former system the gearing of all rewards to the fulfillment of goals specified mainly or exclusively in physical terms failed in providing incentives to maximize profits and to recognize adequately consumer preferences in the determination of the type of goods to be produced. Narrowing the number of success indicators made it possible for individual enterprises to concentrate their efforts on meeting or exceeding these targets in order to qualify for additional financial rewards, such as retention of a greater share of profits.

Maximization of profits is not the ultimate goal of Soviet planning. It serves, rather, as a means of achieving (or exceeding) plan targets of an individual enterprise with regard to productivity and efficient use of various inputs. The principle of profit maximization does not require, or depend upon, ownership: profit and profitability have long been central in the economic calculus in the Soviet Union, even though in economic plans they appeared as just one of many targets. The Reform introduced as additional indicators of enterprise performance a set of ratios measuring the return on (invested and working) capital and profits expressed as a percentage of total production costs, both called "profitability" (rentabel'nost'), with several accounting variants used.[31] The introduction of a capital use charge required a revision of the entire price structure.

[31]For details, see Korovushkin [49], pp. 81ff., Darkov and Maksmov [23], pp. 9 and 111ff.

The reasons for the 1965 Reform were numerous and complex, and stemmed mainly from the performance of the economy itself. For years, Western critics, as well as some Soviet economists, pointed to various shortcomings in the Soviet economy's performance, and in the early sixties there was widespread domestic concern about the key economic indicators showing less progress than during the fifties. However, there is little doubt that the immediate cause of the Reform lay, rather, in the radically changed situation in the consumer goods market. There a rising per capita real income in the early sixties faced a consumer goods output that had reached a level high enough to satisfy most basic consumer demands. After decades of chronic overall shortages, consumers began to buy discriminatingly and, in some cases, to withhold purchases, confident that more satisfactory goods would ultimately appear on store shelves. For the first time, the consumer could choose, reflect, and postpone, at least in the area of certain important periodic purchases, such as clothing and household goods.

The consumers' refusal to buy shoddy or outmoded goods was one of the immediate influences that precipitated the Reform. By postponing their purchases, they caused a piling up of goods in retail channels—while savings soared. Reports in the Soviet press amply documented this situation, succinctly summarized in an article in a leading literary monthly that made a case for greater reliance on the market mechanism.[32] To convert consumer choice into limited feedbacks, the authorities began experimenting in 1962 with a system whereby production would be guided by actual orders from retail stores rather than by planners' command. The new system made greater allowance for consumer choice without giving recognition to consumer sovereignty.

[32]"The consumer had at his disposal quite a tidy sum of money; on the other hand, an adequate supply of goods was available in retail stores. The problem consisted not in a general shortage of goods, but in a shortage of goods demanded by consumers. The consumer began to ask for a greater variety of goods; he was no longer satisfied merely to have something to put on, he wanted to purchase clothing that was beautiful and stylish. But industry continued to work on the principle 'take what you are being offered'."

Supporting figures quoted show that at the end of 1965, store inventories of cotton, wool, and silk textiles amounted to the equivalent of nearly a year's retail sales, an unusually high ratio. While discussing a similar accumulation of such diverse goods as clothing items, knit goods, sewing machines, and toys, the author points out that in the same year the increase in savings deposits almost exactly matched the rise in retail inventories of all consumer goods other than food. Petrakov [197], p. 173.

Greater emphasis on consumer choice pointed to the need for reforms via several different avenues. For example, the pressure to increase the production of consumer goods by achieving greater efficiency and flexibility in planning and better use of fixed capital investment was one of them.

Finally, maximization of benefits from foreign trade required a more rational price system for optimizing the use of domestic resources in producing for export. Removing distortions required the restructuring of domestic prices and integration of foreign trade with the domestic economy. In this area, the Soviet Reform stopped far short of the fundamental changes introduced in Hungary and the more limited reforms in Poland and Czechoslovakia, which were undertaken to make the domestic producer directly interested in the profitability of exports.

The basic characteristics of the Soviet economy were left untouched by the Reform—state ownership of the means of production, central planning of economic activity, administrative allocation of inputs other than labor, and administrative setting of prices have continued as before. In its all-important state sector, it has remained a one-seller, one-buyer economy. The planning authorities still control the relationship between enterprises and the various state organizations that supply raw materials and certain intermediate goods and direct the distribution of finished products. Contracts merely formalize these relationships and set details; monetary penalties still play a very modest role in enforcing fulfillment of obligations undertaken.

3

Money in a Centrally Directed Economy

THE role that money, credit, and financial flows play in the Soviet Union differs significantly from that in nonsocialist countries. For one thing, official Soviet economic theory has had considerable trouble over the years in defending the very existence of money under socialism and in legitimizing the use of credit and interest charges. For another, ever since the inauguration of the planned economy, Soviet economic policy has been implemented by a combination of planning, direct allocation of resources, and administrative controls that does not include any independent role for money and monetary policy.

Soviet money performs its function in an economy characterized by differentiated markets and by a price system in which price changes depend on administrative decisions rather than on supply and demand factors. To achieve equilibrium conditions and growth objectives, primary emphasis is placed on the administrative allocation of existing, as well as on the development of additional, real resources; monetary management does not go beyond assisting in the implementation of plans cast in physical terms. Credit, too, is issued mainly for carrying required inventories and to facilitate payments. For a fuller discussion of Soviet policy regarding credit and monetary equilibrium, see chapters 6 and 8, respectively.

Soviet Monetary Theory

The economic literature of the Soviet Union has been characterized by a good deal of confusion about the nature of money, the role of the monetary process, and the function of the banking system. Undoubtedly, rigid official adherence to the theories of Marx have hampered monetary analysis. Accepting such concepts as interest charges and recognizing the monetary nature of bank deposits have presented problems for the theoretician and policy maker. In fact, a coherent theory underlying the management of money by the socialist state has yet to be formulated.[1]

Soviet monetary theory has long been inhibited by its refusal to recognize that Karl Marx's pronouncements on gold, circulation of commodities, credit, and financial flows were derived from the analysis of a specific, early stage in the development of the capitalist economy and do not necessarily have the same validity in a socialist economy.[2] Still following Marx, who identified money with gold and was blind to credit creation as a source of deposit money and its equivalence to money of other origin, Soviet theory considers fiduciary money and bank deposits to be merely substitutes for gold. A typical treatise still proclaims that "credit (paper) money in actual circulation in socialist countries merely represents gold. The quantity of money in circulation is, as a rule, limited by the demand of the national economy for real money—gold."[3]

While a review of the early history of Soviet monetary theory is largely irrelevant here, it is worth mentioning that the notion of

---

[1] For a brief review of the rate of economics as a science in the Soviet Union, see Nove [137], Ch. 11.

[2] On this, see the section "Marxian Monetary Theory and Soviet Practice" in Spulber [145], pp. 155–158. See also the interesting discussion by the late Hungarian economist Varga [252].

[3] Aizenberg [1], p. 85. For a recent discussion of the role of gold in communist countries and foreign exchange problems, see also Z. Atlas [162], Altman [214], and Wyczalkowski [255]. In this connection, it is well to remember that under the Tsarist regime, paper currency was called "credit notes" rather than money.

separate payments circuits discussed in Chapter 6 is clearly traceable to the views of Preobrazhenski, perhaps the most influential figure in the early period of Soviet economics. In 1918, he advocated the disappearance of money from the state sector of the economy, but after a brief interlude of War Communism the indispensable role of money in the first state of "building socialism" was recognized, and by 1930, the theoretical basis of the standard system, with its emphasis on the payments and control functions of money, was firmly established.[4]

Soviet monetary theory does not deal with conditions of monetary equilibrium or with models designed to estimate proper growth rates of monetary aggregates. Official descriptions of the role of money and credit have tended to emphasize technicalities rather than substance. Soviet monetary literature deals almost exclusively with the practical problems of controlling currency circulation. Soviet monetary economists denied the monetary nature of deposits at the State Bank, most of them viewing such balances merely as a clearing fund, a liability of the Bank, or a potential claim to currency.

That Soviet banks create credit in the same way as banks in capitalist countries was recognized by L. Shanin as early as 1925,[5] but until the late 1940s Marxist orthodoxy prevailed. The view that bank liabilities may be created also through lending became respectable, if not generally accepted, only toward the middle 1950s. But it was not until the middle 1960s that the theory of the credit origin of money became widely held.[6] After decades of doctrinaire and often hair-splitting discussion, much of which revolved around interpreting Marx's comments on money in the context of a socialist economy, the view that deposits (or, in Soviet terminology, balances of enterprises and of the Treasury at the State Bank) *do* constitute money seems to have prevailed, even though the debate is still continuing.

---

[4]For monetary views of early Soviet economists, see Roussel [248].

[5]His views appeared that year in a series of articles in the April, June, and July issues of *Ekonomicheskoye Obozrenie.*

[6]This theory was advanced by Steinshleger, Pessel', Kronrod, Levchuk, Sitnin, Shwarz, Melkov (see Bibliography) and accepted by the veteran monetary economist Z. Atlas, who is responsible for the section on "The Credit Character of the Creation of Money" in Gerashchenko's textbook [29].

The Monetary Unit

The Soviet monetary system is a classical case of managed fiat money, the volume of which is regulated directly and effectively by state authority through a wide range of controls, including a foreign exchange monopoly.[7] Official claims that all domestic money is "fully backed by material values" or that the ruble is "adequately secured by gold and other precious metals and stones"[8] merely prove the survival of outdated monetary theories of pre-Soviet vintage. The 25 percent cover of gold and other precious metals and stones which bank notes are supposed to have, however, is now given little emphasis by Soviet authorities, while it is stressed that the backing of currency issued by both the State Bank and the Treasury consists in "goods owned by the state and salable at fixed prices."

The monetary unit created in 1922 (see Chapter 2, p. 27) remained unchanged until 1947, when a currency conversion similar to those undertaken by several Western European countries was effected after the war. It was designed to deal with an inflationary situation aggravated by a liquidity overhang created by wartime developments, including war financing. In addition to the general problem of excess consumer purchasing power held in the form of currency hoards, a special distributive problem existed in the Soviet Union: a large part of the excess currency was concentrated in the hands of the peasants as a result of sales of foodstuffs at "free" prices (usually considerably above those fixed for similar items sold in state or cooperative stores on the basis of ration cards issued after 1941 to the urban population). The conversion aimed at a reduction of this overhang of purchasing power with-

---

[7]One of the earliest, clearest, most succinct, and, at the same time, sophisticated statements on the credit origin of money, the nature of cash balances, and the role of money in the Soviet economy may be found in Sitnin's booklet [78]. See also Melkov [61], Ch. 2, for a review of the positions taken by various Soviet economists on the relationship of the money supply to bank credit. Konnik [47], Ch. 4 and Levchuk [53].

In 1971, it was still necessary for an economist of the State Bank to justify the use of the term "loanable funds" and to raise, for the first time since the creation of the monobank system, the question of bank liquidity and its determinants: Levchuk [58], pp. 211–213.

[8]Paper currency was originally issued by the Ministry of Finance (since 1924) as well as by the State Bank. The former issued the smaller denominations (up to 5 rubles prior to the currency exchange of 1961) and the latter, bank notes of larger denominations. Currently, the Ministry of Finance issues only coins. Trubenkev [87], p. 13.

out which the abolition of rationing of consumer goods, promulgated simultaneously, would not have been possible.

In the 1947 conversion currency in circulation was reduced to an amount just adequate to meet payroll requirements for one income period. It was assumed that (a) almost the full amount of wages and salaries disbursed would be spent in trade and service establishments and returned to the State Bank at the end of the period, and that (b) much of the remainder would be recaptured through savings banks, both of which would be available for meeting the next week's wage bill. Analysis of the relevant monetary and expenditure aggregates suggested that the amount of currency actually in circulation[9] was ten times larger than this amount, and a conversion rate of 1:10 was chosen. The conversion was not announced in advance. It was undertaken at the end of a pay period (December 14), when currency holdings in the hands of the population could be expected to be at a minimum.

Given the purpose of the currency conversion, no simultaneous change in wage rates or prices were required. Wage rates remained unchanged and enterprise bank balances were not subject to reduction, since they could be adjusted as needed by administrative action. Balances held by producers' cooperatives and *kolkhozes* were converted at the same one-to-ten ratio that applied to currency held by the general population.

The value of the financial assets held by the population—government bonds and savings deposits—was reduced simultaneously with currency conversion, but at rates more favorable than the currency exchange rate in order to discourage currency hoarding in the future. A relative advantage was given to small savings deposits.

The currency exchange effective January 1, 1961,[10] in which ten old rubles were exchanged for one new ruble, may be compared with the shift to a "heavy" currency (such as the "heavy franc") undertaken by several Western countries. In these countries the exchange for a new currency took place over a period of time, without limitations, and was announced several months in advance. The corresponding reductions in all claims against banks, in other claims and assets, and in wages and prices were not

[9]For details and an independent estimate of a proper conversion rate, see Ames [215] and Baran [216].
[10]See Bornstein [220].

designed to have any real effects on the economy, and particularly not to reduce its liquidity. However, in the Soviet Union, forcing concealed currency hoards into the open was a major purpose of the conversion.

Money: A Passive Planning Tool

From its very beginning, Soviet planning has been based on material balances in which specific kinds of physical resources are allocated in order to achieve goals defined in real units.[11] The basic consumption-investment decisions are made by the state. Production targets are set by the government and embodied in specific directives cast in the form of output plans.

The state-owned sector, which accounts for practically the entire nonagricultural production, consists of administratively independent units ("enterprises") whose manager ("director") is appointed by higher-echelon economic organizations, such as regional or industry branch organizations, currently called *ob'edineniye* (see Ch. 5, footnote 27). The director is responsible for meeting all—including the financial—plan targets after the plan has been approved by the supervisory administration which, however, can make changes after the plan becomes effective. Managers are permitted to increase profits significantly only by raising productivity, but are allowed to have a voice in the allocation of profits. Before the 1965 Reform, only an insignificant part of profits determined by formula was retained by the enterprise generating them. While nominally increasing the enterprise's discretion in disposing of profits, the Reform in actuality did little to increase the firm's autonomy in this area.

Once output plans are set, designated government agencies (typically, ministries responsible for individual industries) specify, for each enterprise or group of enterprises, types and sources of inputs, destination and prices of outputs, and channels of distribution for the outputs. Until limited experimentation with

---

[11]For one of the earliest discussions of this topic, see Montias [245]. See also Hirsch [120]. Hirsch points out that the directive effects of money "are merely derived from the preceding fundamental material decisions, that they achieve nothing but the optimal execution of the prescribed basic material concept of the plan by consistent measurement and by allocation of economic divisible quantities accordingly."

more flexible policies was begun in 1965, individual enterprises had little scope for deciding between alternative inputs and outputs or investment decisions.

While centrally planned economies are quantity-oriented rather than value-oriented, they do require money to avoid the cumbersomeness of barter.

In a socialist economy, money acquires the additional function of a planning tool, albeit a passive one. To use Brzeski's expression, money is "an organization input in the process of social production."[12] Money enters economic planning mostly as a common denominator for the purpose of aggregation. It facilitates planning by making different activities comparable. Associated financial categories, such as credit and interest, are merely technical devices for implementing central command ("planning") decisions.[13]

Shortages of money cannot be permitted to interfere with the attainment of output targets. At the same time, holdings of extra cash must be prevented from becoming effective demand for labor, raw materials, and other ("funded") inputs in short supply. Since some maneuvering within administratively set limits is possible, the general tendency under the standard system was to convert redundant cash balances into inventory.

The fact that an economic process is programmed in terms of real magnitudes does not necessarily mean that it has no monetary aspects whatever.[14] These monetary aspects are important, but only in a global, macroeconomic sense. Once the macromonetary decisions are taken, what remains is implementation. Much of what appears to be monetary action is, in fact, the exercise of administrative functions by the banking system in support of policies formulated elsewhere. Monetary flows recorded by the banking system reveal deviations from planned real flows and mirror any cumulative disequilibria and bottlenecks in the real processes. Actual performance measured by comparing payments flows with plan figures provides a day-to-day check on the economy—indeed, the only overall check.

Money thus performs an important function as a signal, but is

[12]"Forced-Draft Industrialization in Poland," in [118], p. 23.

[13]Typical Soviet textbooks refer to money as facilitating planning, control of production, and unified and universal accounting. See, for instance, Bogachevsky's textbook [14].

[14]See Ames [99], p. 172.

not relied on to any significant degree as an adjuster. Credit policy is not used as a means of affecting aggregate demand through varying the cost and availability of credit or by manipulating quantity of money and its composition. Instead, demand money is controlled by administrative means—this mechanism differentiates the Soviet system from the market allocation of credit. Administrative decisions, rather than market adjustments, are relied upon to correct deviations from planned performance (targets), to remove bottlenecks, and to correct for any disequilibria that might develop. These decisions are made by the various economic planning and administrative agencies (the "economic organs"), not by the monetary authorities.[15] However, all deviations from planned performance are first signalled by the monetary flows recorded by the banking system.

Financial Planning

Soviet financial planning has failed thus far to integrate planning on the microeconomic (enterprise) and the macroeconomic level. Financial plans prepared for individual enterprises and units of the state sector are aggregated for planning and monitoring purposes (by industry branch, intermediate units of the economic administration, and territorial subdivision), but are integrated neither within a comprehensive national financial plan nor the monetary plans of the State Bank.[16]

The monetary plans that provide the operating basis of the two main departments of the State Bank are the "Credit Plan" (Credit

[15]It is, perhaps, significant that in *Economics of Soviet Planning* [103], by Abram Bergson, one of the leading authorities on the Soviet Economy, there is no chapter on money and banking, and only a perfunctory reference to the banking system: "Another major agency concerned with credit and finance after the Ministry of Finance is the State Bank" (p. 38). Even in Nove's widely used *The Soviet Economy* [137], fewer than four out of the more than 330 pages of the revised edition are devoted to banking and credit. In a chart showing the "organization and powers of central agencies for planning and managing the Soviet economy," Zaleski [157], p. 25, does not include either the State Bank or the Ministry of Finance. College textbooks similarly ignore the role of money and banking. See, for instance, Turgeon [150], although the gap was filled in the second edition. Compare Grossman, "Gold and the Sword: Money in the Soviet Command Economy" in Rosovsky [143].

[16]On the possible use of banking statistics and for a detailed review of the information contained in the various payment documents for economic planning and forecasting, see Belkin [12].

Department) and the "Currency" or "Cash" Plan (Cash Department). The first combines short-term lending with long-term credit, which has shown rapid growth in recent years. While the inventory needs of the state sector can be derived from enterprise financial plans, other credit needs are difficult to ascertain (funds needed to finance the collection float, for example). The Credit Plan, on all territorial levels—local, regional, and central—is thus a combination of identifiable credit requirements projected from past inventory patterns and educated guesses by State Bank officials of the additional amounts required to bridge the collection gap, as well as various other unforeseen needs; it is not broken down on a quarterly basis. The annual Credit Plan is roughly comparable to the global credit ceilings established from time to time by some central banks of Western Europe.

The "Currency" Plan provides the basis for the other main activity of the State Bank—control of currency in circulation. It is derived from a sources-and-uses-of-funds account of the household sector. This account, known as the "Balance of Money Income and Expenditures of the Population," has two parts. The first shows income received from state enterprises, various organizations, government units, and transfer payments from the budget; the second, transactions within the household sector (such as purchase of second-hand goods) and between households and *kolkhozes* (mainly the purchase of food in the free market).

Efforts to identify and increase "sources" of State Bank resources, such as *kolkhoz* deposits, which figure so prominently in the official pronouncements and literature, must be interpreted as a survival of misconceptions about the credit-creating power of the banking system, or as an effort to keep to a minimum additional currency issue caused by credit expansion, or both.

As to financial planning on the micro level, each enterprise operates on the basis of a financial plan which summarizes and expresses in value terms the content of an underlying economic plan formulated in physical terms. The director of the enterprise is responsible for the execution of the plan, which details the enterprise's relationship with the national economic plan, including the disposition of its social income, or surplus.

Lack of differentiation makes it impossible to trace separately financial flows going into fixed investment, increases in working

TABLE 3.1

Sources and Uses of Funds of an Enterprise, as Summarized in Its Financial Plan

Uses	Profits from Principal Activity	Profits from Sale of Consumer Goods Produced as a Side Line	Profits from (and Economies Made in) Construction	Savings Realized on Investment Expenditures	Depreciation	Sale of Unneeded Property	Increase in Accounts Receivable	Reduction of (Unneeded) Working Capital	Parents' Contributions to Operating Kindergartens	Resources Received from the Budget	Total Expenditures
1. Fixed investment	372		20	60	56						508
2. Major repairs					80						80
3. Increase in own working capital	40						4	36			80
4. Fund for increasing output	20				24	12					56
5. Consumption fund		64									64
6. Premium fund	15										15
7. Expenses for kindergartens									20	24	44
8. Fund for cultural purposes	10										10
9. Repayment of long-term loans	16										16
10. Interest on bank loans	1										1
11. Profits paid into budget	114										114
Total receipts	588	64	20	60	160	12	4	36	20	24	988

SOURCE: Plotnikov [68], p. 132.

NOTE: Figures are illustrative.

capital, and gross additions to social infrastructure (public investment, in the Western sense). Table 3.1 shows this lack of differentiation at the enterprise level with a summary (using illustrative
figures) of the sources and uses of funds in a typical enterprise
under the standard system as it was before the 1965 Reform.

Financial transfers by the enterprise are shown in rows 9 to 11.
They consist of payments of part of the profits into the budget,
interest payments, and repayments of bank loans (which, prior to
the Reform, were charges against gross profits). Rows 1 to 8 cover
internal uses of funds.

It is peculiar to Soviet enterprise accounting that the difference
between planned and actual expenditures for investment (columns 4 and 5) are considered a source of funds, as are economies
achieved in estimated construction expenditures. These sources
supplement the depreciation allowances available to finance fixed
investment provided for in the central economic plan (line 1,
column 12). Another part of the depreciation reserves, together
with a deduction from profits and the proceeds from the sale of
redundant equipment ("unnecessary property"), is used to
acquire equipment and to finance minor construction projects not
provided for in the plan. These sources of "decentralized investments" are channeled through one of the special funds (row 4)
that the enterprise freely used before the Reform as part of the
less differentiated "enterprise" or "directors" fund. Rows 5 and
8 show funds that channel part of the profits into collective
consumption of the enterprise, while row 6 represents another
special fund, also derived from retained profits, which provides
incentive payments (premiums) for the staff. In the case illustrated by Table 3.1, working capital is increased by profits, by a
rise in economic receivables, and a reduction in unneeded working capital (columns 2, 8, and 9, respectively). Note that no use of
short-term credit is shown, although the use of long-term credit is
illustrated.

Since monetary and credit flows are planned as the counterparts of physical flows, financial plans are by necessity derivative.
On the one hand, they register and project the effects of planned
changes in the level and structure of output and prices on money
supply, credit, and investment financing. On the other, they
indicate, through the actual changes in the financial variables, the

"financial plan fulfillment"—to what extent plan targets are being met. Where "real plans" are the result of compromises among the various central and regional economic and political agencies, the related financial plans reflect automatically the goals set and the compromises struck in these original plans.[17]

In the broadest sense, the unified budget is the most comprehensive financial planning document, since it specifies the amounts of investment grants and credit through the intermediation of the banking system. The other financial plans are, in effect, little more than statements of sources and uses of funds. Some are nothing more than incomplete projections of prospective operations, frequently for periods no longer than one quarter, subject to continuous review and adjustment. Except for the budget, all financial plans are internal documents, so that no outside analysis of their relationship to actual performance is possible.

Adjustments in financial plans, for the longer run as well as in midstream, are made through administrative decisions. They may include changes in growth patterns, as well as adjustments to deal with dislocations and bottlenecks in situations where some enterprises (or economic or geographic sectors) fail to meet plan targets while others manage to exceed them.

The Reform of 1965 has not abolished financial planning, but has made it more flexible and less detailed. Central planning of the broad categories of credit use continues, with the aim of preserving monetary equilibrium by balancing availability of resources and demand.[18]

---

[17]Financial planning serves a number of specific needs, but so far it has not resulted in the creation of a comprehensive, all-encompassing financial plan that would serve to guide and monitor the progress of growth and the preservation of overall monetary equilibrium. One of the obstacles to the construction of such a plan is the fact that the *kolkhoz* sector remains outside of central financial planning.

The precise role of financial plans in economic planning remains an area of controversy and considerable confusion among Soviet economists, and views differ as to their practical significance. See, for instance, Alexandrov [2], Ch. 2; Allakhverdyan [98]; Batyrev, Kaganov, and Yagodin [11], Ch. 4; Margolin [59], Ch. 1; Shenger [74]; and Zverev [93].

[18]For details, see Allakhverdyan [98] and [161], Isaev [42], Lyando [56], Margolin [59] Plotnikov [68], Ch. 3, Slavnyi [79], and Usoskin [89]. For an official Soviet presentation in English, see Dundukov, "Financial Balances," in [151]. See also Berliner's pioneering study [218], Lushin [55], and Garvy [117] and "The Role of the State Bank in Soviet Planning in Degras" [110]. For a brief history of monetary planning by the State Bank, see Melkov [61], pp. 92–97.

The Limited Role of Prices

Prices depend on administrative decisions rather than on supply and demand factors.[19] They are manipulated by the government as a means of distributing the social product within a broad framework of economic policy.

The authorities set all consumer prices as well as transfer prices for producers' goods and raw materials. They arrive at their price determinations by adding centrally set (average) profit margins and (mostly average) distribution margins to production costs, with no regard to demand or depletion. Goods, from raw materials to final products, are traded on the basis of price lists issued by central planners (the Price Committee attached to the State Planning Committee), which contain about five million individual prices. In 1972 alone the Price Committee had reviewed about 400,000 individual prices.

Since stable prices facilitate planning and an orderly distribution and redistribution of the national product, major revisions are undertaken reluctantly and only at infrequent intervals. A systematic review is usually undertaken to implement new major policy decisions regarding costing and pricing, or to maintain or change price relationships between individual goods or commodity groups. The basic price revision following World War II resulted in wholesale price lists issued in January 1949, which were revised in 1955. The next and more sweeping revision was not undertaken until 1967, after the Reform, which introduced a charge on capital assets, was launched. Individual price adjustments are made typically to cope with shortages of specific goods (and, in some cases, with consumer dissatisfaction) rather than as a systematic reaction to economic impulses received through the market. Occasionally, individual prices are changed and profit margins on certain categories of products adjusted, primarily in order to reduce differentials that are obviously illogical and cause misallocation of resources.

Export prices are divorced from the domestic price level and may be specified in a convertible currency (usually the U.S.

---

[19]For the rationale and technique of price setting, see Malafeev [57], Smirnov [81], and Zverev [93]. See also Bornstein [222] and Denis and Lavigne [111].

dollar) or in rubles. In the second case (usually in trade exchanges with other socialist countries) applicable prices are differentiated according to various factors characterizing the particular transaction—whether subsidies and premiums are involved, the time at which the original transaction was entered into—and in some cases, depend on the particular export (or import) organization (usually a ministry or its subordinated or special-purpose organization) responsible for the transaction.

Goods are exported at prices that make them competitive abroad. When such prices are lower than domestic costs, the difference is absorbed by a special fund which receives the difference between the price the domestic purchaser must pay for imports and their foreign costs (converted at the official rate). If the required price-equalization export subsidies exceed the amounts accumulated from corresponding payments by importers, the domestic cost of balancing foreign payments is ultimately borne by the budget.[20]

The Soviet price system is thus an inadequate guide for a rational allocation of resources between domestic consumption and exports, or for determining the pattern of trade. Indeed, some Soviet economists have long recognized the existing price system as one of the impediments to an optimal allocation of resources. Therefore, restructuring prices to allow for the cost of capital and, to some extent, for natural rents constituted a significant part of the 1965 Reform. The basis for price setting has been shifted from a literal interpretation of the labor theory of value to factor cost pricing with fixed and largely uniform markups. However, recalculation of prices to allow for the capital use charge and quasi rents did not lead to a restructuring of the entire price system.

Broad adjustments were made during the 1967 general review of wholesale prices and again in 1970, resulting, as in previous general price revisions, in the issuance of new official price lists. But no changes were made in the principles and procedures of central price setting; instead of the introduction of flexible prices that would respond to supply and demand conditions, a set of

---

[20]Only the net receipts from, or cost of, foreign trade (and service transactions) enter the domestic payments circuit. For further discussion of the impact of foreign trade on the Soviet economy, see Pryor [141].

fixed and immutable prices remained applicable until the next cycle of systematic general price revisions. The new cost factors were allowed for, without revising the basic approach to the pricing of other factors and without correcting the numerous distortions embodied in existing wholesale prices. Neither did raising the average profit markup to 15 percent of prime costs (with greater variations by industry, industrial branch, and even individual enterprise) constitute a significant change, although the resulting increase in wholesale prices (not passed on to retail level) did reduce the number of enterprises requiring subsidies.

One argument for not departing from the principle of fixed prices—in contrast to freeing some price categories either entirely or within stipulated ranges, as in Hungary and some other socialist countries—has been to contribute to a stable environment in which managers of individual enterprises can learn to operate without detailed direction from the central authorities. Frequent administrative changes in prices can play havoc with the planning process. Thus, price lists reflecting revisions effective January 1, 1970 were issued too late to be taken into account in developing the economic plan for that year. The plan was formulated in 1969, with the result that the structure of production in the 1970 plan did not reflect the new price relationships. Interenterprise sales were complicated by the need to carry supplementary accounts to adjust for the differences in the two sets of prices. All billing was in 1969 prices to permit control of plan fulfillment, and the difference between new and old prices required additional settlements between buyer and seller that were entered in separate accounts.[21]

One significant objective of the Soviet price system has been to keep prices of producer's goods low in relation to those of consumer goods. This policy, rooted in a doctrinaire application of the Marxian analysis, has been pursued consistently since the first Five-Year Plan. It was not modified by the Reform beyond the indirect effects of allowing for the cost of capital. In some cases, however, this change had far-reaching effects, since capital-output ratios are typically high in producer's goods industries and many extractive industries. The question of applying the turnover

[21]See Komin [183], p. 21.

tax to producer's goods has also been raised, but so far the Reform has not gone beyond recognizing capital as a cost factor. Nevertheless, the increase in machinery and equipment prices can be viewed, together with the introduction of the capital use tax, as an essential move to counteract one of the most basic weaknesses of the Soviet economy—the wasteful use of capital goods and the general tendency to plan for, and carry, excess capacity.

Before the Reform, when no charge was made for capital because it was public property, considerable misallocation and wasteful use of investment funds resulted, as greater investment per unit of output was not automatically reflected in higher costs. Introduction of quasi rents and of differentiated capital charges has frequently resulted in narrowing the considerable differences in profit rates within the same branch of industry and among its individual products.[22] By introducing a capital use tax and rental payments, the Reform changed the *relative* as well as the absolute cost of goods.

The introduction of markdowns on slow-moving consumer goods was an innovation which acknowledged that inferior or out-of-fashion items could no longer be forced on goods-starved consumers. It became part of the State Bank's lending policy to exert pressure on retail organizations to trim inventories, which in some cases results in sales at a loss (a typical concomitant of relatively low retail markup margins).

The failure of the Reform to come to grips with the problem of price formation sets definite limits on the ability of planning authorities to optimize resource input and of all branches and levels of the economic administration to evaluate performance by individual enterprises and industries.[23]

[22]Shortly before the Reform was initiated, it had been planned to reduce freight tariffs by 20 percent, since under the old system of cost accounting the 1964 profits of the Soviet railway system amounted to 67.2 percent of direct costs. When allowance is made for a charge for fixed and working capital, this profit ratio drops to 12.6 percent, less than the national average for all state-owned enterprises. (It was eventually decided to leave freight tariffs unchanged.) See Kondraschev [184]. See also Mitel'man [193].

[23]In the words of the director in charge of the credit department of the State Bank prior to and after the Reform, "The fact that prices for many products of industry and agriculture do not correspond to the amount of required social labor is a serious obstacle to the use of cost accounting, as audited by the staff of the State Bank, as a tool for analyzing economic processes by the Bank." Barkovsky [168], p. 40.

4

The Banking System

The State Bank

THE State Bank is an "adjuster," not a "steerer"; its role—to
borrow Robert V. Roosa's terminology (coined in a different
context)—is defensive rather than dynamic. The Bank is an
administrative, not a policy making, agency which, unlike central
banks in nonsocialist countries, does not use such indirect tools as
rediscounting and open market operations. Indeed, it cannot
exert any significant influence on enterprise behavior, since enterprises are unable to change their prices, can adjust other terms of
sale only marginally, and vary output and its composition only
within narrow limits to correct deviations from the planned
path. The Bank is not expected to make any overall contribution
by changing credit conditions other than preventing spending in
excess of stipulated amounts, granting individual enterprises
credit or special terms to help break a bottleneck (or meet some
other specific situation), and promote productivity through differential credit terms related to efficiency.

The State Bank is responsible for the regulation of note circulation, and for servicing the currency, credit, payments, and household savings needs of the country. In close cooperation with the
Ministries of Finance and Foreign Trade, it also manages the gold
and foreign exchange reserves and foreign payments.

The role of the State Bank is discussed within the larger framework of the entire money and credit picture in the Soviet Union in
Chapters 3 and 6. In this chapter the structure and the main
activities of the State Bank other than extension of credit are
discussed, as well as the role of the Savings Bank. The activities
of the Bank for Foreign Trade—the second specialized bank,

considering Savings Banks as part of the State Bank—are described in Chapter 7.

The ultimate responsibility for money and credit rests with the Council of Ministers, which appoints its board of managers, approves its operating plans, and issues all regulations regarding money and credit, including those involving technical operating procedures of the Bank. Overall direction and supervision is exercised by the Ministry of Finance, which also supervises the Investment Bank and from which the State Bank was dependent directly prior to 1954.

While the monobank is thus essentially an implementing agency, it is an active participant in all phases of national and regional economic planning. It has a close relationship with such government agencies as the industrial ministries and the State Planning Board, which develops and coordinates financial and physical plans. Bank representatives participate in all major economic discussions and in the work of such policymaking bodies as the price-setting boards. The chairman of the board of the Bank attends meetings of the Council of Ministers.

In sum, the State Bank performs macroeconomic as well as microeconomic functions wherever planning and administration involve value aggregates and payment flows. As far as the overall economic performance is concerned, however, the State Bank's contribution has been only marginal, even since the initiation of the Reform.

This, of course, does not detract from the Bank's key position in the administration of the economy. Its close and continuous contact with the entire socialized economy gives it an advantage over the various ministries and *glavks* which are organized on a segmented industry basis.

As the fiscal agency of the government, it performs all the usual functions of the central banks in nonsocialist countries. The collection, allocation, and disbursement of government revenue (called the "cash execution of the budget") represents one of the main activities of the Bank.

As the all-encompassing center of the nation's settlements and clearing mechanism, the State Bank keeps track of all payments flows involving credit transfers.[1] It also allocates individual pay-

---

[1]For a description of the head office, see Poskonov [70].

ments between special-purpose funds, thus acting as a social accounting center. Finally, its control function—supervising the financial performance of all socialized enterprises—makes Gosbank the key agency in monitoring the performance of the entire economy.

The organizational structure of the State Bank reflects the centralized nature of the Soviet economy. A strong headquarters organization is the apogee of a network of local offices numerous enough to bring bank officials into intimate contact with all state enterprises (including state farms), *kolkhozes,* and municipalities.

All policies originate at the head office and are uniformly applied throughout the entire national territory. Regional and local offices merely apply regulations and directives issued at the center, and make loans and issue currency within the overall and specific quotas assigned to them. More than a year after the Reform was launched, B. Chlenov and V. Rybin wrote in Izvestia (Feb. 5, 1967): "The basic shortcoming of the present system is that it requires from the offices of the State Bank merely close following of instructions and, as a practical matter, does not induce them to seek out possibilities for a more effective use of credit. In fact, local offices of the Bank are transformed into technical executors of instructions emanating from higher-level offices and they can only signal conditions existing in the economy, instead of using the granting of credit as a means of improving the production performance." In Holesovsky's words, the Soviet banking official is a "civil servant at the instruments of control."[2]

The territorial structure of the State Bank involves two levels of supervisory offices—"principal" and "regional." There is a principal office in the capital of each of the fifteen constituent republics (the "Republican" Office), and there are several such offices in the largest republic, the Russian Federation. Each principal office supervises several regional offices. Principal offices are concerned only with industries and services of national signifi-

---

[2]In Grossman [118], p. 97; see also [116].

cance, while regional and local offices deal with enterprises of regional or local importance.

Regional offices are staff organizations concerned mainly with credit planning and supervising of local offices. Regional offices have been given greater flexibility in credit policy in recent years, for instance, they may be made responsible for reallocating unused credit lines (quotas) among local offices.

Since all activities of the Bank are directly related to the socialized sector's administration, any organizational changes there lead to corresponding changes in the Bank's internal structure.[3]

The numerous activities of the State Bank require an extended network of branches. Normally, there is at least one State Bank in each of the lowest territorial units (*rayon*). On January 1, 1971, 4,134 offices were in operation, virtually the same number as ten years before; in the earlier post-World War II years, the number reached close to five thousand.

The policy of the State Bank and all its activities are directed by a board (*upravleniye*) consisting of a chairman and several vice-chairmen and other members, including heads of the principal departments of the head office. The savings bank system, while a part of the State Bank, maintains a separate, but parallel, organizational structure, and—since 1973—has its own board.

The internal structure of the head office contains four major subdivisions: policy departments, concerned with such matters as credit and foreign exchange planning;[4] loan departments, structured to correspond to the administrative structure of the economy, each division supervising credit extension to a given economic sector or territory; other operations departments (currency issue, fiscal function, et cetera); and staff departments

---

[3]Thus, the 1957 reorganization of the administration of the economy required a restructuring of the Bank to tie it to the newly organized territorial economic organizations (*sovnarkhoz*). In each *sovnarkhoz*, one bank office was designated as the principal office of a given economic region, and made responsible for financial planning. During the entire period 1957–1965, in which planning and economic administration were organized on a territorial principle, the State Bank remained an important organ of central control and enforcement. See Barkovky [167].

[4]These are concerned primarily with planning and operations rather than research. Creation of a research institute within the State Bank that would deal with problems of monetary circulation has been advocated in recent years by several Soviet economists, among them Levchuk (a member of the Bank's staff) [53], p. 213.

(personnel, legal, building operations, et cetera). Through the entire organizational pyramid, down to the local branches, State Bank offices duplicate, in a simplified form, the internal structure of the head office.[5]

THE BANK AND ITS CLIENTELE

The relationship between the State Bank and its clientele bears little resemblance to the corresponding relationship in nonsocialist countries: it is administrative rather than contractual. The State Bank is, in effect, the representative of the state as well as an agent of the depositor. It protects the interests of the state by debiting the depositor's account—in most cases, automatically— with the various payments due the Treasury. If necessary, it extends credit to assure that such payments are made on time.

The individual client has no banking alternatives. He can obtain from the Bank standard services only. For state enterprises, the use of bank deposit facilities is not a matter of convenience but an obligation; it carries with it constraints and rules of behavior designed to enforce compliance with centrally determined plans. Bank control of economic activities is further facilitated by the requirement that each enterprise, unit of government, or membership organization keep its accounts with one designated banking office in whose territory it is located. This arrangement, however, does not exclude the use of (temporary or permanent) auxiliary collection or disbursement accounts at other branches in locations where the given enterprise receives or makes a large volume of payments, but control over these payments flows remains with one single office.

While, on the one hand, the bank is one of the central authorities' enforcement agencies, it serves, on the other, as a channel through which the individual enterprise may, under certain circumstances, obtain relief and assistance. This is true, in particular, in the case of local industries, enterprises, and organizations whose operations significantly affect the economy of a given area. It is, indeed, quite usual for a local or regional branch of the State Bank to intercede for enterprises located in its jurisdiction (to back up their requests for additional credit or more lenient treat-

[5]Further details on the organization of the State Bank are given in Appendix A.

ment) and otherwise to operate as an important channel through which local or regional problems, complaints, and aspirations filter through to the central authorities.

The State Bank maintains four broad categories of accounts:[6] for economic units whose activities involve business accounting to achieve economic self-reliance *(khozraschet);* for the government; for collective farms *(kolkhozes)* and other cooperatives; and for organizations of a public ("social") character, the expenses of which are met from public funds ("budgetary") or from membership fees and similar contributions ("voluntary organizations"). Collective farms (and other cooperative and membership organizations) may keep their free funds at the State Bank, in savings bank accounts, or in currency.

About two-thirds of all deposits are held by state enterprises engaged in production and distribution. These deposits represent the bulk of their cash resources, since they are permitted to hold only negligible amounts of currency; no time deposits or other near-money assets are available to them. Balances of manufacturing enterprises at the start of 1967 totaled 10 billion rubles, for an average of roughly 40,000 rubles per account (if the total is allocated in full to clearing accounts only). These are very low in comparison with balances maintained by U.S. corporations at commercial banks in terms of percentage of output. They are equivalent to a wage bill of about two weeks or to 5 percent of the value of the enterprises' annual output at factory prices. An annual volume of domestic trade exceeding 177 billion rubles is supported by deposit balances (if the beginning of the year can be taken to approximate average balances) averaging less than one billion rubles.

Since the post-Stalin remonetization of agriculture in early 1953, collective farms have been receiving a considerable amount of cash payments from the sale of their output. As a result, at the end of 1969, the *kolkhozes* held close to one-third of all deposits at

[6]Considerable detail is available on the number and structure of accounts carried by the State Bank, but their analytical value is limited, since changes over time mainly reflect changes in the rules and procedures of the Bank and in the organization of the economy. Such data are summarized, for selected years, in Tables 1 through 3 in Appendix A.

Reserves of the Social Security Fund as well as of the State life and property insurance corporations are deposited with the State Bank rather than invested in Government securities.

the State Bank (see Appendix Table A.3), partly as a result of a relentless campaign to induce them to make maximum use of banking facilities.

Deposits of clients are equivalent to only a small fraction of the loans outstanding. (See Appendix A.) The main counterpart of loans issued by the State Bank consists of current deposits of the budget, accumulated past budget surpluses (including gains from currency conversions), funds deposited by the budget for long-term lending to collective farms and to compensate the Bank for loans canceled or reduced by government order, and, most importantly, currency issued.

Banking authorities place considerable emphasis on "improving the payments discipline" of enterprises, since failure to pay on time is tantamount to obtaining inter-enterprise credit and disrupts the circular flow of funds (see Chapter 2). When an enterprise's balances with the State Bank are inadequate to meet all obligatory payments, a strict and complex system of priorities comes into play. The use of a small amount (up to 5 percent of daily receipts) of the cash flow for meeting "urgent needs" is permitted. Otherwise, currency withdrawals for wage payments usually have first priority (provided these are within the limits of the planned wages fund, or are related to the above-plan-production). Next in priority are payments to the state, followed by payments into depreciation reserve accounts, loan repayments, and, finally, all other claims, including those of suppliers.

The structure of deposit rates reflects a mixture of policy considerations and bureaucratic convenience. Thus, government deposits draw interest at a lower rate, and those of collective farms at a higher rate, than enterprise deposits. Similarly, voluntary organizations are paid a lower rate by savings banks than individual depositors.

Rates paid on deposits (on current account) were originally established at the time of the 1930–1932 reform at relatively high levels (5 percent for state-owned enterprises and 6 percent for collective farms). They were reduced sharply by 1936, and ultimately abolished for state-owned enterprise and reduced to ½ percent for collective farms. After World War II deposit rates were raised again. In 1965, the State Bank paid ½ percent on balances in settlement and current accounts of enterprises and other holders of such accounts, and 2 to 3 percent on sight and time deposits held by the population, depending on the nature of the account. To encourage collective farms to use banking facilities, their deposits are credited with a ¾ percent rate of interest. Indeed, since the deposit level of state-owned enterprises is largely determined by outside authorities, it is difficult to find a rationale for paying even very low rates of interest on their deposit balances.

The difference between the State Bank and the banks of the nonsocialist countries is reflected in the structure of their balance sheets. In addition to an undisclosed amount of gold and foreign exchange, the State Bank's assets consist almost entirely of loans to the various segments of the socialized economy and contain no government or private securities whatsoever. Liabilities consist of currency and deposits by enterprises, collective farms and other cooperatives, government units, and public organizations. The only counterpart of the interbank balances in nonsocialist countries are the working balances of the two specialized banks.

A discussion of the available estimates of the balance sheet, together with a table showing the structure of the liabilities of the State Bank between 1929 and 1938, is provided in Appendix B.

THE FISCAL FUNCTION

The State Bank collects and disburses all government revenues—or more than half (51–54 percent in recent years) of the national income as measured in the Soviet Union[7] (largely because the bulk of capital formation still is reflected in budgetary flows). Over half of the unified budget is spent by the central government, while the fifteen republics and their various administrative subdivisions, down to the local soviets (municipalities), account for the remainder. As the government's fiscal agent, the State Bank carries accounts for nearly fifty thousand separate units of government, the operation of which involves complexities, such as interaccount transfers of revenues, far beyond those known in Western countries.

To be sure, some of the fiscal techniques used in the Soviet

---

[7]For a definition of the concept used, see Studenski [148], Ch. 25.

Union (such as revenue sharing, grants to lower-level units, and current collection of taxes based on estimated income with subsequent adjustments) are also found in other countries. As a general principle, revenues are shared in such a way as to provide adequate funds for meeting all expenditures of each republic, avoiding the need for subsidies from the budget of the Soviet Union. Some federal republics directly collect the entire amount of the turnover and income taxes in their respective territories and receive, in addition, transfers from the central budget.[8] What is unique in the State Bank's fiscal function is the volume of auditing (including individual enterprises) involved in the collection of government revenue, and the frequency with which the various types of revenue originating in the state sector of the economy are paid into the budget.

The considerable amount of paper work arising from the verification of documents required for enterprise payments which constitute about 90 percent of budgetary receipts is further swelled by a variety of subsidy and compensatory payments to enterprises with above-average costs. The budget also absorbs all inventory losses resulting from any lowering of prices and, conversely, benefits from any upward revaluations. Similarly, the transportation of certain consumer goods, ranging from flour to vodka, to distant points served by state or cooperative retail outlets, is subsidized. Such retail outlets and reusers of containers must submit claims for reimbursement from the budget once or even twice a month. Moreover, retail outlets, wholesale organizations, and manufacturers of goods affected by a price change must submit detailed claims for offsetting subsidies whenever any given product is being repriced. All such payments require prior verification; obviously the resulting transfers on the books of the State Bank result in a staggering amount of paper work.[9]

THE CONTROL FUNCTION

With few exceptions, all major economic decisions, including those in the field of banking and credit, are originally embodied in resolutions of Communist Party organs, while the specifics are

---

[8]For specific examples, see Konstantinova [185], p. 28.

[9]See D'yachko, Makhov, and Freiman [24] for details and procedures. The State Bank handles a large variety of additional subsidy payments, such as subsidies to canning factories for the cost of collecting reusable containers.

spelled out in government decrees and operating plans of the State Bank approved at the highest levels of government. Controls by the State Bank (and the Investment Bank, in its sphere) are exercised on behalf of both the government and the party. Bank officials report to both, on the local as well as on the national level. When sanctions available to the State Bank prove inadequate, it has recourse to intervention by government or party authorities.

The purpose of the monobank is not to adjust the level or direction of monetary flows in order to achieve appropriate results in economic activity, but to make sure the funds collected, disbursed, borrowed, or repaid coincide with the figures appearing in the applicable financial plan. Since all financial planning represents a translation of material targets into monetary terms, it is assumed that fulfilling the goals set in financial plans is identical with achievement of the targets in real terms. The financial, administrative, and coercive dimensions of controls are closely integrated.

In a centrally planned economy, where lines of authority are complex and sometimes confused, where directives and information flow through multilevel administrative channels, and where performance is evaluated via a multiplicity of badly coordinated indicators, the monobank is in a singularly advantageous position: it is the country's single, all-encompassing accounting center. Deposit money is essentially a tracer of real flows. By analyzing accounts on its books, the State Bank is in a position to have a full and continuous picture of the financial position of each enterprise and of its progress in meeting plan targets set for it.[10] Changes in production and distribution as measured by one common denominator, money, are almost instantly reflected in great detail on its books. Thus, the State Bank is in fact the main source of current information on how the economic plan targets are being met by the entire state-owned sector of production and distribution, and how operating goals of the unified government budget are being achieved in all their details and ramifications. It is thus a major channel through which any failures in the meshing of

---

[10]Hirsch characterizes money as performing an "evidence function": "Money makes evident the overall significance of individual purposes and means for economic fulfillment of purpose and thus facilitates consistent economic choice." [120], pp. 46 and 73. For a Soviet view of the relationship between real and financial flows, see Lushin [55].

gears and in achieving plan targets come to the attention of the authorities. It raises the flag without cracking the whip: when the signals it transmits call for corrective action, the required policy measures normally emanate from the higher authorities of the state.[11]

The scope of the Bank's control, already broad as a result of the credit reforms of 1930–1932, was widened significantly in 1954, when it was made responsible for evaluating the success of enterprises in fulfilling their economic plan with regard to such key indicators as output, profits, reduction of unit costs, and working capital.

Under the standard system, the strategic position of the State Bank was enhanced by the fact that an enterprise (or any other economic unit) could use its "own" as well as borrowed funds only for the specific purposes detailed in its production-financial plan; the Reform has not significantly modified this principle. Control by the ruble applies to loans as well as to payments from any bank balances and thus to the entire flow of funds (currency payments as well as credit transfers) in the state-owned sector of the economy and at all levels of government. Control by the ruble is facilitated by a complex system of subaccounts designed to separate working capital from amortization and other capital account payments. The widespread use of separate loan accounts helps to insure that funds are disbursed for the specific purpose for which credit was obtained.

One of the main responsibilities of the Bank is to enforce the "financial discipline" of all enterprises in the state sector by making sure that they meet their financial obligations to the Bank and the Treasury and keep all expenditures within limits set by the plan. In fact, an important reason why the "own" (allocated) working capital of economic units is kept low is that they are thereby forced to borrow, thus affording the Bank a better opportunity for monitoring and, when needed, directly influencing their day-to-day activities.

All deposit transfers, cash withdrawals, and credit extensions involve verification that each transaction conforms with the

---

[11]Note, however, that some of the "financial controls" of the State Bank are comparable to independent audit by certified public accountants and by the bank supervisory authorities in most nonsocialist countries. The best detailed study of the control function by a Western economist is by De Maegh [131].

underlying authorization. The State Bank makes sure that the flow of funds through individual enterprises (and higher-level economic units) is in line with economic plans, and that all required payments, such as those for taxes or loan payments, are made in full on the date due, even from accounts maintained with it voluntarily, such as those of collective farms.

Perhaps the most important area of control entails cash withdrawals for the payment of wages, originally instituted in 1939–1940.[12] Control over disbursements from the wages funds is usually very elaborate, as it is intended to keep labor costs down and prevent a "wage drift." The payroll account ("wage fund") of each enterprise is programmed in great detail, but actual disbursements are contingent on the fulfillment of production goals. This arrangement gives the Bank access to a broad range of production and cost data, since unit cost is one element that is taken into account in establishing the eligibility of the enterprise to obtain additional payroll funds.

Some of the control activities of the State Bank and of the other banking institutions merely involve continuous checking of actual performance, as reflected by the Bank's records, against the financial plans of the individual enterprises and the budget of the various units of government. Others require on-the-spot inspection, performed by a corps of outside inspectors or auditors, whose work involves verification by visual inspection, actual count, or other means.

But the Bank's control function goes beyond mere verification. Payments from, and transfers between, depositors' separate accounts may not be made without their order, approval, or even knowledge. The Bank acts to protect the interests of the state (as to collection of taxes or other payments into the budget), and automatically applies a variety of rules and regulations pertaining to certain interenterprise transfers or payments to third parties. Indeed, in some respects control amounts to the assumption of managerial responsibility—with Bank officials deemed to be better guardians of the state's interest than the state-appointed manager of an enterprise.

The State and Investment Banks are not the only agencies that

[12]For details on bank controls over payrolls, as functioning in 1959, see Batyrev, Kagznov, and Yagodin [12], Ch. 6. For the earlier history of these controls, see Holzman [121], pp. 35–38.

exercise financial control functions. As a rule, financial records of an enterprise are subject to multiple audits, conducted by ministries (in particular the Ministry of Finance) and agencies on various levels of government.[13] These are not only burdensome and time-consuming, but also result in overlapping responsibilities, without necessarily raising the quality of audits.

Savings Banks

Savings banks were started in Russia in the last third of the nineteenth century as government-sponsored institutions. The same Soviet decree which shortly after the October Revolution canceled all debts of the Tsarist regime also proclaimed the inviolability of savings bank accounts. However, the hyper-inflation that followed wiped out the value of savings, and the savings bank system was liquidated in the two years following the Revolution. In the wake of the currency reform of 1922, however, a government savings bank system was recreated in the same year under the name of the "Workers' Savings Banks."

The savings bank system has developed considerably since the end of World War II. In addition to stimulating household savings, it offers the population a certain minimum of banking services. Since its incorporation into the State Bank in 1963,[14] the savings bank system has been administered as a separate department of the Bank. An official monograph identifies the savings bank system as "a component part of the government apparatus."[15]

The savings bank office is the only banking facility available to the population.[16] Its services are much more limited than those

[13]For details, see Plotnikov [68], Ch. 9. See also Shevelev [76].

[14]For a history of savings banks, see Zverev [94], Eremeeva [26], and Illinich and Tkachenko [39]. Current developments are reviewed in articles by Chetverikov, the head of the Savings Bank system, which appear annually in *Den'gi i Kredit*. The latest data used in this section are from [173].

[15]Eremeeva [26], p. 19. On the ideological underpinning of stimulating savings, see Chetverikov [172].

[16]Individuals may obtain "deposit passbooks" from the State Bank for demand and time deposits. They are used mainly by a small number of individuals with high incomes, such as artists, and, probably because the minimum deposit is fairly high, are of very limited significance.

available from commercial banks and savings institutions in Western countries. For example, it does not offer any generalized deposit transfer facilities comparable to postal, personal checking, or giro accounts. In contrast to most other socialist countries, savings banks in the Soviet Union do not make loans.

In organizational structure and procedures the savings banks are more similar to their counterparts in the nonsocialist world than any other part of Soviet banking. The savings bank system consists of a central office for each republic, attached to the State Bank office, and a pyramid of regional and local offices and agencies. It combines a network of full-service offices with a postal savings system and with limited-service facilities at the place of employment. However, 80 to 85 percent of all deposits are concentrated in the larger, fully staffed branches.[17]

Of the about 74,000 offices in operation in the autumn of 1973, most were facilities located in post and telegraph offices. They are operated on a part-time basis by the regular employees of the postal adminstration who received from the savings bank additional compensation for these services. Others are operated as part-time agencies for the benefit of employees in factories, offices, and collective farms, and offer only limited facilities (very much like credit unions in the United States). However, about 35,000 were fully staffed offices and a considerable effort has been made in recent years to convert more facilities into such agencies. For the sake of simplicity, in the following pages all categories are referred to as "savings banks." However, not all savings bank offices offer the full range of services discussed below.

Encouragement of personal savings has been much emphasized in recent years as an important means of reducing excess consumer demand. Newspapers, periodicals, radio, and television are used to advertise account services. Promotional literature stresses the absolutely confidential nature of savings deposits and their liquidity, including the privilege of withdrawing term deposits before maturity by accepting the lower demand deposit rate. Payroll deduction plans for workers and members of collective farms were introduced in 1955, while arrangements for direct

---

[17]Mechanization of savings bank operations is still in the early stages. There are relatively few automatic machines for passbook entries and many offices are still not even adequately equipped with adding machines.

deposit of certain nonwage payments, such as honoraria and fees, into depositors' accounts had become available even a few years earlier. In 1971, about one-sixth of the total amounts received came from such automatic deposits.

Until recently, the volume of savings deposits has been low (see Table 4.1). By the outbreak of World War II, aggregated deposits amounted only to 720 million rubles, the equivalent of about 135 million dollars at the official exchange rates applicable at that time. The insignificance of this amount, given a network of more than 41,000 offices carrying 17.3 million accounts, reflects low average income and the lack of such incentives to save as the availability of consumer goods of high unit cost. Significantly, the average turnover period of savings deposits was only seven months at that time. Since the savings bank system provides banking services for the population, including transfer and payments services, all (or at least some) of the savings bank deposits should be considered part of the active money supply.

Indeed, the bulk of personal savings is still of a temporary nature, funds being accumulated in savings accounts for the purchase of specific, relatively expensive items (which could be a winter coat or a motorcycle), or to finance a vacation trip. The preferential treatment given to savings accounts at the time of currency conversion in 1947 contributed greatly to their popularity.[18]

The volume of savings deposits has been on the rise since the discontinuance of forced government bond purchases in 1957. Nevertheless, total balances in 1961 were still less than 11 billion rubles despite a significant increase in the number of savings bank offices. The number of accounts did triple between 1950 and 1961, however. The sixties saw a rapid rise in savings as a result of a higher standard of living, the increased availability of durable consumer goods and the official encouragement of cooperative housing construction in the cities and of private construction in the countryside (see Table 4.1). With a growth of 15–20 percent a year between 1965 and 1971, deposits exceeded 46.6 billion rubles at the beginning of 1971, or an average passbook balance (with 80

[18]The paucity of information and analysis on the subject of savings patterns in the Soviet Union has been discussed by Gekker in [149], particularly p. 21, footnote 11.

TABLE 4.1

Savings Bank Deposits, Selected Years
(in millions of rubles at end of year)

	Total	Urban	Rural
1940	725	576	149
1950	1,853	1,647	206
1960	10,909	8,728	2,181
1965	18,727	14,028	4,699
1970	46,600	34,053	12,547
1971	53,215	38,744	14,471
1972	60,400	—	—

SOURCE: [86] 1972; p. 313.

NOTE: Savings deposits in the State Bank proper declined from 181 million rubles in 1950 to 154 million in 1971.

million account holders) of about 510 rubles. Of the total volume of deposits, about one-fourth were in offices located in rural areas.

Several types of accounts are available, ranging from passbook demand accounts and limited checking accounts drawing 2 percent to term accounts on which 3 percent is paid.[19] Accounts participating in a twice-a-year lottery drawing (on which no interest is paid) are also available. About two-thirds of all deposits are term deposits. Savings banks issue letters of credit to their depositors which are honored by any office throughout the Soviet Union (similar to our travelers' checks), as well as special passbooks from which withdrawals can be made at any office within a specific region and, since 1973, checks which are used mainly to make payment for large purchases, such as motorcycles.

In addition, savings banks also maintain current accounts for the benefit of collective farms, the lowest-level municipal entities (such as village Soviets), and trade unions branches and other organizations.[20]

[19]For a description of the various types of accounts (which may not be fully up to date), see Zverev [94], pp. 244–245.

[20]Accounts of hospitals, children's homes and camps, municipal housing, and mutual aid societies and similar associations are frequently held at a savings bank office. In fact, at

Collection and payment activities on behalf of the government form an extensive part of savings banks activities. This includes payment of old-age pensions and various social security benefits, such as aid to dependent children, and collection activities for various communal services and membership organizations.[21]

Finally, the savings bank system is in charge of placing the national 3 percent lottery bonds, the only security available to the Soviet citizen since the obligatory subscriptions to government loans or "mass loans" were discontinued.[22] No financial assets other than those bonds, savings deposits and money are available to Soviet citizens. Only 2.6 billion rubles of these bonds were held by the population at the beginning of 1971. More importantly, savings banks are in charge of redeeming the consolidated bonds (see Chapter 8, page 166). Savings banks also sell tickets for lotteries that various republics, municipalities, and official organizations have been operating since 1958. The total value of such lottery sales in recent years amounted to roughly two-thirds of (gross) purchases of the 3 percent bonds in 1970 (or 300 million rubles a year—$1.50 per head of the population).

Prior to the transfer of the savings bank system to the State Bank, the net inflow of savings represented a source of budgetary revenue. Now, however, savings deposits have become one of the sources of bank funds, while the relative importance of cumulative Treasury surpluses, previously accounting for 40–50 percent of the Bank's resources, has declined.[23]

---

the beginning of 1970, the savings bank system had 415,000 accounts belonging to organizations rather than to persons. Furthermore, in remote locations, savings bank branches with a full-time staff frequently provide not only limited banking facilities for the local administration (Soviet), but may also act as agents for the State Bank in servicing enterprises of local scope which are normally supervised by municipal authorities (for instance, by providing currency for payroll purposes).

[21]Rent and utility bills and trade union dues and various contributions and fees, even Communist Party membership dues, can be paid at savings banks offices. Efforts to provide better banking services to the population include widening of the range of payments which can be made at full-service branches. Depending on the classification or location of the office, these may include payments for certain educational facilities that are not free (such as music schools), for municipal nursery schools, and for the state insurance institution (*gosstrakh*).

[22]The only other security held, but no longer purchasable, by Soviet citizens is the 2 percent loan into which all previously issued "mass loans" have been consolidated.

[23]Barkovskiy and Kartacheva [9], p. 203. Purchases of small amounts of government bonds were made by the savings bank system in the fifties, but discontinued subsequently. These are examples of switches in the Soviet financial circuit which have little, if any, policy significance but complicate meaningful long-term comparisons of financial flows.

The Investment Bank

The role of banking in providing long-term credit prior to the 1965 Reform is best described as marginal. In fact, shifting financing of capital investment to the banking system and to self-financing was one of the chief objectives of the Reform.

Prior to 1959, long-term investments were administered by four separate banking institutions, designed to serve industry, agriculture, trade and construction, respectively. In 1959 these banks were consolidated into a single bank—the All-Union Bank for Financing Capital Investment (Stroybank); it is now the only bank authorized to finance capital investment, except certain agricultural investments handled through the State Bank.[24] In recent years the bank maintained accounts for over 100,000 clients and disbursed about 300 billion rubles a year. (For comparison of sources of financing centrally directed fixed investments in the years 1959, 1966 and 1971, see Table 4.2.)

All "centralized" funds for financing fixed capital formation in industry, transportation and communications, trade, educational, health, and recreational facilities, construction of municipal housing, and all research facilities are channeled through the Investment Bank. In 1959, roughly 70 percent of disbursements for centralized investment were received from the Treasury and the remaining 30 percent were funds accumulated by the investing enterprises themselves, including depreciation reserves. In some previous years, the share of the budget was even higher. The overwhelming bulk of these funds goes to projects included in the "project list" *(titularnyi spisok),* which is an integral part of the economic plan for a given year. The Investment Bank also administers and disburses certain funds for "decentralized investment" (formed by individual enterprises and considerably enlarged as a result of the Reform) for projects financed through budgets of municipalities and of the federal republics, and funds for stimulation of housing construction. The Bank is, in fact, the depository of all funds that individual enterprises are allowed to retain from profits and depreciation reserves for "decentralized investment." Since enterprises participate with the Treasury in

[24]Some writers abbreviate the title as "Construction Bank" rather than "Investment Bank." See also Zavalishchin and Shor [211].

TABLE 4.2

Sources of Financing of Centralized Fixed Investment Disbursed
by the Investment Bank
(selected years, billions of rubles)

	1959		1966	
	Amount	%	Amount	%
Resources of enterprises				
depreciation allowances	2.8	14.9	7.9	27.9
profits	2.5	13.4	3.0	10.5
other	0.4	1.9	1.0	3.7
Total	5.7	30.2	11.9	42.1
Budgetary appropriations	13.2	69.8	16.4	57.9
Grand total	19.0	100.0	28.4	100.0

SOURCE: Poskonov [70], p. 255 for 1959 and 1966.

NOTE: Total may not add up because of rounding. Figures are smaller than gross investment because some part of expenditures from depreciation reserves spent on "capital repairs" is not included with reported investment.

the financing of housing and various social amenities, disbursement of funds through one single agency facilitates coordination and control. As late as 1966, "decentralized" investments were still equal to less than 10 percent of centralized investments; this percentage increased significantly as the changes in investment financing introduced by the Reform gathered momentum.

The Investment Bank deals almost exclusively with the construction industry. Its clientele includes enterprises specializing in the construction of public works, factories, and all other structures, and those that specialize in site preparation and the rigging and installation of all types of machinery and equipment.[25] About two thirds of the Bank's disbursements go to the first group of construction enterprises and about one third to those supplying machinery and equipment. The Bank supervises delivery of and makes payments for all machinery and other equipment installed. It also disburses all funds for project development and for research benefiting the construction industry.

The Investment Bank has regional offices (149 at the beginning

[25]The State Bank carries the accounts of some construction firms and extends short-term credit to them, although in principle all construction firms must deal with the Investment Bank.

of 1967) that supervise a network of local offices (355), many of which are located near areas of substantial construction activity, such as major power projects and industrial complexes. When the volume of construction does not justify a local office, agents of the Investment Bank are attached to State Bank offices, which disburse about 15 percent of all funds for which the Investment Bank is responsible.

The control powers of the Investment Bank are far-reaching. They are exercised even before a project is started: for example, the Bank can reject a project even after it has received final approval by the highest authority if the estimates submitted are insufficiently detailed or if financing of the project is not fully assured by funds already deposited with the Bank or to be received according to an approved time schedule. Original cost estimates are analyzed by the Bank to ascertain that all charges conform to applicable Government-established prices. (Comparative cost studies of similar projects and various standard ratios, or "norms," are used to arrive at such judgments.) The Bank can also reject the financing of a project if it expects it to be unprofitable or to fall short of technical efficiency standards. Rejection, on whatever grounds, apparently merely establishes the right of the Bank to participate in the revision of the original plans to meet its objections.

In addition to auditing bills from construction firms and suppliers of machinery and equipment, the Bank's main activity is to verify that bills conform to approved cost estimates, thus preventing cost overruns in cases where some flexibility exists, and placement of equipment orders in excess of planned amounts. In addition, the Bank also oversees the progress of construction by sending its inspectors to building sites frequently to make sure that no waste of materials and labor takes place. In general, it analyzes the performance of construction enterprises with a view to enforcing high standards of performance.

The shifting of at least part of plant and equipment financing from a grant to a loan basis under the Reform makes the Investment Bank the manager of a growing revolving fund, continuously augmented by additional budgetary appropriations as well as by its own earnings. Instead of being almost exclusively a disbursing agency, it has become considerably more involved in project appraisal, and is more concerned with the prospective profitability of the projects to be financed, with lending terms (including maturity and rates), and with cash flow projections of enterprises. The shift toward partial loan financing and the changes in the method of payment for construction work have required considerable alterations in the *modus operandi* of the Investment Bank.

Long-term financing is now more evenly distributed between the Investment Bank and State Bank with the second accounting for about 40 percent of all long-term credit in 1969. While its new long-term lending activities, previously limited to agriculture, required considerable changes in the State Bank, the spheres of activities of the two banks are not clearly delineated and properly coordinated. So far there is no indication that the Soviet Union plans to follow the example of some other socialist countries which have abolished investment banks and transferred their functions to the state banks. This puts all credit activities within a single institution and makes it possible to assess the global credit needs of each individual enterprise by making the financing of its fixed and working capital the responsibility of the same institution.

Changes in the Role of the Banking System as a Result of the Reform

The State Bank has followed the official line of de-emphasizing the Reform, in particular in recent years. This shift is reflected in statements by its officials and in its publications. In the period immediately following the October 1965 "Plenum," the publication of the State Bank referred to the new policies in terms of an economic reform. Subsequently, the term disappeared from the publications, and by 1971 the word "reform" was eschewed completely. Thus, the usual lead articles in two successive issues of *Den'gi i Kredit* (April and May 1971) following the XXIVth Congress define the objective of the financial and banking authorities as "a fuller mobilization of reserves in industry and increasing its efficiency; broader use of the financial-credit mechanism to accelerate technological progress and intensification of production." The achievement of the State Bank during the 8th Five-

Year Plan following the introduction of the Reform is summarized as having "provided for the regulation of circulation of money in the country, extension of credit and financing of the economy and clearing of payments, and also for the control by the ruble of the economic and financial activities of enterprises and organizations"—a statement that could have been made twenty years earlier. The term "reform" appears nowhere in these articles.

The Reform has increased the role of the banking system in channeling investment funds, without changing its other procedures to any significant extent. Even though credit has been elevated to the position of a key "economic lever" and is expected to play a major role in improving the performance of the economy, it is to be a tauter string rather than a looser leash, to be used under a modified set of objectives and criteria. Under the old system, the extension of credit on the basis of uniform, centrally determined criteria (designed to facilitate the fulfillment of production plans rather than influence the allocation of real resources) resulted in almost automatic credit availability. This, again, encouraged wasteful use of resources through the accumulation of excessive stocks of materials and parts. Under the new system, the effectiveness of credit was expected to increase and its volume to expand. The broad categories of credit used continue to be centrally planned in order to maintain a balance between resource availability and demand for resources and thus to preserve monetary equilibrium. Financial planning has not been abolished, but has been reduced with regard to details and made somewhat more flexible.

Although the new policies give greater latitude to the local bank official, they have by no means changed his position as an agent of the state. His power remains limited, as most important decisions require approval by higher-echelon offices.

Greater flexibility in granting short-term loans has reduced the rigidity of credit planning. Basically, the quarterly credit plan remains the operational document, but the response to credit requests is no longer automatic. Now the State Bank may refuse to extend loans for carrying inventories of items for which consumer demand has shrunk or is nonexistent, thus compelling the enterprise to change the composition and quality of its output to increase consumer appeal. On the other hand, the Bank may also grant inventory loans to stimulate production of additional quantities of articles in great demand, or to initiate production of new articles, above the limits set in the plan, provided the enterprise has actually received orders for such additional output. The greater discretion given the Bank tends to increase the scope of its activities at the lower levels.

When the cost of a given project exceeds the amount of the enterprise's funds available for investment purposes, the Bank may and normally will grant long- and medium-term credit to state-owned enterprises as well as to *kolkhozes*. The State Bank and the Investment Bank now have more latitude in dealing with loan applications even for centrally approved projects of state enterprises; individual enterprises have to justify the profitability of the projects to be financed.

It is not yet clear to what extent the elaborate mechanism of financial controls is to be ultimately dismantled. The emphasis on the use of credit as a means of controlling operations of individual enterprises remains undiminished. No doubt the rigidity of control exercised by the State Bank has been relaxed somewhat. For instance, within certain limits, individual branches on their own can now determine the frequency as well as operational detail of various audits and verifications to be undertaken.[26] The degree to which administrative interference by the State Bank, the ministries, and the other supervisory organizations has been reduced and controls shifted from the center toward organizations in closer touch with the production process (*ob'edineniye*, other intermediate organizations of enterprises, bank branches, et cetera) is a measure of the true significance of the Reform, but little information on this is available.

The role of banking controls is still conceived as pre- and post-auditing. It continues to be conducted according to centrally determined, uniform procedures, and enterprises remain accountable to a number of separate supervisory authorities. Simplification of accounting and reporting procedures introduced as part of the Reform (for example, quarterly instead of monthly determination of profits to be transferred to the budget) is of a marginal nature. Altogether, the role of the State Bank under the Reform

[26]See report on decisions of its Board of Managers in *D.K.*, December 1966.

falls far short of what those advocating the use of economic stimulation instead of administrative methods have proposed.[27]

However, in the new "system of economic steering" the importance of banking is bound to grow, with the rechanneling of financial flows and with the banks' increased authority in dealing with requests for financing investments as well as working capital needs. But will bank officials be able—assuming that they are given greater latitude—to undergo the mutation from inventory checkers to project and risk appraisers? Will they have sufficient incentives to make the changes necessary to optimize the use of bank resources? One of the issues raised by the Reform is how to make the State Bank and its staff directly interested in the profitability of the enterprise to which it extends credit.[28]

[27]See, for instance, Belkin and Iventor [13]. The authors discuss in detail how data internally available to the State Bank could be used to improve planning. Their earlier articles (*Pravda,* December 21, 1966 and *Novyi Mir,* December 1967) had attracted considerable attention and were interpreted by some to go so far as advocating replacement of the State Planning Commission by the State Bank, rather than merely giving more scope to the latter. The authors also advocate creation of state commercial banks for major industry branches and transformation of the State Bank into a true central bank.

[28]In discussing financial means for obtaining desirable economic results, it has been proposed to make State Bank officials financially responsible for shortfalls and losses sustained due to their negligence or bad judgment. See Tatur [84].

5

Payments and Financial Flows

The Separation of Payments Circuits

IN the Soviet Union, household money (currency) is differentiated from enterprise money (bank deposits), and household banking from enterprise banking. All payments are separated into these two different circuits, which correspond to the separate markets for consumer goods and producers' goods.[1] Their focal point is the State Bank, whose staff (particularly at the local branch level) devotes much of its time to their management. A further institutional separation of the flow of payments under the standard system was the assignment to the State Bank of all payments relating to current production, while the accumulation and disbursement of all funds relating to fixed capital formation in the state-owned sector went on the books of the Investment Bank.

The difference between the two kinds of money is both physical and functional. For the population at large, currency alone serves as medium of payment, except for a relatively small amount of payments via savings accounts. By contrast, all payments among enterprises, economic and civic organizations, and government agencies (except for petty cash disbursements) involve deposit transfers on the books of the banking system. Currency and deposit money are not interchangeable. Deposits are exchanged for currency almost exclusively through payroll withdrawals.

Separation of payments flows, in the Soviet Union as well as in other socialist countries, is a basic mechanism for avoiding excess

[1]See Chapter 4, "The Investment Bank."

demand. A necessary condition for macroeconomic equilibrium in the household sector is that the amount of income paid out equal the value (at set prices) of all goods and services available for household consumption plus voluntary household savings. The total bill for consumer goods is determined by the combined effect of output plans, factory prices, and the turnover tax applicable to each product. Turnover taxes are differentiated by product, and are designed to raise prices for consumer items sufficiently to prevent effective demand from exceeding available supplies.

Once the major macroeconomic decisions are made concerning the apportionment of the social product between private consumption, on the one hand, and collective consumption, investment, and the cost of general administration, on the other, the share of net output earmarked for the population determines the size of the wage fund (after allowing for other sources of income, such as stipends and pensions, as well as for the small amount of personal taxes paid by the population). To achieve the goal of matching these two magnitudes, wage rates and total payroll costs of individual enterprises are strictly controlled.

Separation of payments into two circuits facilitates financial planning as well as central accounting control over the flow of resources within the socialized sector and prevents leakages of goods and services from there into private consumption. It also facilitates detection of bottlenecks and shortfalls in the execution of economic plans. Finally, it gives consumers some choice within the range of goods and services offered by planners (which may guide future production), while preserving the planning authorities' control over inputs and outputs in the enterprise sector. After the abolition of wartime rationing, which was made possible in 1947 by the increased flow of consumer goods, the range of available options widened and household money gradually acquired a higher degree of "moneyness." Options have been limited by the planners' choice of the "assortment" of goods produced and by the lack of a workable mechanism to feed back consumer preferences into production planning. While availability of options does not guarantee rational choices, the limited nature of these options prevents the system from developing procedures for evaluating preferences and demand elasticities.

THE CURRENCY CIRCUIT

Wages and other monetary income are paid in currency, except for a relatively small amount paid directly into savings accounts. Consequently, virtually all consumer expenditures are also made in currency.

Through currency withdrawals, note liabilities are substituted on the books of the State Bank for liabilities to enterprises and to the Treasury: thus, creditor balances are reduced to only a fraction of loans. Indeed, because of cumulative currency withdrawals resulting from the continuous increase in aggregate loan volume, deposit balances of enterprises at the end of 1969 were equal to only about one-tenth of their aggregate loan balances.

Collectivized farmers now receive a very large part of their income in cash, but prior to 1953 payments in kind were prevalent. The remonetization of relations between the *kolkhozes* and the state, and the subsequent changeover of the members' remuneration from an annual distribution on the basis of work performed to periodic money payments, have increased the circulation of currency as well as its rate of turnover among the rural population. Members of collective farms and workers on state farms, as well as the small number of independent farmers still in existence, also receive currency through direct sales of crops and animal products from their privately farmed plots.

Consumer goods and services are obtained almost entirely from state-owned retail stores (the network of "cooperative stores" in villages is, de facto, state-operated).[2] As a result, currency normally returns to the State Bank after only one transaction—when currency paid out as wages is spent in retail stores and is redeposited by them—but some part changes hands within the population itself, with one group purchasing goods from another. In addition to the free-market sales of farm products, such transactions include sales by artisans and cooperative producers, sales of second-hand goods, and payments for services to domestics and other individuals (including moonlighters) and for various forms of illicit transactions. Of all these transactions, farm prod-

[2]Capital goods cannot be acquired by the population at large, but a limited amount of building materials has become available in recent years for repair purposes and new construction.

ucts purchased directly from the rural population are by far the most important. Farmers use the proceeds of their sales to the urban population to acquire goods and services from the socialized sector. As long as claims on the socialized sector are merely transferred from one group of the population to another, few problems arise for planners and controllers of currency flows, even though the resulting shifts in the structure of demand require adjustments in the bill of goods produced for the consumer sector.

The bulk of the demand for currency is met from the supply of currency returning to the monobank when individuals make retail purchases as service expenditures, pay income taxes, and add to their savings accounts. State-owned and cooperative retail stores or service establishments are required to make daily deposits of all currency receipts in excess of a stipulated amount of petty cash.

Prompt recovery of as large an amount of currency put into circulation as possible is one of the shibboleths of Soviet monetary management. Continuous efforts are made to prevent consumers from hoarding currency which might spill over into black market and other illicit activities and make possible sudden surges of spending that typically create shortages in retail stores. Much emphasis is placed on channeling the cash receipts of trade and service establishments into State Bank offices as promptly as possible and on minimizing the amount of till cash that such establishments, as well as industrial establishments, are permitted to hold. Any inflow of currency that results in vault cash holdings ("operational reserves") at a local bank office in excess of stipulated maximum levels is transferred to the centrally controlled "general reserves," from which notes and coins can be released only on specific orders from the head or regional offices of the State Bank. Conversely, elaborate precautions are taken to prevent issuance of currency to enterprises and government units except in strict conformity with the cash plan.

THE DEPOSIT TRANSFER CIRCUIT

The deposit transfer circuit ("noncash circuit," in Soviet terminology) encompasses all payments related to the production and disposition of the gross national income not paid out in currency to the population, as well as transactions relating to the extension and repayment of credit.[3] (Only payments up to a small specified amount—currently 100 rubles—may be made in currency.) Trade organizations are authorized, in strictly circumscribed situations, to make cash payments for certain direct purchases made locally, and state procurement agencies pay for their purchases from *kolkhozes* largely in currency. With those minor exceptions, only amounts needed for meeting payrolls can be converted into currency.

The deposit transfer mechanism is designed to place payments between economic units on a semi-automatic basis while assuring prompt fulfillment of all obligations to the state budget. A primary task of the banking system is to provide a smooth deposit transfer mechanism that will promptly return to every enterprise all working capital spent in producing the output delivered to the next link in the chain, and to provide credit for bridging any payment gaps.

Claims among socialist enterprises arising from production and distribution give rise only to settlements through deposit transfers between the accounts of the buyer and the seller, or through mutual offsetting of claims. Payments are made as goods move through production and distribution channels for purposes determined by the planners according to rigid schedules.

Goods must normally be paid for, in accordance with a fixed time schedule, shortly after documentary drafts (the main means of settlement) are received by the purchasers. One of the frequently criticized aspects of this procedure is that (particularly where shipments to distant points are involved) the buyer's account is sometimes debited before he has received and examined the shipment. Monthly or other periodic billing has not been used until recently; hence each individual transaction requires a separate payment to facilitate control.[4]

---

[3]The use of deposit transfers is obligatory for the socialized sector only. *Kolkhozes* are obliged to use them in their dealings with the budget, with state-owned enterprises, and with the credit system, and for all accounts related to capital formation which they must keep at the State Bank, but otherwise they may use currency and keep their cash assets either in currency or in savings accounts. Although great efforts are made to induce *kolkhozes* to bank their cash receipts, only 20 to 70 percent of such receipts, depending on the region, are actually deposited.

[4]The requirement that each freight bill be settled separately on receipt illustrates the

Also, for certain categories of transactions, specified payments instruments are prescribed, while in other cases the payer has a choice. But as a rule, the nature of the transaction and the location of the parties involved determine the way in which payment must be made. Whatever payment instrument is used, all types require documents establishing the purpose of the transaction.

A variety of techniques is employed in making interenterprise and other payments involving transfers of deposits, including arrangements for mutual offsets of claims. These techniques grow out of a continuous search for the best methods to combine optimal control with speed. Arrangements frequently are different for local and out-of-town payments.[5] The form and frequency of transfers have been changed from time to time by administrative action aimed at specific categories of transactions, types of payments, or industries.

The use of money as a tool of administrative control as well as a means of payment has ruled out widespread use of checks, as well as the development of a nationwide check-clearing system (as in the United States) or a centralized deposit transfer (giro) system (as in most countries of Western Europe). Instead, it has created a complex and cumbersome payment system in which documentary drafts and other payment orders are used in preference to checks and which requires processing a large volume of documents. In recent years, steps have been taken to automatize the payments mechanism, but progress has been slow, partly due to shortages in electronic equipment.

Even before the 1965 Reform, there was a growing tendency to widen the choice of available payments instruments and procedures and to let the enterprises involved agree directly on settlement procedures. However, in the Soviet Union even relatively

---

extreme to which the general principle is pushed. Delinquent payers are penalized for the benefit of the payee by a fee of 0.03 percent a day for the amounts past due (only 0.01 percent before the Reform). This fee is automatically collected by the bank and credited to the account of the payee.

[5]Clearing arrangements to offset counterclaims differ for local and out-of-town payments. On clearings and compensating arrangements, see Baskin and associates [10], Boguslavskiy [14], Gindin [178], Piletskiy [67], Shenger [74], Shvarts [77], and Taflya [83]. See also Mitel'man [194]. In the late sixties, about half of all payments were offset by various clearing arrangements (with only residual balances credited or debited), but this proportion declined between 1965 and 1970.

minor changes, which elsewhere would be made routinely by management on the advice of efficiency experts, are considered to be of such importance that they are frequently the subject of formal decisions by the Council of Ministers.

Delays in settling for goods occur mainly when consumer goods reaching retail outlets are selling slowly or not at all. This is the point in the deposit transfer circuit where the greatest "unplanned" use is made of short-term bank credit. It takes the form of an automatic (but not unlimited) extension of loans, either to the seller to bridge the settlement gap, or to the purchaser to enable him to make payment on the date due.

The volume of payments related to the production of goods is geared in large measure to the degree of vertical integration of industry. On the whole, the number of intermediate transactions is presumably smaller in the Soviet Union than in the nonsocialist industrial countries because raw materials and intermediate products reach manufacturers more directly and because final products pass through fewer stages of distribution before reaching ultimate purchasers. Also, no debits are created by payments related to trading in financial assets. On the other hand, the Soviet economy generates payment flows peculiar to it, such as those related to its budgetary system and reimbursements for various kinds of containers—returned to shippers. Deposit transfers in 1970 amounted to nearly 1½ trillion rubles, several times the value of GNP, just as bank debits in the United States are a multiple of the dollar value of GNP.

Financial Flows

In the Soviet economy, financial flows arise in the course of the central authorities' disposition of the social product (surplus value—in Marxian terminology, that part of the gross product that exceeds expenditures for labor, raw materials, and capital consumption) and from credit operations. In contrast to nonsocialist economies, flows related to investments never represent an exchange of money for financial assets through specialized institutions or instruments, but merely deposit transfers on the books of the State Bank and the Investment Bank.

Before the 1965 Reform, financial flows consisted essentially in one-track intermediation via the unified budget, which centralized all social income and redistributed it among the various levels of government and the economy. Financial flows also included loans and their repayment. The size, direction, and form of financial flows were determined by inventory norms, the allocation of "funded" commodities, the investment financing mechanism, et cetera. Any changes in these arrangements were automatically reflected in the financial flows. The amount of bank credit that might be required to facilitate and speed up planned flows depended on rules and regulations spelled out in considerable detail and changed infrequently (see Chapter 6).

The financial system of the Soviet Union, as depicted in a recent Soviet text book,[6] is summarized in Figure 5.1. Some of its components, such as social, personal, and property insurance and finances of consumer cooperatives, are outside the scope of this study.[7] Numerous Western students of the Soviet economy, such as R. W. Davies,[8] have also constructed schematic presentations of Soviet financial flows.

Note that the bulk of the social income, except for the growing portion retained by enterprises since the Reform, goes into the national budget, which distributes it to various lower-level units of government as well as to the various ministries and other economic organizations that undertake new investments; a smaller portion is transferred directly to special investment accounts of individual enterprises at the Investment Bank. Before 1965, about 90 percent of the social income was channeled through the budget, but the Reform inaugurated a multi-channel system of distribution of the social product, discussed more fully in the following section.

The fact that more than half of the national income flows through the budget—a much larger proportion than in the United States and other leading industrial countries—primarily reflects two decisions made early in the development of the Soviet eco-

---

[6]Ipatov [41], p. 7.

[7]Textbooks on Soviet finances, including those listed in the bibliography, provide detailed descriptions of the institutional arrangements in these areas, but availability of financial data is very limited. See Sitnin [78], Slavnyi [80].

[8]See [228].

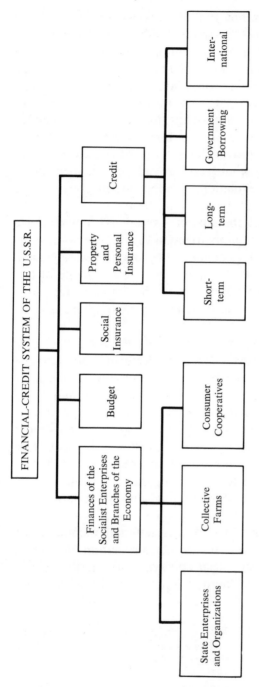

FIGURE 5.1

nomic system, once the currency was stabilized and an efficient fiscal system established. First, it was decided that the problem of obtaining adequate financing for state-initiated investment should be solved by direct pre-emption from the social product. Prior to the abolition of the machine-tractor stations, even the bulk of the fixed capital in *kolkhozes* was largely financed by the state. Only producers' cooperatives (mostly engaged in handicraft production) remained outside the area of state-planned and state-financed investment.

Secondly, nearly all expenditures of the lower governmental units are financed from a single, unified budget through transfers and, to a small degree, by certain categories of revenue allocated to them. Budget-financed expenditures, in addition to "ordinary expenditures" typical of the budgets of nonsocialist countries, cover the bulk of "collective consumption," which includes—in addition to free education—health, and other services subsidies for housing, transportation, and the like. Flows which in nonsocialist countries are normally channeled through separate social insurance funds are an integral part of the Soviet budget, from which all social security and social assistance payments are met. The only significant financial circuits outside the budget are a separate reserve fund for meeting casualty losses of state enterprises, and a nationwide state-operated personal property and life insurance organization.

Investment, largely in plant and equipment, is a major component of government expenditure at all levels. This constituted before the Reform about 50 percent of the funds spent by the central government, an average of 25 percent of the budgets of the constituent republics, and about 30 percent of the funds of municipalities, with particularly heavy expenditures in major cities. Municipal governments not only provide the various utilities and public services but also operate a variety of enterprises which supply the population with bread, milk, and other staples, as well as with repair and similar services, which all require investment in fixed plant.

The relative importance of the expenditures at the various levels of government has changed over time due to administrative reorganizations. The creation in 1957 of regional administrations *(Sovnarchoz)*, which placed a large number of enterprises under the supervision of the fifteen republics, automatically expanded at this level since enterprise profits create revenue for the supervising government unit. The subsequent reorganization, which returned individual industries of national importance to the supervision of national ministries, left a larger number of enterprises of local or regional significance under industry ministries of individual republics (or lower-echelon administrations) than before. Thus, some decentralization was carried over into the system now in effect. As a result, and largely because of increased spending for the economy, the 1969 share of the republics in the unified budget was 45 percent, as compared with about 25 percent between 1940 and 1955, and close to 60 percent between 1959 and 1965.

Some revenues, such as the turnover tax, are apportioned between the national budget and the budget of the republic in which they are collected. A variety of systematic and specific transfers of funds from higher-level to lower-level administrative units is required to balance the budgets of some units whose assigned fiscal resources are normally inadequate to cover all expenditures. This typically occurs in areas where spending on new investments is particularly heavy.

Budget receipts in 1971 reached almost 166 billion rubles, nine times the level of 1940. The main source of budgetary receipts and the distribution of expenditures between financing the economy and the other main categories of expenditure are shown in Table 5.1.

Nine-tenths of the budget receipts are obtained from enterprises. Nearly all revenues of the state enterprises in excess of prime costs (which, prior to the Reform, did not include the cost of capital) are siphoned off into the budget, either by transfer of the bulk of profits or through the collection of "turnover" (sales) taxes which are imposed on most consumer and some producers' goods. In 1971, the turnover tax alone accounted for 33 percent of total budgetary receipts, even though its relative contribution has been declining in recent years (to some degree due to an upward revision of factory prices for producers' goods in 1966 undertaken as part of the Reform). As late as 1950, enterprise profits provided only a little more receipts than the turnover tax, but since 1964 they have been exceeding its contribution by a rising margin. Periodic payments into the budget are based on estimated profits,

TABLE 5.1

The Budget of the USSR, Selected Years, 1940–1971
(in billions of rubles)

	1940	1950	1960	1970	1971
Receipts					
Turnover taxes	10.6	23.6	31.3	49.4	54.5
Payments from profits of state enterprises[a]	2.2	4.0	18.6	54.2	55.6
Social security taxes[b]	0.9	2.0	3.8	8.3	8.8
Income taxes paid by *kolkhozes,* other cooperative organizations and enterprises operated by organizations[c]	0.3	0.6	1.8	1.2	1.4
Individual income taxes and other receipts from the population	0.9	3.6	5.6	12.7	13.7
Government loans	1.1	3.1	0.9	0.5	0.3
Miscellaneous	2.0	5.4	15.1	30.4	35.7
Total	18.0	42.3	77.1	156.7	166.0
Expenditures					
Economy	5.8	15.8	34.1	74.6	80.4
Social and cultural purposes	4.1	11.7	29.4	55.9	59.4
Defense	5.7	8.3	9.3	17.9	17.9
General administration	0.7	1.4	1.1	1.7	1.8
Government loans[d]	0.3	0.5	0.7	0.1	0.1
Miscellaneous	0.8	3.6	8.5	4.4	0.6
Total	17.4	41.3	73.1	154.6	164.2

SOURCE: For 1971 [86], p. 481; for earlier years, various earlier volumes.

NOTE: Items do not add up to totals because of receipts and expenditures not specified. Footnotes added by author.

[a] For capital used, rents, charges against profits and remaining profits.

[b] Paid by employers.

[c] "Organizations" include trade unions, voluntary associations, etc.

[d] Amortization, interest, and administrative expenditures.

and so are substantial proportions of depreciation allowances and deductions for various special-purpose accounts (called "funds") of the generating enterprise. They are normally made automatically by the State Bank at frequent intervals (in some cases, every five days or weekly) from the general enterprise account to which sales proceeds are credited. If the accrual of funds in the enterprise's accounts is not adequate, obligatory payments into the budget are financed through bank loans.[9]

[9]See Chapter 6, footnote 7.

The expenditures side of the unified budget plays the key role in the redistribution of the national product. It embodies all major macroeconomic decisions, the division of current output between investment and consumption, the size and structure of collective consumption, and the apportionment of public spending between the various levels of government. The national budget thus fulfills a most important allocative function[10] with regard to investment flows (between industry and agriculture, among manufacturing industries, and between regions), which, in nonsocialist economies, is performed largely through the capital and credit markets.[11] Investment expenditure, mainly for plant equipment, rose from exactly one-third of total expenditures in 1940 to 47 percent in 1960. They have stayed close to this level through 1972, in spite of the much-emphasized claim that decentralization of investment financing was one of the main objectives of the Reform.

Kolkhozes are the only sector in which virtually all financial flows involve debtor-creditor relationships, and in which self-investment does not involve circuitous routing via the budget and its agent, the Investment Bank. Indeed, since the agricultural reforms of 1958, financial flows in the only sector of the Soviet economy that has no counterpart in any nonsocialist country have become quite similar to those generated by the agriculture sector in capitalist countries.

Financial flows not related to current household expenditures generated by the population are relatively small. Since the discontinuance of forced sales of government bonds in 1957, they involve mainly transactions in savings accounts.

---

[10]Konnik has estimated that, while only 56 percent of the turnover tax was collected from basic producers' goods industries in 1964, 88 percent of all capital investments were made in that group of industries [48], p. 98. See also Hahn [119], Lavigne [128], Leptin [130] and Seidenstrecher [144].

[11]At the same time, a large volume of transfers of investment funds between individual industries may by-pass the budget. Thus, in 1969 the automobile industry required transfers of funds amounting to 575 million rubles from other industries, while 800 million was siphoned off from the electric power industry. These are large amounts compared with total net fixed investment in industry.

Depreciation reserves not spent for capital maintenance and repair, profits and turnover taxes periodically transferred into the budget, together with retained enterprise profits, constitute what is known in Soviet planning as "financial accumulation." The concept is of limited analytical value since it does not include all funds, such as those of the *kolkhoz* sector, household savings, and a number of other sources available to meet investment needs.

Financial Flows of Enterprises

The restructuring of financial flows is the only significant change that has occurred in the financial area in forty years.[12] The Reform has given the enterprise somewhat more autonomy in the use of the profits it generates. Another important aspect of the Reform is the role assigned to profits.

PROFITS SINCE THE REFORM

Profits are now expected to depend increasingly on decisions of the enterprise manager and not on the proper execution of detailed plans handed down from above. Profitability has become a key criterion for the distribution of incentive rewards, but as a guide for resource allocation it has acquired only limited significance.

A lively discussion has been under way in the Soviet Union on whether the profit ratio determining the size of the social product should be related to labor inputs, to fixed capital only, or to different variants of total production costs.

Higher profit retention is a related aspect of the Reform. One of its main purposes is to induce individual enterprises to design schemes for additional compensation that would offer meaningful incentives to management and workers. The other is to enlarge, within limits, the investment independence of individual enterprises.

When actual profit and sales targets are exceeded the attached rewards are relatively large, as payments into the government budget on extra profits are at reduced rates and decline with the rise in "unplanned profits." Profits in excess of the planned targets expand retained earnings, permitting the manager to undertake additional minor investments to spur productivity and, within set limits, to raise the real income of workers through improved fringe benefits and additional cash payments in the form of various premiums.

However, a higher profit retention does not influence directly the distribution of investments. In particular, on a macroeconomic level, the higher profit rates in consumer goods have not

---

[12]There have been some minor changes, such as the introduction of loans to finance small-scale mechanization discussed in Chapter 6, "Medium-term Credit."

resulted in a rechanneling of funds into this sector from producer's goods industries, since overall economic targets are set independently of profit considerations. The notion that investment decisions should be related to enterprise profits remains irrelevant for the Soviet Union.

With regard to prices, the only flexibility available to plant managers is to discontinue production of profitless or low-profit items and to replace them with virtually identical products embodying minor modifications, entitling the enterprise to submit to the price-fixing authorities a request to set a higher price on the "new" product. For example, by replacing a wooden frying pan handle with a plastic one, or by moving a zipper on a blouse from the back to the side, the enterprise can obtain a reclassification of the product, and thereby a higher price tag. Thus, over time, the price index is protected (since it is ostensibly based on standard merchandise), while the enterprise improves its profitability.

With prices of inputs and outputs still fixed by outside authority, improving productivity is the only way to increase profits. Since the technological equipment of existing plants tends to be frozen largely at the level of initial construction, although the new system makes it easier to allocate funds for the acquisition of superior and new technology, most of the improved productivity must come from labor inputs, better management, and avoidance of disruption in production due to such factors as breakdowns in the flow of physical inputs and in equipment and unbalanced inventories. Given these limitations, it is understandable that the Reform was presented largely in terms of a new system of management rather than as a new approach to the restructuring of the basic mechanism of the Soviet economy.

Furthermore, ministries and other higher-echelon administrative units are not interested in enterprise profits alone but in the performance of the whole set of overall indicators. Those expressed in physical quantities remain of key importance, since the goals of administrative units in charge of the economy, on the national, regional, and local level, continue to be set in terms of physical targets. Profit targets continue to be administratively set as a percentage of total factor costs, and there is relatively little fluctuation in this percentage among, and practically none within, industries. While the range of key indicators designed to guide the enterprise's activities has been reduced, with financial indicators gaining prominence, higher economic authorities continue to issue various kinds of binding directives to the enterprise, including indicators *(direktivnye pokazately)* stipulated in real rather than monetary terms.

In fact, the redefinition of targets appears to be a mere formality for a large segment of output. This is particularly true of goods contracted for in advance (typically, producers' goods and defense industries), and of staple items (such as basic raw materials, fuel, building materials, and most food products) where supply shortages are the rule and demand growth is secular. The area in which the new system has led to greater responsiveness to final demand, with the recognition that not all of the output may be salable, or that it is salable only with price concessions, does not seem to extend much beyond semidurable and durable consumer goods.

Indeed, with factory prices fixed, total sales targets are actually identical with targets previously specified in quantitative terms. The important difference arises from calibrating the target on goods actually sold rather than produced, and from the greater flexibility in the composition of output. Enterprise managers have been reluctant, however, to introduce new products requiring radically new technology, while at the same time they have been eager to make small changes in design that may enable them to obtain upward price revisions. To combat management inertia in promoting technology innovations, additional measures were taken in July 1972 requiring enterprises to set specific sales targets for new products "corresponding in technico-economic terms to the highest domestic and foreign achievements."

Before the Reform, virtually all of an enterprise's profits went to the budget, except for a very small statutory proportion retained for designated special-purpose funds. Now profits are distributed via three main channels according to their three main functions: as a fiscal source, a source of fixed and working capital for the enterprise, and a source of various special-purpose funds "for stimulation" controlled by the enterprise. The distribution of profits under the new system is summarized in Table 5.2.

The budget's share consists of three parts: charge on invested capital, quasi rent ("fixed payments"), and a residual remaining

TABLE 5.2

Use of Profits After the Reform

Payments into the budget	Charge on fixed investment and allotted working capital
	Fixed payments (rentals)
	Residual profits
Planned expenditures of the enterprise	Financing of centrally planned capital investment
	Increase in working capital
	Reserves for giving temporary financial assistance
	Amortization of loans for financing fixed investment
	Amortization of loans for temporarily supplementing own working capital
	Absorption of losses in operating factory housing and other facilities for the benefit of the staff
Formation of funds for stimulation	For material stimulation
	For socialist competition
	For socio-cultural projects and dwelling construction
	For stimulating output of consumer goods
	For development of production

NOTE: Profits are from the sale of output and some other sources, such as the sale of redundant equipment. This list is adapted from Darkov and Maksimov [23], p. 103.

after all statutory deductions for funds that the enterprise can retain are made. On the whole, in many enterprises this residual is still quite large in relation to total profits. (It is, of course, nonexistent in the case of enterprises with planned deficits which receive subsidies, including those designed to nourish some of the statutory "funds for stimulation," discussed below.)

A second major portion of the profits goes to finance certain categories of fixed capital investment or to increase working capital. As illustrated in Table 5.2, such funds can be used either (see Chapter 6) for projects that are centrally planned but financed from retained earnings, or to repay bank loans obtained in previous years for such projects. Profits of a given year can be used to finance not only current and past investments but also future investments by building up balances at the Investment Bank.

Other uses of retained earnings are for bridging temporary flow gaps in special funds for the payment of subsidies for housing and other facilities built by the enterprise for the benefit of the staff, and, finally, to expand working capital or repay loans obtained in previous periods for this purpose.

The various "funds for stimulation" replace the "directors' fund," which had existed before World War II, was reinstated between 1946 and 1956, and was subsequently renamed the "enterprise fund." Earlier attempts at using part of enterprise profits to stimulate productivity by providing limited financial incentives had little success. Payments into the directors' or enterprise funds depended largely on overfulfillment of the plan. Enterprise managers were understandably interested in inducing planners to set low targets in order to receive bonuses for "plan overfulfillment." Even so, payments into the fund depended on the simultaneous achievement of a large number of specified targets, and failure to achieve even one of them reduced, or even completely removed, the prospects for a bonus. Finally, the fact that diverse purposes such as financing investment not provided for in the plan and expenditures for collective staff benefits, were met from the enterprise fund reduced its effectiveness as an incentive to increase production.[13] Prior to the Reform, depending on the industry, 1 to 6 percent of any additional profits were available for this fund.

Two of the new incentive funds initiated under the Reform are designed to distribute additional monetary rewards to management and workers either (a) on the basis of a specified formula, or (b) as a reward for exceptional performance entitling winners in "socialist competition" to receive additional rewards (see Table 5.2). The distribution formula is set by each individual enterprise and may vary from department to department. In some cases, special criteria, different from those applied for the fulfillment of plan targets, are used in determining an individual department's claim for bonus payments, and shadow prices rather than official prices may be used.[14] Such bonus payments may, in certain cases, result in significant additions to basic wages and salaries. Moreover, the new arrangements also widen the distribution of

[13]See Alexandrov [4], pp. 44–45.
[14][4], p. 48.

such additional compensation to benefit the entire work force, not only management and the professional staff, which had been largely the case under the old system. Another fund provides for fringe benefits in the form of staff facilities like factory housing, kindergartens, children's camps, and vacations for workers at nominal cost.

The third "development fund" can be used by the enterprise itself for research expenditures, some limited product development activities, and certain specified types of investment not provided for in the plan.

Finally, enterprises are encouraged to make the widest possible use of remainders and by-products that are likely to help overcome shortages and that can be disposed of locally. The additional profits resulting from such operations are treated in a way to stimulate their production further. The use of incentives is discussed in more detail in a following section of this chapter.

The order in which profits are distributed among the budget, the various funds, and the other recipients continues to be determined by administratively set priorities and allocation formulas. The differentiations between the rules applying to planned profits and those governing additional profits, as well as the special procedures set up for enterprises requiring subsidies since their plans anticipate losses rather than profits, were unaffected by the Reform.

PAYMENTS TO THE BUDGET

As illustrated in Table 5.2, a portion of enterprise profits goes to the budget as interest payments. Interest, under the name of "charge on capital," is now charged on both fixed and working capital. To equalize the cost of new and existing fixed capital originally supplied on a grant basis, a charge has been imposed on the depreciated value of capital assets in use at the time the new system became applicable to an industry following the 1965 Reform. Enterprises that require subsidies ("planned deficit units") are exempt from the capital use charge. The ancestry of this charge can be traced to discussions during the NEP period. In 1922–1923 a proposal was made by the Commissariat (now Ministry of Finance) to introduce a capital use tax for all state-owned enterprises as a means of improving the use of fixed and working capital. A rate of 4 to 5 percent was discussed at the time.[15] While the charge on capital is applied to gross profits, it is a cost factor in setting prices. It may be regarded as a property tax, or, alternatively, as the minimum socially acceptable rate of return on productive assets (capital use tax), or as the minimum share of government in enterprise profits.[16] Its introduction affected the rate of profits in individual industries and for the economy as a whole.

The question of what the proper level and structure of charges on invested funds should be is far from resolved. In the first full year of the Reform rates were set uniformly at 6 percent, but in the following year (1967) they varied within a range of 3 to 10 percent for individual industries.[17] The whole problem of the proper charge for capital, its relation to planned profits, and the disposition of such profits, including the determination of the share to be retained for the "funds for stimulation," is still being hotly debated, and competing schemes are being put forward,[18] including proposals for differential rates between branches of the same industry and even between individual enterprises.

The existence of quasi rents is recognized by the introduction of a rental ("fixed") payment with a rate set for fairly long periods in advance in each case when it is levied. Given the divergence of profit rates in individual industries, the ratio of this rental payment to total costs varies widely. Differential rents are fixed either as a percentage of sales or as a fixed amount per unit of output, and tend to equalize the production cost of each enterprise.

In effect, these fixed rents are akin to the turnover tax, except that they are imposed on an enterprise (or entire industry or industry branch) rather than on a product basis. They tend to equalize net profits among individual units within the same industry, where otherwise, with pricing on the basis of average industry costs, enterprises enjoying natural, locational, or technological advantages would obtain a higher profit rate and therefore retain a greater share of profits.

The introduction of the capital use and rental charges, while reducing the amount collected under the heading of "remaining

---

[15]See Mitel'man [194] and Decaillot [228].
[16]Ipatov [41], p. 20.
[17]Tulebaev [88], p. 13.
[18]See, for instance, Brazovskaya [170] and the literature quoted therein.

profit," has not changed the total share of profits in the economy going to the budget. Payments for capital use and quasi rents are a relatively small part of profits as calculated prior to the Reform. They do not depend on changes in sales or profitability which affect "remaining profits" only. The share of profits retained by the enterprise is determined under the new system by the net profits, defined as profits measured by "accounting profitability," from which fixed rental payments and capital use payments are deducted.

The Reform had only a very slight overall effect on the sources of budgetary income and on the structure of expenditures. In 1971 the share of national income channeled into the budget was essentially the same (52.7 percent) as in the year the Reform was initiated (52.9 percent in 1965). The budgetary receipts derived from payments by the socialized sector of the economy remained very close to the old level (91.1 percent, compared with 91.8 percent in 1965); and the expenditures for the economy, overwhelmingly for investment purposes, rose (from 45.7 percent in 1965 to 48.9 percent in 1971), in spite of all the emphasis on decentralized investments from profits retained by individual enterprises.[19]

FINANCING FIXED CAPITAL INVESTMENT

Financing fixed capital investment from budgetary resources on a nonreturnable grant basis under the standard system had involved considerable misallocation of resources and costly delays in the completion of construction projects. Since the Reform, the financing of fixed investment has been gradually shifting toward a combination of retained enterprise profits, depreciation reserves and bank loans. If and when this process is accelerated, the proportion of national income redistributed through the budget will tend to decline, and that of self-investment and bank loans, to increase.

The ultimate objective of the new arrangement is to achieve a more rational pattern of investment in productive capital and a reduction in investment in relation to output. If the Reform is to be more than a substitution of control mechanisms, financial

---

[19]Vinokur [209]; for 197, computed from [86], 1972, p. 481.

processes must acquire new functions. The significant question is, therefore, whether the functional relationship of the financial system to resource allocation and profit maximization is being changed. Thus far, central accumulation and allocation of investment resources has remained largely unimpaired, though implementation is shifted to a multichannel system of fund flows which, among other things, reduces the circuitous flow of resources between the units that generate them.

Changes in the flow of investment funds (including depreciation reserves) and credit are bound to have some effect on patterns of real investment, inventory behavior, and the producers' price structure, and thus on consumer welfare. The broad question is, therefore, whether reforms in the area of financing will tend to raise efficiency of investment, accelerate the rate of real output growth, and improve the relative apportionment of the increased output between consumers and the state.

One change that received considerable publicity when the Reform was announced involved (a) shifting fixed investment financing from grants to repayable loans,[20] and (b) permitting individual enterprises to retain a greater share of profits and depreciation reserves in a move toward greater decentralization of investment. However, greater decentralization of investment funds does not necessarily mean greater decentralization of decision making. Investment decisions remain largely centralized in the bureaucratic hands of the planning agencies, industrial ministries, and the *glavks* and their organizational successors. Even most of the resources of the decentralized enterprise funds must still be spent on centrally planned investment.[21] The state continues to control the level and the broad distribution of investments. (Since 1971, the upper limit of investment is set by the relevant ministries of the various republics, depending on who supervises the individual enterprise. In the new scheme of things, there is no more room than under the old system for anything even remotely resembling a capital market. The principal channel for enterprise initiative is "arguing it out" with the supervisory and planning

[20]Partial shifting to loan financing of investment in fixed capital had been under discussion since at least 1957.

[21]In 1965, for instance, 38.7 percent of all centrally planned investment was financed from enterprise resources. See Poskonov [70]. For a detailed discussion of the various kinds of enterprise funds which, under the standard system, could be used to finance decentralized investments, see [93], pp. 37–41.

authorities. The bulk of investment designed to increase existing plant capacity and investments involving a variety of minor projects remain centrally planned but no longer necessarily grant-financed. Loan financing of part of all such projects by the state and by the Investment Bank will gradually lead to the formation of revolving loan funds by the latter and reduce the need for giving them additional resources from the national budget.

Grants from the budget continue to be made not only for social overhead investments like schools and hospitals, but also for such priority projects as new industries, large plants (such as those in the automotive industry), and major programs for the development of national resources. In principle, they are to be limited to large *de novo* projects, designed to change the structure of production and the geographic distribution of industry, to introduce new technology, to open up major new sources of raw materials, and to construct important hydro-electrical projects. Needless to say, all defense-related investments, as well as those connected with atomic energy and space programs, continue to be budget-financed. While these expenditures are never mentioned in Soviet literature, they are no doubt subject to rules different from those applying to other investments, and what changes, if any, the Reform has brought.

The change in the channeling of investment funds between 1965 and 1971 can only be described as modest. In 1971, 59 percent of total profits in all branches of the economy still went to the Treasury, as against 70 percent in 1965 (and only 64 percent in 1960). During the same period, the percentage retained for investment purposes rose from 10 to 13 percent—not much above the 1960 level of 12 percent. In money terms, the increase amounted to about 8 billion rubles. Depreciation allowances rose from 18.8 billion rubles to 32.1 billion, of which half were retained by enterprises each year for plant maintenance. Thus, the total fund for investments available internally rose. Some part of retained profits had to be invested in centrally planned projects, however. As a result, the amount that individual enterprises can expend independently for capital projects, including those required to upgrade technology, and even for maintenance and repairs has not been significantly increased. It remains to be seen whether profits put at the disposal of the newly created associations of enterprises *(ob'edineniye)*, in fact, horizontal or vertical combinations of enterprises which retain a large amount of independence, will contribute to greater decentralization of fixed investment decisions.

Long-term loans (outstanding at year's end) for investment purposes in the six-year period rose only by 6.3 billion rubles despite their tenfold increase from the 0.7 billion level at the end of 1965.[22] This roughly 21 billion expansion in retained profits, depreciation allowances, and loans compared with an increase by 35.5 billion in budgetary expenditures for the economy, over-whelmingly for fixed investment purposes. Thus, so far, the gap between announced objective and actual performance remains very wide; the share of centrally directed investments may have actually increased rather than decreased since the Reform was launched.

During the last ten years prior to the Reform, retained profits available for "decentralized investments" amounted to only about 2 percent of total new investments in the Soviet economy.

While the Reform undoubtedly gave enterprises greater finan-cial control over their own capital investment, it did so without simultaneously improving the availability of real resources to implement this more decentralized investment. This fact consti-tutes one of the principal limitations of the Reform. For it is clear that the one major reason for changes in investment financing had been to help solve one of the main problems of capital formation in the Soviet Union—the chronic immobilization of resources in uncompleted construction projects and hoarded building sup-plies[23] and the lack of pressure to complete individual projects as rapidly as possible.

---

[22]Computed from [86], 1972, pp. 465, 466, 480, and 486. These figures relate to the entire economy, excluding *kolkhozes,* and thus include state farms, municipal enterprises, et ce-tera. Separate data for manufacturing are not available.

[23]In many cases, plant managers have been unable to find contractors willing to take on additional jobs since their resources were already fully committed to major projects approved by central authorities and were included in lists of eligible projects. See Petra-kov [197], p. 181. Thus, in the third full year after the initiation of the Reform, enterprises which had switched to the "new system of economic steering" were able to spend only 47 percent of the funds earmarked for housing and the construction of social and cultural facilities such as clubs and movie theatres. Only 58 percent of their *total* "funds for economic stimulation" were spent in that year. In 1969, only 85 percent of all construction scheduled to be completed was actually finished. Lack of funds and other shortcomings in planning and execution account for the shortfall. See Kartashova [179]. At the beginning of 1971 incomplete construction of retail stores in rural areas exceeded the value of a full year's investment. See Sotnikov [205].

Project completion was delayed by many factors prior to the Reform. Since performance was measured in terms of gross value of work performed (construction put in place) rather than value added, subcontracting construction firms tended to give preference to those operations that yielded the largest "work performed" figures, with the result that the flow of many projects was much delayed.[24] Another factor was poor coordination between construction and equipment delivery schedules, as well as the tendency to place contracts for equipment in excess of financial resources available.[25]

To remedy this situation, the Reform has instituted moves designed to increase financial incentives for the completion of projects. Prior to 1965, payments were made as a rule for each individual job (in 1954, for instance, to the extent of 95 percent of all disbursements) irrespective of whether it resulted in additional operating capacity. One of the ways in which the Reform began to use financial levers was to make partial progress payments dependent on the percentage of scheduled operating capacity completed. In a more radical step, in some cases progress payments on each phase of a construction job completed have been replaced by a system under which the Investment Bank pays the contracting firm only after the completed plant is ready for delivery, but by 1972 only a small part of all projects financed was subject to this procedure.

Other shortcomings of the standard system, such as interruption of construction because of inadequate financial planning, [26] are to be remedied in a variety of ways. Projects requiring bank financing must now submit flow-of-funds projections to document availability of funds over the entire period of construction and loan amortization and penalty rates are charged when loans are not amortized on schedule.

Despite these measures, there is little evidence that the Reform

[24]Belkin and Inventor [13] have estimated that projects in process of completion absorb 50 percent more resources than would be required if their average time of construction was comparable to average U.S. performance.

[25]For a fairly candid discussion of reasons behind the inefficiency of the construction industry and of the attempts of the Investment and State Banks to foster improvements, see Yunik [91], pp. 13ff. and pp. 133–135.

[26]Poskonov [70], p. 260. Immediately prior to the Reform (1964–1965), the average cost of projects sponsored by local Soviets exceeded estimates by 18.9 percent. Alexandrov [4], p. 89.

has succeeded in improving the chronic problem of failure of investment projects to be completed on time.

ENTERPRISE FINANCES AND THE REFORM

Has the enterprise made real strides toward greater autonomy under the Reform? There are no easy answers to this question. It is not clear to what extent any of the moves toward autonomy have been actually implemented in various industries. The creation of associations of enterprises (*ob'edineniye*) [27] represents a substitution of administrative authorities interposed between the enterprise and the industrial ministry (such as *glavk*). Their creation does not necessarily mean more autonomy for the enterprise, since they can possibly also result in the transfer to the association of some decisions previously left with the enterprise manager. It is not clear as yet whether enterprises have, on balance, won at the expense of the top and intermediate levels of the economic hierarchy.

Reducing circuitous channeling of investment funds means an increase in funds retained by enterprises, and a shift to credit on turnover simplifies their short-term credit relations with the State Bank. It must be kept in mind, however, that the financial flexibility of managers in dealing with the funds retained by the enterprise has been increased only within narrow limits.[28] Furthermore, retained enterprise funds can still be transfered to other enterprises (decree of February 12, 1966) under ill-defined conditions at the discretion of higher-level economic administrations.[29] Nevertheless, funds subject to management control are normally accumulated in segregated bank accounts pending disbursement, and enough of these temporary accumulations seep into the gen-

---

[27]*Ob'edineniye* is an association of enterprises, usually within the same industry and region. It represents a standard administrative level between the *glavk* and an individual enterprise. (It corresponds to the "trust" in earlier periods of administrative organization.) On the arrangements for the extension of credit to associations, see Stundyuk [206].

[28]For example, with trade union approval, up to 20 percent of funds allocated to the bonus fund can be used for fringe benefits (such as factory housing construction), and vice versa. See Chistyakov, "The New System of Stimulation Funds and their Role in Increasing Efficiency of Production," in Alexandrov [4], p. 56.

[29]Eidonova, "Profits, Rentability, and Their Role in Increasing Efficiency of Production," in Alexandrov [4], p. 36. Examples are given where profits were transferred in their entirety to other enterprises supervised by the same ministry.

eral cash balances of the enterprise to offer various possibilities for escaping constraints imposed by planners and controllers.

Moreover, ministries and other economic authorities (such as *glavks*) can act as intermediaries, borrowing from the Bank and making credit available to individual enterprises for the purpose of retiring funds borrowed to bring working capital up to required levels. The same authorities can also remove the need for borrowing either by replenishing working capital through transfers from other enterprises under their supervision or by simply lowering the working capital requirements (norms) they impose.[30]

As a result of the Reform, funds of enterprises designated as "internal resources" have increased in relation to their working capital. Such "temporarily available funds," which are not considered part of the "owned working capital," include, in addition to retained profits earmarked for various specific purposes but not as yet actually expended, also (a) profits payable into the budget but not yet actually transferred (these transfers, as well as those to the Investment Bank for the financing of centrally planned investments, are being currently made only three times a month, at roughly ten day intervals), as well as (b) a large part of accounts payable. It was estimated at the beginning of 1971 that such "internal resources" constituted about one-fifth of the *total* working capital of state enterprises; less than one-third of these internal resources were at that time actually taken into account in financial planning (as *ustoichivye passivy*—"stable liabilities"), so that the individual enterprises had a certain flexibility in using the remainder. A special investigation conducted by the Central Statistical Office (TsSU) as of January 1, 1971, revealed that 70 percent of these "unplanned internal financial resources" were actually used for bridging various shortages in funds resulting from situations not foreseen in financial plans, thus obviating the need for unplanned bank loans or other outside assistance. Typical uses of such resources included financing of inventories not eligible for bank loans, meeting expenditures for which resources provided in the enterprise's financial plan did not actually materialize, and reducing accounts payable.[31]

[30]See Kartashova [43].

[31]See Agraponov [160] and Shermenev [75].

Enterprise balance sheets also show a certain amount of resources provided by creditors even though inter-enterprise lending is prohibited. Some of the amounts shown in this

Greater profit retention and the extension of credit on turnover have increased average cash balances of enterprises with the State Bank (which prior to the Reform averaged 4 to 5 percent of working capital). They have somewhat reduced the need for short-term credit, and have provided enterprises more opportunity for maneuvering in spite of the existing safeguards against the use of funds accumulated for purposes other than those specified. The level and structure of bank interest rates apparently do not encourage loan repayment before maturity, while abolition of the payment of interest on free balances encourages their use for unauthorized purposes if the vigilance of the controllers of the State Bank can be circumvented.[32]

FINANCIAL INCENTIVES

Before the Reform, enterprises had very limited opportunities for technical modernization, and few incentives existed to stimulate efforts in that direction. The Reform recognizes that financial incentives on an individual as well as on a group (team or enterprise) basis are indispensable for increasing efficiency and stimulating initiative leading to cost reductions and generally improved performance.

Bonuses can be paid for a variety of reasons. The precise basis on which such payments are made is fixed by the director of the enterprise, ostensibly with the participation of the trade union committee. The premium schemes of individual enterprises may cover individual workers and members of the technical and managerial staff as well as groups of workers, such as departments or teams ("brigades"), including premiums for winners of intrafactory competition for superior performance, known as "socialist competition." The resources for such premiums are derived from savings achieved in "planned" payrolls as well as from the various premium funds (see section above, "Profits Since the

---

category are float (bills in the process of collection), contested bills, as well as bills due for which settlement credit was not available to the buyer and which may be considered as trade credit. The percentage of total amounts due from creditors (including drafts in the process of collection) in total working capital varies by industry, over time and for individual enterprises within an industry, but usually averages between 8 and 12 percent.

[32]This is shown by Lisitsian [188] and [189] on the basis of several sample surveys. One survey of machine building enterprises shows that the special funds for the stimulation of the staff and for decentralized investment accounted for 15 percent of total "nonplanned expenditures" on January 1, 1966, but for as much as 47.3 percent on October 1, 1969.

Reform"). All premium schemes require approval by the supervising economic administration and must be within the limits set by the Council of Ministers for each industry.[33]

To increase the effectiveness of incentives, the profit funds earmarked for additional employee compensation are made available, although in reduced amounts, even if individual plan targets are not achieved, while under the old system no premiums were payable unless all targets were met.[34]

There is little evidence to indicate that the main objective of the new financial incentives has been achieved. After nearly a decade of discussion and considerable experimentation, no satisfactory way has been found to find a workable bonus system that would heighten the staff's interest in raising productivity and introducing new technology. The new system of determining bonuses retains the earlier procedures. No mechanism has emerged that would automatically make factory workers and various levels of technical, managerial, and administrative personnel strive for more efficient use of existing equipment, the introduction of superior technology, and for the elimination of bottlenecks due to resources immobilized in construction or the distribution process. Instead, a new, rigid system of bonuses has been combined with the previous one. Moreover, neither the bureaucracy of the higher-level economic administrations (*glavks,* for example), on whose initiative, or at least approval, technological and managerial progress depends, nor the staff of the State Bank and the Investment Bank participate in the new system of incentives. These groups may derive some satisfaction from the fact that the targets they set, the norms they determine, and the repayment schedules they impose are possibly met with greater regularity than before. But their interest remains in playing safe by setting targets low enough to show "overfulfillment," and by refraining from innovations that contain the risk of something going wrong.

One of the generally recognized effects of the Reform has been a greater seepage of profits into labor compensation. With profit-related bonuses becoming a significant part of money income,

---

[33]Up to 20 percent of the resources accruing to the three individual funds for stimulation can be reallocated during the year. See Belobzhetsky [169]. See also Leeman [243].

[34]Slavnyi [79], p. 35. On the rules governing the formation of funds for stimulation in enterprises with planned losses, see Tarsov and Utkin [208].

control of payroll disbursement has proved an insufficient means of planning and balancing real flows of consumer goods and of money incomes. As a result of the broader use of bonuses and other changes introduced by the Reform, in some industries labor income has increased more rapidly than productivity. To counteract the resulting inflationary pressures, measures have been taken to transfer to the "fund for social and cultural purposes" at least part of the funds that should have automatically become available for individual bonus payments under the Reform, or, alternatively, to postpone their disbursement to the following year.[35]

By 1971, manufacturing enterprises were distributing more than 4.1 billion rubles in bonuses, and, if the "funds for stimulation" were distributed proportionately in the other branches of the economy, the total disbursed by all state enterprises must have been near 5.4 billion rubles. Interestingly enough, the amount accumulated for this purpose but not yet disbursed at the end of 1971 in manufacturing alone amounted to nearly two-thirds of the sum actually paid out. By comparison, the two funds carried over from pre-Reform years (premiums for "socialist competition" and for creating and introducing new technology) yielded only 36 million and 586 million rubles, respectively, in all state enterprises.[36] Once the provisions of the Reform are fully and generally implemented and the financial incentives have had their full effect on productivity, as much as one-fifth of the total compensation of employees is expected to come from the incentive fund, with perhaps a more than proportionate share going to the engineering and management group.[37]

[35]There are indications that, despite the new emphasis on consumer goods, their output has been lagging behind effective household demand, and shortages for specific geographic areas persist. This was particularly true in 1968 and 1969, when payrolls increased at a more rapid rate than productivity, partly as a result of a general upward revision of wage scales. The various old and new problems slowing down expansion of services to consumers also revealed themselves again. See Smirnov [81], p. 84 and Zverev [93]. While during the three years preceding the Reform (1963–1965) annual increases in consumer services exceeded that in consumer goods by about 15 percent, in 1967–1969 the value of services grew less than that of goods available to consumers. See Slavnyi [203].

[36][86], 1972, pp. 478 and 479.

[37]The new provisions for worker compensation affect almost exclusively production workers, whose share in the labor force has been declining mainly as a result of the growth of nonmanufacturing industries. The percentage of nonproduction workers in the labor force, only 11.7 percent in 1940, had risen to 20 percent by 1965 and has doubtless increased since. Slavnyi [79], p. 15.

6

The Role and Structure of Credit

THE state in the Soviet Union has complete control over all types of credit, operating chiefly through a single agency, the State Bank. The aggregate volume of credit is determined by the production and distribution goals set in real terms.[1] When physical plans are revised, related credit plans must be modified accordingly. Under the pre-Reform system, the primary role of banks was to provide working capital to the state-owned sector of the economy.[2] Prior to the 1965 Reform, the significance of bank credit was only marginal in fixed capital formation, and in a slow uptrend in the farm sector.

Volume and Composition of Credit

The total volume of credit is considerably smaller in the Soviet Union than in the United States, and the range of end uses for which credit is available is much narrower. The contrast is high-

[1]"The basic function of Soviet credit is in the planned use of the resources of the socialist economy and in speeding up the tempo of the enlarged socialist production" is a standard statement in textbooks, speeches, and articles by Soviet government and State Bank officials.

The private segment of the economy, which sells its output at free market prices, is smaller than in any other country in the socialist bloc. It is ignored by Soviet economists, official statistics, and the State Bank.

[2]For a discussion of ambiguities of "working capital" as used in the Soviet Union, see Becker [101]. See also Bychkov [20], Campbell [106], and Podolski [139]. For a further discussion of working capital, see Mitel'man's review of Melkov's book [61] in *D.K.,* October 1970.

lighted in Table 6.1, which compares credit outstanding at the end of 1969 in the two countries.[3]

In the Soviet Union, the total amount of credit outstanding at the end of 1969 was equivalent to about one-fifth of the gross social product. By contrast, the amount of credit in use in the United States was nearly double the value of GNP. Even adding an estimated 35.7 billion dollars for de facto trade credit available to state enterprises, total credit outstanding in the Soviet Union comes to less than $165 billion, or only one-eighth of the comparable U.S. figure.[4] In the United States, the overwhelming bulk of credit is extended by deposit institutions. The credit not evidenced by credit market instruments ("other credit") mainly represents trade credit, which alone is almost double the amount of all loans extended by the Soviet banking system.

Loans to the federal government are excluded from both totals. In the Soviet Union the bulk of such borrowing consisted of bonds placed with the population, while in the United States, government securities are held by business firms and financial institutions as well as by individuals. The bulk of the total working capital of the Soviet economy (excluding *kolkhozes*) consisted of amounts due to various creditors. This category mainly includes accounts (including those past due) payable to other state enterprises rather than merchandise purchased on credit terms, as well as amounts due the Treasury (and usually payable within a few days) and other creditors.

Short-term lending still accounts for the overwhelming bulk of all credit, as illustrated in Table 6.2, hovering around 90 percent in recent years. The authorities set the uniform standard rules for the issuance of credit, specifying in great detail the activities qualifying for credit financing (i.e., collection of drafts, or payment of taxes). Before 1959 short-term credit extended directly to

---

[3]Comparative statistics like those presented in Table 6.1 are subject to a variety of limitations. For instance, U.S. figures include loans to foreigners, while Soviet foreign indebtedness, limited to foreign governments and extended solely by the Treasury, is omitted from the data in Table 6.1. Melkov [61], Ch. II contains a brief but valuable historical review of the credit activities and of the liabilities of the State Bank.

[4]Note that ruble figures are converted into dollars at the official rate applicable at the end of 1971.

TABLE 6.1

Credit Outstanding in the Soviet Union and the United States, 1969
(billions of dollars, outstanding at end of year)

	USSR				U.S.[a]		
	Bank Credit	Trade Credit	Total		Credit Market Instruments	Other	Total
Kolkhozes	12.4		12.4	Farming[b]	45.1	8.9	54.0
				Nonfarm, noncorporate business	70.1	−1.2	68.9
State enterprises[c]	106.1	35.7	141.8	Nonfarm corporations	335.3	194.3	529.6
Households				Households[a]	440.6		461.9
Mortgages	2.7[e]			Home mortgages	260.4		
Consumer credit	3.7		6.4	Consumer credit	122.5		
				Other[f]	57.6	21.3	
Cooperative and official organizations	3.8		3.8[g]				
Local government	—		—[h]	State and local government	137.1	5.9	148.0
				Federally-sponsored credit agencies	30.6	4.5	35.2
Total	128.7	35.7	164.4	Total	1,058.8	233.7	1,292.6

Notes to Table 6.1

SOURCES: [86], 1969, pp. 774–779; and Federal Reserve Board, *Flow of Funds Accounts: Financial Assets and Liabilities Outstanding, 1959–1971*, Washington, D.C., 1972.

NOTE: Components may not add to totals because of rounding. Rubles are converted at the rate of 1 ruble = $1.1.

a Excludes financial business and loans extended to foreigners.

b Includes farm business other than farmers.

c Includes state farms, excludes credit to retail trade for financing household purchases.

d Includes nonprofit organizations.

e Covers construction cooperatives and individuals.

f Includes "other mortgages," security credit, and miscellaneous bank loans.

g Long-term only.

h Very small amount of loans to municipalities for improvements included with state enterprises.

---

the agricultural sector was financed almost exclusively via state procurement organizations outside the credit system.[5] The uses of short-term credit, by major economic sector and by main purpose, are illustrated in Tables 6.3 and 6.4.

While the relative importance of long-term loans has been on the rise since 1965, their share in the total credit volume at the end of 1971—at least about 17 percent—was roughly the same as in 1940. The increase from 1965 to 1971 was mainly due to a larger credit flow to collective farms and cooperative housing. In contrast to the pre-1959 period, when the volume of long-term credit granted to *kolkhozes* had been very small, total long-term lending to agriculture, including credit for the acquisition of livestock, averaged close to 6.5 billion in the 1959–1965 period, and rose to 8.4 billion in 1968.[6]

While it makes credit available to municipal governments for financing municipal services, the Bank does not extend credit to the national government[7] and to the relatively small number of farmers not on collective farms.

[5]See also Parchenko and associates [64].

[6]For more details on long-term lending to agriculture, see Yunik and Miseyuk [91], pp. 153ff and Pzybyla [247]. Golev [36] and Katsenelenbaum [44] review the situation prior to the changes made in 1958. Both sources contain a considerable amount of statistical data; Golev includes a valuable historical introduction.

[7]Credit to enterprises for financing their payments to the budget in effect constitutes indirect credit to the national government: the budgetary surplus resulting from such payments is, in effect, a counterpart of bank loans. This type of credit arises from the

TABLE 6.2

Loans by All Banks, Selected Years
(in billions of rubles, outstanding at year's end)

	1933	1940	1950	1960	1965	1970	1971
				Short Term			
Industry		2.1	7.0	14.6	23.6	35.5	37.2
Agriculture (including							
kolkhozes)		0.2	0.6	3.0	4.6	9.5	12.0
Kolkhozes		*a*	*a*	0.7	0.4	2.5	3.4
Wholesale trade[b]		1.6	6.1	16.3	25.7	35.1	38.6
Total[c]	1.1	5.6	17.3	42.7	68.0	108.2	115.4
				Long Term			
Collective farms	0.1	0.2	0.7	2.4	3.9	10.3	11.6
State and cooperative							
enterprises and							
organizations[d]		0.5	0.7	0.4	1.3	7.1	9.4
Households		0.1	0.6	1.0	0.8	0.6	0.6
Total	0.1	0.8	2.0	3.8	6.0	18.1	21.6

SOURCE: [86], 1971, p. 486; 1967, pp. 891 and 893; 1968, pp. 779 and 781.

NOTE: Details may not add up to totals because of rounding. Wholesale trade organizations of industrial ministries are included under "industry."

[a] Less than 100 million.

[b] Supply and purchase organizations, including those purchasing farm output.

[c] Includes other segments of the economy.

[d] Includes cooperative housing, which rose from 0.02 at the end of 1952 to 2.3 at the end of 1971.

In the household sector, credit for financing purchases of consumer goods is not available from the banking system at all, in contrast with several socialist countries where savings banks make loans to finance such purchases. However, since 1958 stores of the state retail trade organization have been selling certain goods on credit.[8] (See Table 6.5.)

Installment buying of consumer goods was introduced at a time when supply conditions had improved sufficiently to make cer-

peculiar accounting arrangements that are a feature of socialist economies. For example, in each accounting period (which may be as short as five days), the proportion of the profits the given enterprise should achieve under its plan is automatically paid into the national budget. If this profit has not been earned, the depletion in working capital may have to be offset by a bank loan.

[8]For details, see Il'in and Koryagin [240]. See also Novoselov and Blyukova [196] and, on pawnshops as a source of consumer funds, Churkina [174].

TABLE 6.3

Short-term Loans of the State Bank, 1926–1971, by Major Segments of the Economy

(in millions of rubles, outstanding at the beginning of the year)

	1926[a]	1933	1941	1951	1961	1966	1971
Industry[b]	85	414	2,844	7,606	14,805	23,692	36,132
Agriculture (including *kolkhozes*)	15	77	211	498	2,964	4,899	9,431
Kolkhozes		7	12	43	666	365	2,452
Procurement of farm products		118	328	624	2,890	4,900	8,059
Transportation and communications	15	41	116	326	477	681	1,428
Wholesale trade	[c]	61	449	1,535	3,508	4,199	8,854
Retail trade	25	293	1,446	5,547	15,288	23,589	31,084
Total[d]	150	1,045	5,530	16,670	41,195	64,689	100,062

SOURCE: *D.K.*, April 1970, p. 87, and September 1971, p. 44.

[a] October 1.

[b] Includes distributive organization of industrial ministries.

[c] In 1926 distributed among other segments.

[d] Includes segments of the economy not listed separately.

TABLE 6.4

Short-term Loans of the State Bank, by Purpose, 1941–1971,
Selected Years
(amounts outstanding at the beginning of the year, in billions of
rubles)

Purpose	1941	1951	1961	1966	1971
Carrying of inventory	3.3	10.2	30.2	48.6	75.9
Production expenditures	0.1	0.3	0.6	0.8	2.6
On payment documents in collection channels	1.8	3.9	6.7	8.8	11.5
To meet payment obligations	0.1	0.9	1.0	2.0	2.3
For other purposes	0.2	1.3	2.1	3.1	3.7
Total	5.5	16.7	40.6	63.4	96.0

SOURCE: [213].
NOTE: Detail may not add up to totals because of rounding.

tain relatively expensive items amply available. These were put on the list of goods eligible for credit sales, a list that has gradually lengthened over the past several years. Variations may occur among cities and regions, depending on supply conditions and on the accumulation of excess stocks for certain items. In 1960, annual credit sales amounted to not much more than three rubles per capita; a decade later, they were about five times as large. The share of all nonfood commodities sold on the installment plan increased from 1.8 percent in 1960 to 5.7 percent in 1967.[9] The importance of consumer durables, including motorcycles, has grown at the expense of clothing and footwear items, which still represent substantial expenditures in relation to the average Soviet income.

Terms available to individual purchasers depend on salary, level and structure of family expenditures, and other household characteristics, as well as on supply conditions. Differentiation in interest rates is related to maturity, the rate varied from 1 percent for loans up to six months to 2 percent for twelve-month loans (the maximum maturity available) in 1960. Loans are repaid either directly at the store from which the purchase was made, or by the

[9]For retail sales in 1961 and 1963, and details on share of credit sales for various consumer goods, see Il'in and Koryagin [240], as well as Goldman [236].

TABLE 6.5

Credit Sales of Consumer Goods, by Category, 1960, 1965,
and 1971

(in millions of rubles)

Year	Clothing	Household Goods[a]	Other	Total
1960	364	223	47	633
1965	1,152	1,631	588	3,372
1971	1,146	2,187	1,434	3,766

SOURCE: [86], 1972, p. 395. No earlier data available.

NOTE: Data cover goods sold in state and cooperative stores. Details may not add up to totals because of rounding.

[a] "Goods of a cultural and household character" (TV, refrigerators, etc.).

employing enterprise, which may remit the full amount and then deduct installment payments from the purchaser's paycheck, possibly on more liberal terms than those extended by stores. Some large enterprises borrow from the State Bank in order to make immediate settlements with retail organizations for all purchases of their employees.

Housing shortages have plagued the Soviet economy since its beginnings, especially after the large-scale destruction of housing stock during World War II. Yet credit was not available for multiple dwellings until the early sixties. Indeed, prior to 1962, credit was available only for the construction of individual dwellings in rural areas and small towns. Since that year, however, the Investment Bank has been making long-term loans available to cooperatives formed for the purpose of building multidwelling apartments for their members in urban centers. This is an important change, given the long waiting periods involved in obtaining apartments in municipal housing and in dwellings erected by factories or various other large employers, such as government offices. Residential construction undertaken mainly by municipalities is financed via their budgets, and that by large enterprises, via their "enterprise funds."[10] The importance of cooperatives shows rapid growth in the housing picture: in 1966, about 6 to 7

[10]Since 1966, enterprises can obtain credit for the construction of dwellings for their staff in amounts matching the funds available for this purpose from retained profits allocated to the "fund for staff benefits" (see Chapter 5).

percent of all housing space was provided by housing cooperatives, and by the end of 1971, loans outstanding to cooperatives,
at 2.3 billion rubles, had more than quadrupled their 1962 volume.

Construction of individual homes is permitted in rural areas on
land made available by municipal authorities. Though credit
granted for this purpose has been microscopic by U.S. standards,
in the 1955–1966 period such construction accounted for no less
than 27 percent of all dwelling space built.[11] In the years between
the reforms of 1930–1932 and 1965, more than nine-tenths of the
credit extended or outstanding each year was to the state-owned
enterprises. The balance of this chapter deals with credit to the
socialized sector, which, even after 1965, consisted overwhelmingly of short-term loans.

Credit Policy

The closest that official Soviet doctrine has ever come to formu-
lating a credit policy is the set of "five principles of socialist
credit," spelled out in numerous monographs and textbooks.
These stipulate that such credit should be planned, specific,
secured, repayable, and with a fixed maturity. In actual practice
provision is also made for supplementary "unplanned credits,"
extended in excess of the planned volume where a refusal to
exceed set limits would merely aggravate the underlying difficulties. The requirement that each loan be made for a specific
purpose and be identifiable as to end use resulted, under the initial
modus operandi of the system, in the granting of separate loans for
different specified purposes. The principle that the loan must be
repayable serves to stress the distinction between credit and
nonrepayable grants. While the bank is also expected to determine whether the expected flow of payments will be adequate to
retire the loan, this is a purely formal rule, given the automatic
nature of most categories of loans granted.

These principles provide the rationale for detailed administrative control, but no basis for a credit policy to regulate aggregate

---

[11]For details, see Gerashchenko [29], p. 343, Plotnikov [68], pp. 159–160, Yunik and
Miseyuk [91], pp. 195ff, and Usoskin [89], Ch. 16.

demand. Soviet monetary theory denies that in a socialist economy there is room for credit policy. The *Finansovo-Kreditnyi Slovar'* (Financial and Credit Dictionary) was published in 1958 and 1962 by the official publishing house specializing in financial literature. It defines credit policy as a "system of measures in the area of credit designed to secure the economic interests of the ruling class." "Credit restrictions" are described as "limitations or reductions in the volume of credit, which are put into effect by capitalist banks and bourgeois states," and "credit expansion" is "enlargement of credit, put into effect by capitalist banks and the bourgeois state, which exceeds the growth of production, stimulates overproduction and the coming about of economic crises."[12] The dictionary is silent about its role in a socialist economy except to state that "in the Soviet Union credit policy corresponds to the tasks that the government places before the country in each phase of the construction of socialism and communism." Indeed, circumstances may make it necessary to tolerate modification of these principles as indicated, for instance, by the large amount of past-due loans or to ignore them altogether by using credit for payrolls and collective farm payments to members, for example.

In practice, the actual implementation of these five principles has resulted in arrangements whereby, once certain targets or conditions stipulated in the applicable plans are met, credit is available almost automatically and at a fixed cost. The enterprise obtains a loan by filing a request, which the bank official processes by merely ascertaining whether the nature of the underlying transaction qualifies the applicant for obtaining credit accommodations within the limits set in the underlying plans. These arrangements obviously provide no incentive for management and personnel of the banking system to improve service. On the other hand, the Bank cannot close an unprofitable account, either.

Before the Reform, access to bank credit did not depend on profitability; indeed, credit-worthiness is a concept hardly applicable to state-owned enterprises. In extending credit, the State Bank does not have to be concerned with risk exposure and risk

---

[12][27], Vol. I, pp. 584–585 and 591.

appraisal. Neither its clients nor its own liquidity are relevant factors. Its criterion for measuring a borrower's performance is his success in meeting production, inventory, unit cost, profit, and various other real and financial targets stipulated in the economic plans.

A working capital shortage in any given enterprise can be remedied either by granting it more credit, or by adding to its working capital via transfers from the budget from other enterprises under the same ministry or from "higher echelon" organizations in the economic administration. Provision is also made for access to bank credit in order to finance unforeseen expenditures for real assets, such as bulges in raw materials inventories which occur when deliveries are ahead of schedule or above planned targets.

Geared to the flow of material output, actual changes in loans outstanding almost automatically reflect deviations from planned targets, shortfalls as well as "plan overfulfillment." On the other hand, accumulation of balances in the account of an enterprise may result in a request to repay a loan before maturity, or in the transfer of such "redundant" funds (by order of a supervisory administrative organization—a *glavk* or *ob'edineniye*) to some other enterprise or economic organization.

Rationing of credit, like that of material resources, operates via administrative decisions that filter down to individual borrowers through a pseudo-banking process. When aggregate credit demand exceeds the amount of credit provided for in administratively determined "credit plans," the State Bank determines the order of queuing.[13]

Changes in credit availability in the Soviet Union, which in nonsocialist countries are typically signaled by changes in the discount rate, have, instead, generally involved the addition of specific activities to the list of those eligible for bank financing, as well as other liberalizations of procedure. None of the instruments and techniques used in nonsocialist countries, such as fractional reserve requirements or the discount mechanism, are use. In fact, variations in the availability of credit over time have depended as much on the degree of flexibility in credit administration, including "bending" of rules, on the laxity of bank officials in apply-

---

[13]See Garvy in [110] and [117].

ing the rules, and on their readiness to respond to local and outside administrative pressures as on formal quantitative changes embodied in financial plans.

The principle of rewarding exceptionally efficient enterprises was established in 1954, while credit sanctions against poorly operating units date back to the credit reforms of the early thirties.[14] Successful enterprises are eligible for favorable treatment, which consists of reduced red tape and lenience in applying restrictive rules rather than lower rates. They may receive loans on favorable terms to meet contingencies (arising through no fault of their own) that result in a diminution of their own working capital, and may now also obtain additional loans for wage disbursements and inventories above plan limits under certain specified conditions.

Granting a privileged status, additional credit facilities, or more liberal terms involves assessment of the quality of an enterprise's performance. Before the Reform, this meant meeting the physical targets of production plans and the degree of success in maintaining the planned levels of costs per unit of output, as well as in achieving increases in labor productivity in accordance with targets set.

Credit sanctions, on the other hand, are direct administrative measures applied by the State Bank (and the two specialized banks) to loans as well as to current (clearing) accounts when the enterprise's overall performance is unsatisfactory. They are used to assure fulfillment of the economic plan rather than merely to safeguard the interests of the bank as a lender. The usual purpose of sanctions is to reduce the enterprise's volume of indebtedness to conform with the applicable norms. However, whenever this conflicts with the need to keep the particular enterprise operating, sanctions are unlikely to be pushed very far. Indeed, higher-echelon economic and local political authorities frequently intercede with the bank on behalf of enterprises in danger of being subjected to more stringent lending terms. Also, concrete measures for remedying the situation that caused the borrower to become a problem case is normally initiated by the economic organization supervising the enterprise's operations, such as a

---

[14]For details, including statistical data on the application of credit sanctions by the State Bank, see Shenger [74], essay XI.

ministry, or by the political authorities, if the enterprise is controlled by a local government unit.

A widely used form of sanctions is to put poor performers on a special regime including typically, pressure to liquidate excessive inventories or to complete production held up for lack of parts, increased control over all transfers of funds, and imposition of a rigid system of priorities for payments from the bank account. In some cases the Bank may require, for future loans or renewals, a guarantee by the higher-echelon authority supervising the enterprise, such as the ministry of the local administration, as the case may be. There are only few cases, however, where the guarantor actually has to make good on the obligations of the enterprise; more frequently, direct administrative action is taken to improve the delinquent's performance.

More extreme measures involve suspension of access to all liberal forms of credit, the take-over of collateral (goods), complete withdrawal of all credit facilities, and, as a last resort, the forced sale of the collateral and, ultimately, declaration of bankruptcy.[15] The more severe the sanction, the higher the level of bank authorities from which authorization to apply it must be obtained.

Short of extreme measures, credit sanctions, particularly penalty rates, have proved largely ineffective under the standard system. Where fulfillment of physical production goals and other "real" targets constitute the main success indicators, with management having only limited interest in the size of profits, payment of penalty rates is clearly not much of an inhibition. Moreover, in the last analysis, the increased interest cost is borne by the national budget and affects neither the most relevant success indicators (set in physical terms before the Reform) nor the income of the management group. Contrary to expectations, the Reform has not provided the machinery through which penalty rate payments can affect the compensation of managers and the fringe benefits of the staff.

However, a trend toward greater flexibility in credit administration has been developing since the mid-fifties. This includes a very gradual shift from the multiplicity of separate "objects" for credit extension (specific purposes) toward credit for broader

[15]Malein [58], pp. 113–132.

purposes, giving greater latitude to the managers of the local State Bank offices. Also, a gradual simplification in accounting has been taking place through merging the various special loan accounts and channeling receipts more directly into loan repayment transactions. Since the 1965 Reform the consolidation of subaccounts has made considerable progress. Logically, its ultimate outcome would be the complete consolidation of the current and separate loan accounts into a single account for each enterprise. This would facilitate the determination of the efficient allocation of a given unit's working capital and its overall need for bank financing. Proposals along these lines are currently under discussion.

Finally, even before the inauguration of the Reform, bank lending was used to achieve greater responsiveness to consumer preferences. Increasingly, the Bank has sought to induce retail trade organizations to reduce or liquidate low-quality inventories (if necessary, by cutting prices), by means not unknown in the rest of the world, such as refusal to renew loans or renewal at a penalty rate. Thus, as early as 1959 restrictive measures were introduced against trade organizations accumulating finished products for which there was insufficient demand. A year later, provision was made for the extension of special credits to trade organizations that take losses by marking down prices of goods which have become outmoded or whose quality has deteriorated.

On the whole, the increased lending flexibility introduced in the last years prior to the Reform mainly served to facilitate adjustments where discrepancies arose between physical plans and actual performance. Availability of credit continued to depend essentially on high-echelon administrative decisions rather than on negotiations between the borrower and the lending officers of a State Bank branch, so that application of the more liberal credit techniques remained of limited significance until 1965.

Credit to State Enterprises

SHORT-TERM CREDIT

Under the standard system, short-term credit performs three basic functions: it reduces the need for working capital by automatically financing peak working capital needs (mostly through inventory credits); it assures prompt replacement of working capital after completion of production (through semi-automatic crediting of collection float); and it provides an added means for controlling not only the financial performance of each borrowing enterprise, but of many other assets of its activities as well.

During the entire period between the credit reforms of 1930–1932 and World War II, the growth of short-term credit exceeded the increase in output.

Two basic types of inventory loans are made: one is geared to the level of stocks and the other to the flow ("turnover") of goods. Credit geared to the level of inventories, which was the predominant form through the early fifties, involves a separate application for each loan and is granted up to a "limit" set for each enterprise (comparable to a credit line granted by commercial banks in the West).

The proper amount of total working capital and the proportion in it of the enterprises' own resources, designated as "own funds," are determined by central authorities for each individual industry. The proportion of inventories of raw materials and of goods in production to be financed by the enterprises own working capital is governed by "norms" (*normatifs*) worked out in great detail for all industries, products and locations. Norms may be varied for individual enterprises and are revised from time to time, usually for specific industries. They are usually calculated in such a way as to require seasonal peak needs as well as some part of the basic year-round inventory to be financed by bank credit. Thus changes in the volume of credit are for the most part the counterpart of changes in the volume of inventories, unless planning authorities decide to change the relative share of enterprise funds and bank credit in the carrying of inventories. The setting and modifications of these norms are used as a means of achieving specific operating goals, such as a decrease in the inventory-output ratio or optimal degree of administrative control over the activities of individual enterprises. Indeed, much of the discussion in Soviet publications about credit tends to revolve around the proper determination of the proper share of credit in the financing of various types of inventories.

The original requirement that extension of credit be for a

specific purpose involved compartmentalization of loans by purpose, with a rigid definition of the purposes that were permissable. As new purposes for granting credit ("objects of crediting") were added, the number of separate loan categories multiplied.[16] For each newly eligible "object" there was still detailed stipulation of the conditions under which the loan could be obtained, and of the mode of repayment. Credit could not be extended unless its purpose was specifically mentioned on an approved list. Actually, of course, the rigor of logic was frequently circumvented by the necessities of practice, and thus, in addition to the categories of loans that neatly fitted the planned movement of goods, various categories of "transitional," "special," "interim," and "extraordinary" credit were introduced. Basically there was no alternative to providing such funds if a chain reaction was to be avoided; whether they were provided under special headings or merely changed to an overdue credit account mattered little. The fact of the matter is that in spite of the lofty principles and elaborate procedures of "socialist credit," automatic extension of credit was required under the standard system to validate any distortion, whether it resulted from uncontrollable causes, administrative failures, misjudgment in planning, or mismanagement of real resources.

Flexibility of credit administration has been somewhat increased, since the late fifties, by authorizing bank offices to transfer unused credit quotas among territories and among enterprises of the same industry. Also, 5 percent of the total volume of planned credits earmarked for any major geographic area or ministry has been placed in an unassigned fund, from which loans are made to enterprises that perform exceptionally well.

The alternative method—gearing credit to output—was first tried in 1936. "Crediting on turnover," originally introduced in 1934 (but little used in the following thirty years), which requires establishment of a "special loan account," is similar to a revolving line of credit.[17] The bank pays the seller when shipping documents are forwarded to it by the buyer, and sales receipts, or a stipulated part of such receipts, are credited to the special loan

[16]According to Melkov [61], pp. 129–130, a pharmacy can obtain loans under 17 different purpose headings and an alcohol factory under not fewer than 23.

[17]For details, see Melkov [61], Chap. 3, and Pessel' [65], pp. 6–13.

account. The proportion of credit in the total working capital remains constant, but it fluctuates seasonally while the volume of credit changes over time depending on working capital needs.

Loans geared to turnover made very little headway until 1957, but in recent years they have accounted for 70 to 80 percent of all short-term inventory credit. Despite the Bank's efforts, and despite the all encompassing planning and the absence of cyclical fluctuations, the accumulation of excessive inventories has been a chronic problem, more severe at some times than at others.

Settlement credit (credit on shipment documents in anticipation of payment by the buyer) is closely geared to the shipments of goods, whether raw materials or finished products. Its granting depends almost entirely on whether the goods received (in the case of raw materials) or shipped (in the case of finished goods) conform to the production plan applicable to the given enterprise. The volume of settlement credit depends on the ability of the enterprise to ship goods produced in accordance with the plan; its extension on the basis of shipping documents is automatic.[18]

Some loans which the Bank issues are cancelled or taken over by higher-echelon economic organizations up to the ministerial level, but the volume of such loans is not reported. Figures for loans overdue refer to a situation in which the borrower's financial prospects have not as yet resulted in the intervention of administrative organizations which supervise.

The State Bank can hardly be left holding bad assets, since, with few exceptions (such as lending to *kolkhozes* and to other cooperatives) a higher-echelon organization can be asked to take remedial action and to guarantee the credit granted or past due. But bank assets can be slow, and the volume of overdue loans, resulting mainly from the inability of individual enterprises to control inventories of raw materials as well as, in the case of retail stores, of finished goods, has been a continuous problem. The

---

[18]In the early sixties, about 14 percent of all bank loans were advances or drafts and other payment documents in collection channels, while an additional 3 percent went to enterprises whose balances were inadequate to pay drafts received within the applicable time limits. Poskonov, [70], p. 111.

need to reduce the volume of overdue loans is a recurrent theme in financial periodicals and official statements.[19]

MEDIUM-TERM CREDIT

In spite of the very limited use of medium-term for the financing of plant and equipment on the state-owned sector, the experience gained through the use of this technique has no doubt contributed to the shift from grant to loan financing which constitutes an important aspect of the reforms begun in 1965.[20]

"Loans for small mechanization" were introduced in 1932, but numerous restrictions surrounding their use prevented such lending from attaining much importance. In principle, only investments designed to improve technology, rather than break bottlenecks or increase capacity were eligible for credit financing. The specific purposes for which investment loans were available under the standard system include acquisition of machinery or equipment (1) embodying advanced technology (including automated equipment) and (2) to increase the output of consumption goods, mainly on the basis of locally available raw materials or by-products, and (3) for which, for one reason or another, no provision was made in the plan ("afterthought projects"). One frequently heard complaint was that investment loans were available to buy, for instance, an automatic lathe, but not to build another freight elevator which would have cut costs by a much larger amount.

In the five years immediately preceding the Reform (1960–1964), about one-third of all medium-term loans were for automation, and one-third for machinery replacement and acquisition of additional equipment. The remainder went largely for investment connected with the introduction of more advanced technology. However, some medium-term loans were also made for purposes not related to improving or enlarging production. For instance,

---

[19]For a discussion of past-due loans based on data for the Russian Federal Republic, see V. Zakharov [210]. The author remarks that while the Bank's statute provides for the foreclosure of collateral, this is very rarely done, even when loans long overdue are involved.

[20]For a detailed discussion of these loans, see Grossman in [143]. For a comparison of terms and conditions between 1938 and 1966, see Lavrushin [52], p. 56.

such credit served in the decade preceding the Reform to build movie theaters in numbers far exceeding those financed from budgetary (mostly local soviet) resources.[21] Stringent requirements were, and still are, attached to such loans, primarily to prevent consummation of projects which were rejected by the higher echelon economic and planning authorities for inclusion in investment plans. The provision that construction expenditure cannot exceed 15 percent of the total cost of the proposed project to be bank-financed serves the same purpose. Loans for investment purposes have a maximum maturity of up to three years, depending on industry; in practice they are amortized more rapidly, on the average within one year, since they are usually made available only for purposes profitable enough to permit relatively quick repayment.

The growth of modernization loans had been slow until the Reform because there was little inducement to borrow, even at nominal interest cost, as long as investment funds could be obtained free on a non-returnable grant basis (though perhaps only next year or later) by having the project included in the regular investment plan. Further reasons were the delays in obtaining such loans and the difficulties in acquiring materials and machinery from the authorities in charge of their allocation. Thus the use of bank credit to finance fixed investment remained negligible through the beginning of the 1960s and became of some importance only with the launching of the Reform.[22]

The Reform and Credit

The Reform has affected the use of credit in two ways: it has extended loan financing of fixed investment, and it has further simplified financing of working capital along the lines initiated in this direction since the middle fifties. The supply of bank financing for both purposes was eased by making loans available in anticipation of retained earnings and depreciation allowances in future years, thus bridging the time gap between current spending

[21]See Barkovkiy and Kartashova [9].
[22]See Levchuck and Melkov [180].

and future income. However, all basic features of the standard system remain.

Since the Reform, the use of bank credit for carrying inventories is now less restrictive; greater emphasis is placed on credit on turnover. Such credit is made available to cover normally between 40 and 50 percent of the planned level of working capital. This percentage can vary for individual categories of working capital used by an enterprise (raw materials, fuel, parts, et cetera), with stipulated exceptions. By the time the Reform was initiated, the majority of industrial enterprises qualified for the use of such loans on turnover, but did not take much advantage of them. At the beginning of 1966, such loans represented only 3½ percent of all short-term credit extended by the State Bank.[23] Following the example of some other socialist countries, the State Bank had begun in 1972 to experiment with credit contracts with individual enterprises.[24]

While loans on turnover have expanded, they have by no means replaced special-purpose loans. Individual enterprises using loans on turnover may, and typically do, still obtain additional credits for carrying inventories in excess of planned levels (norms), for paying debit balances in clearings, and for other purposes. The amount of credit extended to an enterprise for working capital purposes remains linked to the degree its production plan has been fulfilled, but the total volume of credit available to it is subject to subsequent negotiations as new facts develop.

Such changes in credit practices as increased lending on the basis of total turnover are designed to provide greater flexibility in the use of borrowed funds, and to reduce detailed verifications and other "documentation." They also give plant managers somewhat greater latitude, as the role of the authorities interposed between the individual enterprise and the ministry concerned is reduced. Under the new system, enterprises determine their own working capital requirements, which, once approved by

---

[23]Chernyshova [22], pp. 44 and 66–67. See also Sotnikov and Mezhiborskaya [205], Zakharov [210].

[24]See Garber and Doinikova [176]. Among the voluminous Soviet literature on the significance of the Reform for credit and banking, see Rumyantsev and Banich [71], Bachurin [8], and Dzhavadov [25]. For the impact on credit of reforms initiated simultaneously in other socialist countries, see Atlas [7].

the higher authorities, cannot be changed during the year unless the production plan is modified. If an enterprise's working capital has been impaired because of losses or lower-than-projected profits, the shortfall will no longer be made good through budgetary appropriations but will have to be rebuilt from future profits. Enterprises that have depleted their working capital must now resort to bank credit, on which charges are relatively high and which must be repaid from future profits. Repayment of such bank loans, which have a maturity of up to two years, must come from profits that exceed plan targets. If a given enterprise does not have higher-than-plan profits, up to 30 percent of the resources earmarked for the "development fund" must be used to retire the debt.

All in all, the share of bank credit in the economy's total working capital at the end of 1969 was considerably higher—at 47.1 percent—than at the end of 1950, when it had constituted 40.4 percent (see Table 6.6). This was due more to the sharp reduction in accounts payable during the twenty-one years (from 20.1 percent in 1950 to 12.3 percent in 1969) than to the moderate decline in enterprise funds (from 37.9 to 34.4 percent). While bank credit showed an uptrend in all branches of the economy, the gain in its share of total working capital was particularly significant in manufacturing (at 44.3 percent in 1971, compared with 33.1 percent at the end of 1950), wholesale distribution (at 62.4, versus 52.5 percent in 1950), and organizations purchasing farm products (at 84.0, up from 64.3 percent during the comparable period).[25] The rise in manufacturing presumably reflects the greater use of credit (rather than budget grants) for working capital, one of the most significant developments in the credit picture since the early sixties.[26]

The role of credit in supplying working capital for the economy is still widely debated.[27] One of the problems is that, due to differences in profitability, the rules applying to profit retention

[25]Mitel'man [195], p. 22.

[26]On the changes in the role of credit in trade, see Gryzanov [38] and Orlov and Shimanskiy [63]. See also Podolski [139], Appendix D, for statistical data, 1940–1968.

[27]On the controversy concerning the proper ratio in an enterprise's working capital between its own resources and bank credit, see Seidenvarg [200] and the numerous references cited therein. See also Kartacheva [179], Lavrushin [51] and [52], Levchuk and Melkov [87].

TABLE 6.6

Structure of Working Capital of State Enterprises
(percentage composition at the end of year)

	Total Economy			Industry		Agriculture		Trade	
	1950	1960	1969	1960	1969	1960	1969	1960	1969
Sources									
Own resources	37.9	38.8	34.4	47.7	39.6	57.3	49.3	31.3	26.9
Bank credit	40.4	44.3	47.1	39.2	43.7	32.3	34.9	58.2	60.5
Bills payable	20.1	14.0	12.3	10.6	8.2	5.8	4.5	9.9	11.4
Other	1.6	2.9	6.2	2.5	8.5	4.6	11.3	0.6	1.2
Uses									
Inventory		77.2	78.4	80.4	82.0	87.1	87.8	89.8	87.1
Goods shipped and services rendered		9.2	7.0	11.2	8.5	0.4	0.7	3.9	4.7
Bank deposits		6.2	7.0	4.8	5.6	5.2	7.2	3.7	3.8
Accounts receivable		7.0	7.2	3.4	3.3	3.4	2.7	3.2	4.3
Other		0.4	0.4	0.2	0.6	3.9	1.6	—	0.1

SOURCES: [86], 1968, pp. 750–751 and 1969, pp. 750–751; and [214].

and the policies of supervisory economic administrations result in excesses of working capital in some enterprises while others find themselves short and must borrow from the State Bank.

Credit for Agriculture Under the Reform

Lagging productivity in agriculture—in large measure a result of a half century of neglect on the part of planners and of lack of incentives for those working on the land—has been one of the most persistent problems of the Soviet economy. It is not surprising, therefore, that the first move toward the Reform consisted of a series of administrative as well as policy changes concerning agriculture, announced in March 1965, six months before promulgation of the parallel measures affecting the rest of the economy. In particular, steps were taken to alleviate the credit burden on agriculture. About 1.5 billion rubles of the *kolkhozes'* long-term and over half a billion of their short-term bank debt were written off, and some other obligations were canceled or postponed. The various reforms introduced involved price increases for farm produce, administrative rearrangements, and various organizational changes, including the gradual shift of *sovkhozes* to a business accounting *(khozraschet)* basis. Many of these measures aimed at increasing the responsibilities of the chairman of the *kolkhoz* and the manager of the *sovkhoz* paralleling similar measures in industry, but administrative controls have actually been reduced only to a minor extent. The role of the State Bank in the farm sector, however, has increased[28] with the growth in direct lending to agriculture.

Financial incentives play a similar role in the changes affecting *kolkhozes* initiated in March 1965 as in various state-owned sectors under the Reform. These changes were a logical development of a series of significant modifications in the operations of *kolkhozes* introduced in 1953.[29] The gradual reduction in the use of the *kolkhozes'* own products in compensating members and for purchasing non-labor inputs as well as in discharging obligations toward the state was accelerated. Simultaneously, the income of *kolkhozes* was increased by an upward adjustment of procurement prices paid by state purchasing organizations for various types of farm products, with a 50 percent supplement paid for deliveries above plan targets, and by an increase in the output of individual plots.

A major policy change involved extending working capital credits directly to *kolkhozes* rather than via the state purchasing organizations, thus bringing *kolkhoz* officials into contact with the banking system.[30] Since 1967, all loans to *kolkhozes* have been

[28]See Kotchkaren and Glinsitkiy [182] and Levchuk [189]. Price changes and administrative efforts to raise productivity are, perhaps, of greater significance than changes of a purely financial character, which are discussed in this chapter. The shift toward direct lending by the State Bank has entailed large-scale experimentation with alternative methods of extending credit that involve about 3,000 collective farms differing in size, profitability, and location.

[29]For detailed discussion of Soviet agricultural policy, see Strauss [147] and Karcz and Timoschenko [125]; see also Clarke [226], and Diamond, "Trends in Output, Input and Factor Productivity in Soviet Agriculture," [152, Part II-B], Diamond and Krueger, "Recent Developments in Output and Productivity in Soviet Agriculture" in [153] and Volin [155]. For a review of the situation before 1958, see Golev [36] and Kartashova [43].

[30]Section 21 of the "Sample Statute for Collective Farms" (adopted by the Kolkhoz Conference held in November 1969) deals with relations with the State Bank, including opening of accounts and procedures for obtaining short- and long-term loans.

made from the State Bank's own general resources. Previously such loans were made from special budget appropriations, with the Bank acting merely as allocator and administrator with little interest in their repayment.

Official statistics suggest that a good measure of success was achieved in increasing the use of credit by *kolkhozes* during the first years following the shift to the new policy. By 1969, *kolkhozes* had become heavy users of credit; at the end of the year, 94 percent of them had some outstanding long-term indebtedness to the State Bank. Short-term credit financed more than one-third of all current production expenditures of the *kolkhozes,* including the wages of the membership. In 1969, *kolkhozes* received bank loans amounting to almost 13 billion rubles, including 1.9 billion rubles in long-term loans, which covered 28 percent of all investment in fixed assets and livestock. Fixed investment in *kolkhozes,* only an estimated 5 billion rubles in 1935, exceeded 40 billion rubles in 1969, but only a small part of the increment was credit-financed (bank credit is extended only for a limited range of construction projects).[31]

Greater stress is now placed on increasing the availability to, and the use of credit by, *kolkhozes,* and to provide appropriate incentives to this end. In the past loans were frequently regarded as disguised subsidies, and the State Bank kept many loans to *kolkhozes* on its books long past their original maturity dates by granting extensions irrespective of the effort made by borrowers to repay them. Given the minuscule amount of bank credit extended to *kolkhozes* in the four decades following the forced collectivization, a vast need remains for expanding the use of industry-produced inputs, such as fertilizers and insecticides, and for increasing investment in equipment, livestock, and farm dwellings as well as in such amenities as electric power, telephone lines, movie theatres, educational and recreational facilities.

---

[31]Bank credit is still, for instance, not available for the financing of irrigation, drainage, or the construction of feeder roads or roads entirely within the territory of a single *kolkhoz.* See Kartashova [43].

When medium- and long-term lending to agriculture was shifted to the State Bank in 1958 and the modest program of loans for small-scale technological improvements in industry was revitalized, the distinction between short- and long-term loans was underlined by making appropriations from the budget to the State Bank for dispensing such loans.

To stimulate capital formation from retained funds, taxation of *kolkhozes* was modified in 1966 by shifting the tax base from gross to net income. By exempting profits up to 15 percent of net income from taxation and by lowering the tax rate to 12 percent (instead of 12.5 percent previously applicable to *gross* income), the new system made the income tax, in fact, progressive. It lowered the total tax burden on *kolkhozes* by an estimated half a billion rubles a year, and encouraged modern farming methods.

Greater official concern with making *kolkhozes* conduct their affairs in a businesslike manner (rather than as the lowest administrative unit of a vast bureaucracy running agricultural production) has also led to a number of changes in internal accounting and financing.[32] Among these the allocation of part of the profits for a systematic increase in working capital is, perhaps, the most important.

Sovkhozes benefit from several changes in financing, too. They are now able to maintain two separate funds for financing fixed investments and other expenses designed to improve income in the long run. The "*sovkhoz* fund" and the "fund for the strengthening and widening of activity" receive 4 and 8 percent, respectively, of planned profits and 40 to 50 percent, respectively, of any additional (above plan) profits. These funds can be used for a wide variety of projects not included in the economic plan. The purposes for which these resources may be spent, however, are spelled out in great detail. Therefore, the second fund, for example, may be directed only toward investments in such projects as electrification and telephone and radiocommunications and the erection of field markers. Projects can be initiated only when centrally allocated ("funded") resources are not involved. This excludes a wide range of investment activities; it is not readily clear, for instance, how electrification projects can be financed from these *sovkhoz* resources when wire, transformers, and other equipment are on the scarcity list.[33]

---

[32]For a standard financial plan of a *kolkhoz,* see Solntsev and Fisenko [82], particularly pp. 280–282.

[33]See Yunik and Moseyuk [91], pp. 37–43.

Interest Rates

The rigidity of interest rates reflects the view of policy makers that interest has no regulating function in a socialist economy. Their reluctance to vary interest rates may be traceable to the fact that it is considered a particularly objectionable source of "parasite income" in capitalist countries. As a result, interest is treated merely as a service charge intended to contribute to meeting operating costs of the banking system. No attempt was made before the Reform to use the level of interest rates and their differentiation to influence the aggregate volume or distribution of bank loans and real investment, or to achieve equilibrium between the demand for and supply of loanable funds. The Reform has done little toward moving the use of interest rates in these directions.

Rates are uniform for all loans made for an identical purpose. The somewhat greater differentiation in interest rates since the mid-1950s was not designed to influence the volume or distribution of credit, but, rather, to implement certain preferences as to social targets by the planning authorities.

Changes in lending rates are made infrequently, and are the result of high-level administrative decisions in the Ministry of Finance. Neither deposit nor lending rates are varied in response to credit demands, or in order to influence them; as long as demand for real resources is not dependent in any important way on availability of financial resources (including credit), interest rates do not need to be set at a level designed to clear the market for loanable funds.

The level of interest rates on short-term loans has been reduced significantly since the credit reforms of 1930–1932, when the rate charged ranged from 8 percent for loans for carrying inventories and for advances on drafts in the process of collection to 15 percent for loans past due; penalty rates on past-due loans have been high in order to achieve maximum speed in the turnover of borrowed working capital. (See Table 6.7.) By the end of 1965, the former were reduced to 2 percent and 1 percent, respectively, while the penalty rate was lowered to 5 percent. Since prior to the 1965 Reform interest was included with production costs, with

TABLE 6.7

Annual Rates of Interest on Short-term Loans

Type of Loan	Following the Credit Reforms of 1930–1931	1934–1936	1936	For Firms Operating in 1968 Under the	
				Old System	Reform System
Planned inventory loans	8	6	4	2	6[a]
Loans on drafts covering goods in transit	8	4	2	1	1
Other loans	15	8	6	5	8

SOURCE: [13], p. 85 and Mamonova [190].

[a] Equals or approximates the rate charged on funds owned by a given enterprise and thus differentiated by industry and location. This rate applies to enterprises charged 6 percent for funds owned, which is the case for the majority of enterprises.

profits normally set on a cost-plus basis, enterprises had no desire to lower rates. As a result of the Reform, to induce enterprises to avoid building up excessive inventories interest is now charged against actual gross profits and thus diminishing funds available for bonus payments and other enterprise uses. Later interest rates have been raised for all categories of loans (including inventory credit), except for loans on drafts covering goods in transit.[34]

Since the Reform was initiated there has been considerable discussion about the level at which interest rates ought to be set, and whether and how they should be manipulated. These discussions have yielded little convincing reasoning as to the desirable term structure of rates and differentiation by purpose or branch of industry. Every specific end use, or type of borrower, continues to command one specific rate, determined by the central authorities and uniformly applied without regard to the financial position of the borrower. The differentiation of rates according to purpose has been increased, but not depending on prospective economic effectiveness of the credit.

[34]Several Soviet economists have been advocating a more flexible use of interest rates, as well as a greater differentiation of rates within a wider range, from 2 to 10 percent, for example. Some steps in this direction were taken in 1972. See Sotnikov [205], pp. 8–9 and Mamonova [190].

The rate applicable to any given transaction continues to be determined by the loan's formal characteristics and does not depend on the judgment of bank officials. The new system is merely designed to remove some of the most obvious defects of the standard system and to adjust lending rates to the new fixed charge for fixed and working capital. The only change is that rates are now set at the same level as the capital charges applied to the particular industrial branch concerned. Evidently, loan rates lower than the charge on owned working capital would induce enterprises to seek maximum financing of inventories and other working capital needs through bank credit. The new minimum lending rates for plan-approved uses are equal to the applicable capital charge (normally 6 percent, but for some enterprises as high as 10 percent and as low as 3 percent). The rates for loans carrying inventories in excess of the applicable "norms" are similarly differentiated. Interest costs for various purposes other than carrying planned inventories worked out in 1972 to about 7 percent (as compared with the uniform charge on short-term loans of 2 percent prior to the Reform). Even higher rates apply for loans past due.

In a modest way, the Bank can now also use variations in rates to achieve what before was considered the proper object of administrative action. Thus, poor performers, who previously merely needed the guarantee of higher-echelon authorities to obtain additional loans on which regular rates were charged, now have to pay 20 percent above these rates. Similarly, exceptional loan accommodations to enterprises experiencing temporary financial difficulties will now involve a 1 percent surcharge. Altogether, the Bank's interest in the level and structure of interest rates continued to be greatly reduced by the fact that the bulk of its interest receipts is payable directly to the budget. There is little evidence that any reliance on rate flexibility, as contrasted with rate differentiation, is intended.

7

Banking and the Foreign Sector

GIVEN the marginal importance of foreign trade and the services related to it, such as transportation and insurance, and the absence of financial flows not tied to trade or tourism, the international financial relations of the Soviet Union do not rank among the most important aspects of the Soviet economy.

Foreign Exchange and the Exchange Rate

The basic difference between the role of the national currency of the USSR in relation to international payments and the role of money in countries with convertible currencies is that the ruble is strictly an internal currency.[1] When it comes to foreign trade or other international payments, it is nothing more than an internal accounting unit. The Soviet ruble is not, and never has been, traded on international exchange markets. Fluctuations in the exchange value of the ruble under the present regime of floating exchange rates do not reflect the relationship between demand

---

[1]Discussion in Aizenberg [1] of the role of gold in the Soviet monetary system and the relationship between the balance of payments and the money supply is typical for the treatment of these issues by Soviet writers. It ranges from the pertinent quotations from Marx and Engels to the assertion that "the strengthening of the ruble in the world arena will lead to the gradual displacement of the dollar from the position it still occupies now [in 1946] in the world market" (p. 124).

Export and import prices may be specified in a convertible currency (usually the U.S. dollar) or in rubles (usually in trade exchanges with other socialist countries). In the latter case, different implicit exchange rates apply to individual transactions which reflect a variety of subsidies and premiums, and also depend on the point of time at which the original transaction was entered into and, in some cases, the particular export (or import) organization (a ministry or its subordinated or special-purpose organization) involved.

for, and supply of, various foreign currencies, but are computed cross rates based on an administratively determined ruble-dollar rate. The administratively set exchange rates are practically permanent in the case of socialist countries. For other countries changes are made normally only to acknowledge foreign devaluations and revaluations and, since the advent of floating rates, significant changes in the exchange market.[2] Official exchange rates are neither capable of reflecting a disequilibrium in payments flows involving a trade partner nor can they be interpreted as equilibrium rates. They are, indeed, completely irrelevant for foreign trade as export prices are quoted in a convertible currency, such as the dollar. Foreign analysts and an increasing number of Soviet economists consider the isolation of export and import prices from the domestic price structure as one of the basic weaknesses of the Soviet economic system. Recognizing that feedbacks between foreign and domestic prices are essential for the optimal allocation of resources, they consider foreign trade as a leading candidate for radical reforms.[3]

The external value of the ruble rests on strict controls designed to prevent foreigners from acquiring any negotiable claims (currency, trade bills, et cetera) denominated in rubles. Nothing is revealed officially about the size or management of the gold or foreign exchange reserves of the Soviet Union. The size of its gold production has long been only a matter of guesswork, but in recent years detailed estimates have been made by Western scholars.[4]

The external parity of the ruble was set originally in terms of the U.S. dollar and subsequently (in 1961) in terms of gold

[2]Prices of goods sold domestically for convertible currency by special stores controlled by Vneshposyltorg suggest the real purchasing power of the dollar is several times the official exchange rate.

Tourist rates could not be as completely isolated from domestic prices as goods prices. Therefore, exchange rates available to tourists from socialist countries are set at levels different from those represented to be official exchange rates. In contrast to other socialist countries (East Germany being a special case), the Soviet Union does not now have special exchange rates for tourists from nonsocialist countries.

[3]Aizenberg [1], for instance, while pointing out that in socialist countries the exchange rate is independent of the balance of payments, advocates setting it at a level which would equate export and import prices with world market prices (pp. 102–104 and p. 115).

[4]For earlier estimates, see Zauberman [256] and Altman [214]. For recent estimates, see Kaser [242] and Bush [223].

(0.987412 grams).[5] Official foreign exchange parities, however, have no operational meaning, since the ruble is not convertible into the currency of any other country. Rubles that might come into the hands of foreigners, or are payable to them (for instance, royalties), cannot be exchanged for a convertible currency; only convertible currencies held by tourists and diplomats can be exchanged at the posted rates.

Two changes in the external value of the ruble in terms of the U.S. dollar were undertaken between the end of World War II and the floating of the U.S. dollar. In March 1950 the rate was raised from 5.3 to 4.0 rubles to the dollar in recognition of the decline in the Soviet price level following the currency conversion of 1947. In 1961 a new parity was established in a manner to create the impression that the external value of the new ruble had increased. Actually, however, the ruble was devalued, even though its gold content was set 10 percent above that of the dollar (and, incidentally, above that of the Tsarist ruble). Indeed, the one-for-ten rate at which domestic currency was exchanged would have required setting the value of the dollar at 40 new kopeks rather than at 90. The new exchange rate (1 ruble = $1.11) was much closer to the special rate introduced in April 1957 for "noncommercial" transactions, which applied to tourist expenditures in the USSR and foreign exchange requirements of Soviet tourists traveling to non-Communist countries and thus was more representative of purchasing power parities. While the dual exchange system was abolished at the time of the 1961 revaluation,[6] which raised the cost of foreign travel and similar expenditures in the Soviet Union by 11 percent, the overall effect of the rate unification on the Soviet balance was very small, since export and import prices continued to be divorced from the domestic price level.

The two successive changes of the U.S. dollar's parity in terms of gold, in December 1971 and February 1973, resulted in the establishment of new exchange rates based on the unchanged gold content of the ruble. In fact, since the dollar began to float in

[5]For a review of changes in the official ruble exchange rate between 1917 and 1957, see Holzman [240]. For more recent years, this information is readily available.

[6]For a review of the history of multiple exchange rates to favor tourism and for non-merchandise payments, see [1], p. 105.

March 1973, official rates have been established each month to reflect the changing value of the U.S. dollar in foreign exchange markets. For example, in September 1973, the rate offered in the Soviet Union was 72 kopeks to the dollar.

Foreign Trade and Payments

International financial relations of the Soviet Union are confined essentially to those related to trade and tourism.

Exports are equivalent to only about 4 percent of the gross national product of the Soviet Union. In part as a result of policy decisions made in the formative years of the Soviet Union, and partly as a reflection of the economic blockade following the Bolshevik seizure of power and the political isolation between World Wars I and II, the basic policy of the country has been to consider foreign trade as a means of obtaining goods which were not, or could not be produced domestically. The rich endowment of the Soviet Union in natural resources and the wide range of climatological zones within its territory made such a policy feasible.

After World War II, the emergence of socialist states on its western border, and Communist China to the south, and the creation of the COMECON offered the challenge of integrating the economies of the Soviet Union with those of its allies and planning trade to achieve common development goals. Little progress has been made so far in this direction, even after the adoption of the "Complex Program" in 1971. Nevertheless, since immediately after the war, the Soviet Union's trade with its COMECON partners has represented about two-thirds of all its foreign trade. While the exchange of goods is officially planned to achieve a better coordination of the various socialist countries' industrialization efforts, de facto, the trade partners of the Soviet Union frequently pursue policies influenced by much narrower national objectives. In more recent years, in particular since the advent of the political "detente," the closing of the technological gap with the West has become a major objective of economic policy. In recent years a number of factors have allowed the Soviet Union considerable flexibility in managing its foreign exchange obligations. These include use of the Eurodollar market, the ability of the Soviet-owned banks abroad to attract deposits from a variety of sources, and the temporary availability of foreign exchange resources of other socialist countries using these banks.

Changes in emphasis in policy objectives have not as yet eventuated in a change in the basic structure of international payments and the related mechanisms. The international monetary relations of the Soviet Union are based on direct and complete regulation of trade and all foreign payments flows. Complete control over international payments was established almost from the very beginning of the Soviet regime by introducing a government foreign exchange monopoly in 1918 and by placing all foreign trade in the hands of state foreign trade organizations. All receipts of foreign currency in whatever form are disposed of by the government through the State Bank and its agents.

The mechanics of the financing of Soviet foreign trade are quite simple.[7] In the case of imports from countries with convertible currencies, such finance has been easily handled by traditional banking channels used by nonsocialist countries and through bilateral compensating arrangements. The multilateral clearing of payments among COMECON countries has been ultimately shifted to a specialized institution.[8] The real problem has always been the attainable volume of trade and not techniques of settling international payments. The main difficulty has been the limited availability of goods which could be sold to various trade partners to earn enough convertible exchange in order to achieve import targets set in the successive Five-Year Plans. It always has been a problem of central planning, not of the financial or payments mechanism.

By the same token, the complete isolation of foreign trade from domestic production and prices[9] has deprived the Soviet Union, in every but the purely formal sense, of a link to the world market

---

[7]The author of the first comprehensive monograph on the foreign trade of the socialist countries, F. Pryor [141] did not find it necessary to discuss financing of this trade. Neither did many of the studies published subsequently and dealing with the foreign trade of the Soviet Union or of the socialist countries.

[8]For a short review of the history of foreign payments of the Soviet Union, see Polyakov [199] and Familton [230]. See also Altschuler [5], Meznerics [133], Wilczynski [156], Zwass [159] and Zotschew [158].

[9]On the relationship of foreign to domestic prices, see Chapter 3.

and of all the effects of continuous exposure to the shifting world pattern of demand and prices. It has also prevented the optimal allocation of resources between exports and output for domestic consumption and between alternative uses of domestic and imported materials and finished goods. It has deprived the Soviet economy of a continuing stimulus to improve product quality and technology, two areas in which improvements have been sought through administrative intervention rather than market exposure.

The foreign trade and foreign exchange monopolies, together with their close control over all nontrade transactions, permit the Soviet authorities to balance foreign obligations against expected receipts of convertible and other categories of foreign exchange. It may be said that Soviet imports from Socialist and less-developed countries basically reflect the highest level attainable given supply limitations in the Soviet Union, while those from developed countries, and in particular the U.S., reflect basic decisions of how much of a gap between the imports and exports should be financed by gold exports or foreign credit.

Financing foreign trade and managing international payments flows involve close cooperation between the Ministry of Foreign Trade (which administers the foreign trade monopoly), the Ministry of Finance, the State Bank, and the Bank for Foreign Trade.

The pattern of foreign payments is determined by four institutional factors: the state monopoly of foreign trade, the state monopoly of foreign exchange holdings and transactions, the central planning and control of the balance of payments, and the compartmentalization of foreign payments. More will be said later about each of these factors. The first three institutional arrangements had been introduced originally at the very beginning of the Soviet regime and have been copied by the other socialist countries. It is important to note, however, that these arrangements, while basically inherent in a centrally directed economy, by no means need to be maintained in the rigid form in which they have been continued in the Soviet Union practically without any significant change in over half a century. In particular, several of the smaller socialist countries now authorize some important enterprises to deal directly with foreign customers or suppliers, including those in nonsocialist countries. They also encourage exports by authorizing enterprises to retain a specified proportion of the foreign exchange proceeds of their exports to convertible currency countries. In the Soviet Union, international monetary flows are not only centrally controlled and directed, but they actually pass (with insignificant exceptions) through separate enterprises created to handle various kinds of transactions and to act as intermediaries between domestic enterprises and foreign buyers and sellers. From the point of view of an individual enterprise, there is no basic difference between domestic and foreign sales; export levels are based on targets or quotas set by planning authorities rather than the enterprise's economic decisions.

The Soviet payments system is related to planning and compartmentalization of foreign payments. The balance of payments is planned in advance each year (and projected for longer periods, such as those covered by the Five-Year Plans), country by country.[10] Trade with the COMECON countries is conducted on a cash basis multilaterally, at least in theory, and payments are planned to be compensated in full. Trade with nonsocialist countries is usually conducted on the basis of bilateral agreements, which set specific overall volume targets, with the important, but not single, exception of the U.S. While imports and exports (and invisibles) may not balance for each country, the total balance with countries with convertible currencies is settled separately. Since the ruble is not an international currency, trade between the USSR and the non-socialist countries is invoiced in dollars, sterling, or some other convertible currency, so that surpluses with one country can be used to meet deficits with some other countries.

Skillful management of foreign exchange resources on the basis of projections, formalized as foreign exchange budgets, together with a scrupulously punctual discharge of all its obligations[11]

[10]The task of projecting exchange receipts and commitments and the general strategy of managing foreign trade resources is the responsibility of the State Bank's foreign exchange planning department. It discharges this task in close cooperation with the Ministry of Foreign Trade, which has the power to restructure trade exchanges to fit the Soviet Union's foreign exchange capabilities and to make adjustments for changes in price and availability of commodities. An annual foreign exchange plan elaborated through the cooperation of the State Bank, the Gosplan, and the Ministry of Finance is formally approved by the Council of Ministers; it is, in fact, an *ex ante* balance of payments. See also Neuberger [135] and Kaser [242].

[11]The Soviet Union has never defaulted on any of its obligations to creditors in nonsocialist countries, whether they involved current transactions or credit.

enabled the Soviet Union to expand its foreign trade between the two world wars and to increase it considerably, with socialist as well as nonsocialist countries, after World War II. The world's largest gold producer outside South Africa, it has been able to meet balance of payments deficits arising from extraordinary circumstances (such as exceptionally poor harvests in 1965) by drawing on its gold reserves.

The foreign trade relations, and thus the foreign payments flows, of the Soviet Union have thus developed into three separate, though interrelated spheres: socialist countries, industrial countries with freely convertible currencies, and less developed countries. At present the difference between arrangements involving industrially more advanced and less developed countries lies mostly in the greater survival in the second group of what in fact amounts to barter agreements stipulating balancing of trade and restricting the disposal of credit balances.

SOCIALIST COUNTRIES

Formal multilateral clearing (mutual offsets) of trade and other payments was not undertaken until the formation of the International Bank for Economic Cooperation (IBEC), under the sponsorship of COMECON, which began operations at the start of 1964.[12] However, the ruble has been a unit of account for settling intra-bloc trade since 1951, and arrangements for settling bilateral balances through the State Bank have existed since 1957. As a matter of fact, even before the creation of IBEC, practically all payments between the Soviet Union and the other socialist countries (95 percent in 1960) were made through mutual offsets. Multilateral balancing, one of the main goals of COMECON, has made little progress so far. In 1973, less than 4 percent of the trade was multilaterized. This is partly due to the absence of an interrelated price system, limited coordination of national economic plans, and complexity of the annual negotiations required, and

[12]The IBEC charter, as well as the agreement underlying settlements in transferable rubles, have been published in *The American Review of Soviet and Eastern European Foreign Trade,* January–February 1966. For a description of the history of the settlement arrangement between the Soviet Union and its socialist trading partners, see Gerashchenko [29]. See also *Moscow Narodny Bank* [258], Francuz [230] and Gekker [235].

partly due to the reluctance of individual countries to incur a deficit with any trading partner.

The International Bank for Economic Cooperation. Currently, all payments between the Soviet Union and the socialist countries of Eastern Europe (except Albania and Yugoslavia), as well as Mongolia, are cleared through the multilateral clearing arrangements of IBEC. Cuba became a member effective January 1, 1974. While settlements are multilateral, the underlying trade agreements are bilateral. The intra-bloc trade is conducted, in effect, as barter trade, on the basis of binding delivery contracts and negotiated prices that are frequently completely divorced from both world and domestic prices for identical items. The trade volume is negotiated annually, at prices which apply to longer (normally, five year) periods. Trade between the Soviet Union and the participating socialist countries is conducted on the basis of agreements calling for the balancing of trade payments of each country vis-à-vis all other participating countries. These give rise to balances on IBEC's books in an accounting unit called the "transferable ruble," which is nothing more than a conventional unit of account, inconvertible into any of the currencies of the socialist countries, including the ruble. Neither are transferable ruble balances convertible into commodities, since they originate in the nondelivery of goods contracted for and no free market exists in which such rubles can be spent outside the framework of commodity trade agreed upon in advance.

Trade payments between participants are converted into transferable rubles on the basis of the official exchange rates between a member's currency and the Soviet ruble. However, non-commercial transactions (for example, those arising from tourism and various services) are converted at negotiated rates, designed to approximate more closely the purchasing power of the currencies in the consumer goods markets of the various countries. Such transactions are originally recorded in a separate set of accounts carried in national currencies. At the end of each year, balances in separate bilateral compensating accounts for service payments are reduced by a conversion factor originally set at 3.4 in 1963 and in 1971 reduced to 2.3 and added to balances arising from merchandise trade.[13] Thus, net credit or debit balances that may

---

[13]For further details, see Zwass [159]; see also Babitchev, in [118]. For a history of

result in a given year from the failure of one or both parties to achieve the volume of trade originally agreed upon can be offset (or further aggravated) by service and other nontrade payments, including those arising from joint investment projects. A debtor country may receive credit from IBEC within stipulated limits (in fact, automatically up to 6 percent of the total amount of the trade volume), which can be repaid only by delivery of additional goods acceptable to the other party. Such repayment may be reflected in appropriate adjustments in the following year's trade agreement. A limited volume of credit with fixed maturities of up to five years (with interest rates ranging up to 5 percent) is also available.

In 1973, IBEC's tenth year of operation, clearings exceeded 47 billion rubles and mutual offsets between members were still its main activity. Temporary imbalances between receipts and payments of individual countries required in 1973 extension of 3.8 billion of short-term credits in transferable rubles, or about 8 percent of the payments compensated (95 percent of which were related to trade). These loans carry a nominal interest rate charge which, since 1970, has ranged, depending on maturity, between 2 and 5 percent per annum, with the highest rate charged on loans overdue.[14] Temporarily redundant funds in convertible currencies deposited by IBEC members are invested mainly in Eurocurrency markets (or are re-lent to members).

The balance sheet of IBEC is small compared with its operations. At the end of 1973, total assets of the institution, through which trade and other payments of the socialist countries of Europe are settled, were still less than 2.8 billion transferable rubles (with loans extended accounting for nearly 60 percent of the total, and funds held on deposits for most of the remainder), not much more than the assets of the smallest among the Federal Reserve Banks.

NONSOCIALIST COUNTRIES

Trade relations of the Soviet Union with nonsocialist countries have been expanding rapidly in recent years, particularly with the

---

multiple exchange rates covering non-trade transactions among socialist countries, see Aizenberg [1].

[14]In practice, a large part of credits extended is interest-free. Statutory charges ranged originally for 1½ percent for seasonal credits to 3 percent for amounts past due.

highly industrialized Western countries. In the years immediately following World War II, such trade was conducted on the basis of agreements providing for bilateral balancing, with all payments cleared through an account maintained at one of the central banks. Trade with advanced countries, many of which have in recent years provided a considerable volume of export credits, has gradually become subject to a more flexible payments regime, generally involving payment in convertible currencies of balances in either direction at the end of the year, or else settlement of all payments as they become due in a specified convertible currency. In the sixties, "switch trading" was developed for the purpose of disposing, at a discount, excessive credit balances in bilateral accounts by triangular and other complex transactions. Such trading has shrunk considerably since the late sixties, but has rebounded with the oil crisis.[15]

Foreign trade with most less developed nonsocialist countries (currently about seventy) is still ruled by trade treaties that stipulate the volume and commodity composition of mutual trade, as well as the mode of payment and other details of settlement. In recent years, there has been a growing tendency on the part of the Soviet Union to replace such agreements with treaties stipulating merely the target levels of trade exchanges, with all balances to be settled in convertible currencies.

Typically, trade agreements cover several years and are supplemented with annual "protocols." The underlying negotiations are carried out on the Soviet side primarily by the Ministry of Foreign Trade, which also normally negotiates any extension of foreign credits that might be involved.

Annual plans for international payments (foreign exchange budgets) are prepared by the Soviet Union for each country with which it trades. Such plans are aggregated by currency area, and are ultimately incorporated in overall plans for all convertible currencies and those cleared through bilateral accounts. Obviously, planning of payments involving nonsocialist countries must take into consideration possible price fluctuations and cyclical and other influences relevant to the ability of the Soviet Union to buy and sell in those markets.

[15]See "Back to Barter," *The Economist,* Sec. 14–20, 1974.

Advance planning of trade with each country generally aims at balancing payments flows in each direction (allowing for invisibles), taking into account any available sources for financing imports. Last resort use of monetary gold is reserved for meeting deficits with countries whose imports are essential for implementing Soviet longer-term plans for enlarging capacity and upgrading technology.

While Soviet planning involves advance decisions with regard to each country, a meaningful overall picture is obtained by observing the trade gap with all countries with which Soviet trade is conducted in convertible or "hard" currencies, estimates of invisible payments, and the two sources of financing—loans and gold sales. The overwhelming bulk of trade in hard currency (estimated at 90 percent in 1971) is with developed countries. These estimates may involve significant percentage errors for several minor items. All items other than merchandise trade are estimated on the basis of various types of evidence and assumptions, since the Soviet Union does not publish balance of payments statistics (see Table 7.1).

One estimate of the share of gold sales in settling deficits with convertible currency countries and the level of USSR gold reserves is given in Table 7.2.

Since data on gold production, sales or monetary stock are not released by the Soviet authorities, and private estimates have been frequently revised in the past and do not agree among themselves, the data in Table 7.2 should be considered essentially as indicative of the order of magnitudes involved rather than as a close approximation of year-to-year changes in the various series shown.

Private estimates of Soviet gold production and its use, which differ considerably from data widely used earlier and based on Central Intelligence Agency (CIA) estimates, are given in Table 7.3, measured in metric tons.

As can be seen from Table 7.2, settlement of the convertible currency deficit required gold sales, but estimated sales do not match deficits year by year. In 1960, about one-third of the deficit could be met from net receipts from medium- and long-term loans. Gradually, repayments rose more rapidly than new loans, so that by 1965 loan financing (net) had shrunk considerably.

TABLE 7.1
Estimated USSR Hard Currency Balance of Payments
(billions of U.S. dollars)

	1960		1965		1970		1971		1972[a]	
	Credit	Debit	Credit	Debit	Credit	Debit	Credit	Debit	Credit	Debit
Goods and services		292		211		496		274		706
Merchandise f.o.b.	768	1018	1374	1563	2197	2711	2652	2955	2900	3500
Transportation, net		65		45	35		50		b	b
Travel	25	b	46	9	81	19	96	21	b	
Interest payments		2		17		79		96		106
Payments to U.N.		15		27		40		43		45
Lend-lease repayments		11		11		11		11		12
Medium- and long-term credits	125	37	190	149	700	319	700	387	900	457
Gold	200		550			c	c		250	
									300	
Errors and omissions (net)[a]	30			342	166		15		20	

Source: [154], p. 703.

[a] Preliminary.

[b] Not available.

[c] Negligible.

[a] Includes changes in hard currency holdings and short-term capital movements.

TABLE 7.2

Financing of the Convertible Currency Deficit by Gold Sales
(millions of dollars)

Year	Convertible Currency Payments Deficit (positive)	Gold Sales	Gold Reserves[a]
1960	250	200	2555
1961	161	300	2365
1962	233	215	2550
1963	275	550	1800
1964	483	450	1495
1965	186	550	1095
1966	238	b	1265
1967	95[c]	15	1425
1968	109	12	1590
1969	311	b	1765
1970	514	b	1945
1971	303	b	2135
1972	1100	250–300	2400

SOURCE: [154], p. 702.

[a] Gold sales 1960–1968 and reserves (at year end) are calculated at the official price of $35 per ounce and $38 for 1972.

[b] Negligible.

[c] Surplus.

Foreign Credit and Investments

The Soviet financial system does not permit financial investment or even holding of balances in foreign exchange by foreigners other than diplomats. International flows resulting from lending not directly related to foreign trade and investing are insignificant. Until the end of World War II, Soviet international credit flows, like those of Tsarist Russia, were one-sided. The Soviet Union was a borrower, mainly on short-term capital accounts.[16] It continues to finance a large part of its capital imports through

---

[16]The Soviet government did not have to meet problems arising from foreign holdings of Russian securities, since all such claims (whether denominated in rubles or in foreign currencies) were repudiated after the revolution. No funded borrowing abroad (in contrast to using bank and vendor credit) was ever attempted by the Soviet government.

TABLE 7.3

Soviet Gold Production and Reserves
(in tons)

	Output	Sales to West	Other Uses	Change in Reserves	Year-End Reserves
1940	140				
1950	139	—	5	+123	1446
1951	141	—	5	+135	1581
1952	143	—	6	+143	1724
1953	144	67	6	+ 77	1801
1954	145	67	7	+ 74	1875
1955	146	67	8	+ 70	1945
1956	147	133	10	+ 8	1953
1957	153	231	11	− 85	1863
1958	162	196	12	− 42	1826
1959	173	222	14	− 61	1765
1960	181	178	15	− 5	1760
1961	197	173	16	+ 12	1772
1962	210	191	19	+ 5	1777
1963	222	489	20	−280	1497
1964	237	401	21	+178	1319
1965	254	488	23	−251	1068
1966	268	—	25	+253	1321
1967	283	13	28	+208	1529
1968	299	10	31	+263	1792
1969	325	—	33	+285	2077
1970	347	—	37	+299	2376
1971	360	20	42	+283	2659
1972	379	190	57	+113	2772
1973	398	280	86	+ 5	2777
1975 Plan	441	. .	. .	. .	. .

SOURCE: Michael Kaser, "Comecon," *International Currency Review*, May–June 1974, pp. 60–62. For output only, revised in 1975 (private communications from Mr. Kaser). The revisions are small (not exceeding 10 tons) prior to 1965; they are higher for 1969 and the following year.

"barter-on-time" in which imported equipment is paid for in kind by the additional output which it produces.

In fact, in some respects 1965 represents a turning point in the financing pattern of the trade deficit in convertible currencies. Following relatively large gold sales to help finance imports of grain following poor harvests in 1963 and 1965, gold sales could be reduced considerably as alternative credit sources became available. As a result, and following the more intensive working of old, and the discovery of new, gold fields, the Soviet gold stock, which by the end of 1965 had declined to little more than $1 billion (or by nearly 40 percent in five years), is estimated to have risen by the end of 1972 (measured in tons) rapidly. According to Kaser (Table 7.3) it was at a level considerably in excess of the end of 1960 volume. Since the mid 1960s, greater reliance on (and availability of) foreign loans has rapidly raised the ratio of debt service to convertible currency exports from 5 percent in 1960 to 18 percent ten years later, and 19 percent in 1972, as medium- and long-term debt in convertible currencies is estimated to have risen by the end of 1972 to $3 billion. The Soviet Union, and its creditors, might consider a 20–25 percent debt service ratio as an upper limit.

Foreign credit available to the Soviet Union (apart from the short-term credit normally extended for various raw materials and nondurable goods) falls into three main categories: vendor credit, bank credit, and official loans. These distinctions are less than clearcut in the case of some of the main exporters of machinery and equipment (such as France and Italy) where the principal commercial banks are nationalized, or where some export credits are granted by government-owned corporations. In any case practically all loans are issued by government-sponsored organizations. In contrast to the other socialist countries, the Soviet Union had not as yet attempted until late in 1974 to borrow long-term in international capital markets, such as the Eurodollar market, although Soviet-owned banks have participated in consortia sponsoring such borrowing by banks of several of the smaller socialist countries.

The Johnson Act precludes such borrowing from the U.S. since the Soviet Union has refused to recognize official debts of Tsarist Russia. This contrasts with the ease of almost all of the other countries of Eastern Europe which have reached agreements with the U.S. and other creditors to settle debts of their respective governments made prior to the institution of Communist regimes.

Since the advent of the detente the Soviet Union has endeavored to obtain U.S. and other foreign financing for a variety of large projects, involving mainly natural resources. Such arrangements have been, in fact, barter deals with an extended horizon;

repayment for foreign machinery, equipment, engineering service, and knowhow is to take place over long periods (stretching out as long as the lifetime of a generation) through the delivery of products of these projects. Represented as "self-liquidating credits," these arrangements (few of which have been consummated as yet) are congenial with the Soviet emphasis on the real, as contrasted with financial, aspects of economic processes, since they do not make the interest cost as explicit as in financial borrowing. The acceptability of such projects to private entrepreneurs depends not only on such political factors as assessment of the status of such arrangements under a different Soviet leadership, but also on the anticipated time profile of world market prices for the products to be received in repayment over an extended period and the nature of adjustment formulas and mechanisms built into such contracts. It appears that the various sources of finance for Soviet import surpluses from Western countries discussed have been, or are about to be, exhausted before Soviet trade has expanded to a volume generally considered desirable and feasible. This raises a number of broad questions with regard to Soviet economic policy which are, indeed, beyond the scope of this study.

After World War II the Soviet Union began to grant credit to other socialist countries and to some underdeveloped countries, normally in connection with the export of capital goods. In some exceptional cases it made hard currency loans to countries in Eastern Europe confronted with pressing reconstruction needs or with political difficulties. Export of capital to underdeveloped countries is accomplished largely through supplying goods (including complete factories) and services, partly on a grant-in-aid basis, partly against future deliveries in kind.[17] In fact, with very few exceptions, international borrowing and lending involves product payback schemes, which involve barter on time, the contracts merely being the recording of the monetary value of goods deliveries related to negotiated investment projects. This applies also to investments in socialist countries through the International Investment Bank (IIB) since its creation in 1971 (see

[17]For a detailed historical review of foreign lending to the USSR since 1917 and of credit extended by the USSR to the developing areas and to other socialist countries, see Komissarov and Popov [46], Ch. 18.

below) and prior to that, to the bilateral and infrequent multilateral investment projects.

Shares of the member countries in the Bank's capital of 1,052.6 million transferable rubles (in small part to be contributed in convertible currencies) are related to the relative importance of each in inter-COMECON trade. During the first three years of operations the IIB made commitments to finance 33 projects with loans aggregating 280 million rubles, about half of which was in convertible currencies. Following the example of the International Bank for Reconstruction and Development, the IIB established in 1973 a special fund designated to extend long-term credit to less-developed countries. The first IIB loan to the Soviet Union was granted at the end of 1973, although in the preceding years some socialist countries had participated in large-scale projects in the Soviet Union by supplying equipment and thus establishing "loans" repayable in goods to be produced by the individual projects.

The Soviet Union has not joined any of the international monetary and financial organizations although its delegates attended the Bretton Woods conference in 1944 at which the IMF and the IBRD were established. Despite various statements by Soviet officials in recent years that the Soviet Union might reconsider its position, acquiring membership in the two organizations and, in particular, in the IMF, would involve reporting obligations requiring disclosure of data which so far the Soviet Union has been unwilling to make public. The 1951 breakdown of the monetary arrangements administered by the IMF and the subsequent failure to make significant progress toward establishing a modified or alternative regime have been additional factors in diminishing the pressure on the Soviet Union to reconsider its original position.

Neither has the Soviet Union joined the Bank for International Settlements (BIS), of which all the other European members of the COMECON are members, continuing an association which goes back to the founding of the Bank in the early thirties. In this case, the ownership of shares in the BIS which were acquired by the Baltic states at the time of the Bank's founding, and the status of gold held in their accounts, constitute legal hurdles which need to be, but have not been, resolved to clear the way for membership.

The Bank for Foreign Trade

Although the Bank for Foreign Trade (Vneshtorgbank) was organized in 1922, until 1961 it operated virtually as a department of the State Bank.[18] Its responsibilities were limited to handling foreign exchange operations of a non-commercial character, such as dealings with foreign diplomatic missions, and foreign remittances. All other foreign banking activities were normally carried out by the State Bank.[19] In 1961 the Bank for Foreign Trade was reorganized and given greatly expanded operating responsibilities for the financing of Soviet foreign trade, while remaining subordinated to the State Bank in all policy matters. In fact, the Bank for Foreign Trade is now the point of contact of foreigners for all financial transactions with the Soviet Union.

Foreign operations are conducted by the Bank for Foreign Trade under the direction of the State Bank, which has been in charge of administering the foreign exchange monopoly since 1922. At the beginning of 1964, all correspondent accounts of the State Bank with foreign commercial banks were transferred to the Bank for Foreign Trade, with the State Bank retaining only accounts with foreign central banks. All dealings in the Soviet Union with foreign tourists and other foreigners remain in the hands of the State Bank, due to the very limited facilities of the Bank for Foreign Trade, which operates branches only in Leningrad (since 1968) and in the new Pacific port of Nachodka (since 1970).

The Bank for Foreign Trade now operates very much like the

---

[18]For the statutes of the Bank, see *D.K.*, January 1963. See also Gekker [235].

[19]The State Bank maintains currency exchange facilities at border crossing points, airports and railroad stations and in hotels in which foreign tourists are lodged (those operated by "Inturist," the organization in charge of foreign tourism). The State Bank also provides limited and strictly regulated facilities for nationals and foreigners who maintain accounts in foreign currencies, which can be used abroad or converted into rubles. The State Bank also provides foreign exchange to Soviet citizens travelling abroad.

The State Bank will automatically buy currency of, or checks on banks of, a non-communist country (although those denominated in nonconvertible currencies are accepted only "on consignment"), but it will not freely exchange bank notes of any socialist country. As a rule, funds for travel in socialist countries are carried in travelers' checks denominated in the currency of the country a Soviet tourist plans to visit.

foreign department of any of the roughly 1,500 foreign commercial banks in about one hundred countries with which it maintains correspondent relationships. In order to facilitate business relations with foreign commercial banks, the Bank for Foreign Trade is organized along the lines of a European joint stock bank; the State Bank holds the bulk of its shares while the Ministry of Foreign Trade and some other official organizations hold the remainder.[20]

The Bank's domestic activities include paying (in rubles) domestic foreign trade organizations the proceeds of exports and any service and other foreign payments due them. It extends credit to various state enterprises in charge of foreign trade. In effect, however, in providing short-term ruble credits, it merely acts as an agent of the State Bank. Table 7.4 presents its balance sheet for the end of 1973.

The Bank for Foreign Trade's activities in connection with export and import financing are conducted in close cooperation with several Soviet-owned banks abroad. In addition to the usual activities of banks specializing in foreign trade (such as collections), these banks raise funds for bridging temporary gaps in the availability of convertible currencies, transfer, and convert funds, take foreign exchange positions, and invest temporarily redundant foreign exchange. They maintain wide networks of correspondent banks to service their own needs as well as those of the Bank for Foreign Trade and the State Bank, and of official banks of other socialist countries using their services.

Soviet-owned banks abroad give the Soviet Union (and other socialist countries) a point of contact with the money markets of the West for dealing in gold and convertible currencies and for participation in the Eurodollar market. Indeed, these banks were major participants in the Eurodollar market at its inception. Two

---

[20]In contrast to the State Bank, the Bank for Foreign Trade operates in a competitive environment and its operations abroad must conform to foreign usage. Its operations must adjust continuously to fluctuations in foreign exchange markets, and numerous other changes in conditions over which it has no control. In contrast to the personnel of the State Bank, the staff of the Bank for Foreign Trade must continuously assess markets and trends and make quick decisions to take advantage of opportunities as well as to protect the Bank's interests and to avoid losses. The senior personnel of the Bank for Foreign Trade is given additional training in foreign banking through tours of duty with the Soviet banks abroad.

TABLE 7.4

Balance Sheet of the Bank for Foreign Trade of the USSR as of January 1, 1974
(in millions of rubles)

Assets		Liabilities	
Cash and bank deposits	2,070	Deposits	8,289
Investments	15	Borrowing, guarantees and	
Loans and discounts	11,172	acceptances	4,278
Other assets	2	Capital	594
		Profits and reserves	94
		Other liabilities	4
Total	13,260	Total	13,260

SOURCE: *D.K.*, August 1974.

NOTE: Loans are gross and include acceptances and guarantees offset by a counterentry under liabilities. The various foreign assets and liabilities are presumably converted into rubles at official exchange rates.

of these banks occupy an important position in the cities where they are located: the Moscow Narodny Bank in London and the Banque Commerciale pour l'Europe du Nord in Paris.[21] The Moscow Narodny Bank was originally established in London before World War I as an agency of a Russian Bank for Cooperatives. The Banque Commerciale pour l'Europe du Nord was bought by Soviet interests in 1925 from Russian anti-communist emigrés who organized it. The shares of both banks are owned entirely by various official entities of the Soviet Union. They have been able to attract a large volume of deposits from a variety of sources, including firms doing business with the Soviet Union and other socialist countries, and correspondent banks of the official banks of these countries. Both banks are very active in all kinds of transactions related to the foreign trade of the socialist countries of Europe, as well as of Cuba and China.

While the activities of the Paris bank began to expand rapidly in the early fifties, the growth of the Moscow Narodny Bank in

[21]Other Soviet-owned banks abroad are the Voskhod Bank, organized in 1966, in Zurich, the Ost-West Handelsbank formed in 1972 in Frankfurt, and the Russo-Iranian Bank in Teheran, carried over from the pre-revolutionary days. The Moscow Narodny Bank, which, in the twenties, had branches in New York, Paris, and Berlin, opened a branch in Beirut in 1963. Between the two World Wars, additional foreign banks owned by official Soviet interests operated in several other countries of Europe and Asia.

London after the advent of convertibility of most Western currencies in 1958 may be termed extraordinary. In addition to credit operations related one way or another to East-West trade, it conducts a variety of other operations, including some designed to acquire and maintain the image of a British bank, with the usual commitment to discount operations. By contrast, the Paris bank specializes in foreign exchange operations and various types of financial intermediation.[22] The Moscow Narodny Bank, together with the other officially owned Soviet banks abroad, not only facilitates the trade of the Soviet Union (and the other socialist countries) with the nonsocialist countries, but also serves as the channel for the sale of gold and for managing the foreign reserves of the Soviet Union.

[22]See Gekker [235].

8

Stabilization Policy and Monetary Equilibrium

Sources of Inflationary Pressure

OVER the years, Soviet economic policy has had to deal with a wide range of macroeconomic problems, some of which are similar to those encountered in Western economies. Repressed inflation is one of these, arising from excessive money creation.[1]

The opening of an inflationary gap in the consumer sector may be due to one or several of the following main causes: faulty planning, crop failures, bottlenecks in the flow of materials into consumer goods industries, excessive immobilization of resources in unfinished investment projects, transportation difficulties, and insufficient or defective storage facilities. Such phenomena unbalance the equilibrium between the flow of purchasing power to consumers and the availability of goods provided for in the economic plan. The concentration on goods was justified until recent years because the flow of purchasable services to consumers was very small.

Students from noncommunist countries have been almost exclusively interested in the effect of inflation on the real wages of urban wage earners. Yet, until 1960 the rural population was larger than the urban population, and twenty years earlier it had been twice as large.[2] Another source of inflationary pressures is the excessive immobilization of resources in unfinished major

---

[1]The term "inflation" is banned from the Soviet vocabulary in relation to the domestic economy.

[2]In the smaller socialist countries the importance of services is greatest in part because some services are supplied by the private sector.

capital investment projects.[3] During World War II, another major problem was the accumulation of money in the hands of the agricultural population. This was the unavoidable consequence of several factors: the efforts to achieve maximum availability of farm products in the face of a huge manpower drain; the almost total lack of industrially produced inputs in agriculture, and the general disorganization as the invading armies swept back and forth across the main producing areas of the country.

In the enterprise sector, fixed transfer and end-product prices for producers' and consumer goods, together with the attached administrative controls, have sharply limited the ability of managers to use enterprise balances outside of the legitimate planned channels.[4] Lower-echelon administrative units can obtain funds mainly via the national budget; other sources are marginal.

The fact that the unified budget has always been in balance or shown a surplus (except for one or two war years) eliminates a possible source of inflationary financing which is significant in some nonsocialist countries. However, enough outside pressures from industrial ministries, *glavks,* and various federal and republican authorities converge on the State Bank to result, at times, in excessive credit issuance, prolongation and renewal (if necessary, in disguised form) of loans outstanding, and undesirable over-expansion of currency in circulation.[5]

Policy Objectives

The objectives of Soviet financial policy are essentially twofold: to achieve macro equilibrium in the enterprise sector by securing adequate financing to cover the planned volume of investment,

---

[3]See Brzeski [222].

[4]The Soviet government has not used the various techniques developed in other socialist countries to deal with excess liquidity. Such techniques include the temporary blocking of some part of enterprise accounts (Poland), creation of credit cooperatives in which some part of money held by farmers is immobilized as the members' capital contribution (China), and advance deposits (usually in special savings bank accounts) for cars (Czechoslovakia), cooperative apartments, or imports.

[5]This contrasts with the experience of other socialist countries of Eastern Europe, where overspending by state enterprises and operations of the remaining private enterprise sector have occasionally constituted important sources of inflationary pressures. See, for instance, Podolski [139].

and to avoid—and, if necessary, absorb—any excess purchasing power in the household sector.

In the enterprise sector, "financial balance" is achieved when budget resources available for investment plus retained enterprise profits earmarked for this purpose match planned investment requirements in excess of available depreciation reserves. Equilibria consistent with quite different allocations of resources and rates of growth may be achieved at various levels by successful manipulation of taxes, prices, and credit.

In the household sector, the main objectives of financial policy are to avoid inflationary pressures, both overt and repressed, in the consumer goods market and to prevent consumers from becoming excessively liquid. This must be viewed against the background of the inelastic supply of consumer goods resulting from the forced-draft industrialization since the inauguration of the first Five-Year Plan in 1928. Since the early thirties, banking policy has aimed at preventing loan expansion from raising currency withdrawals above the total value of any additional consumer goods and services the economy is capable of producing.

While overall economic strategy at different times has involved the use of available policy tools in a variety of combinations, Soviet sources (official as well as academic) hardly ever discuss its rationale and actual application.

The Tools

In order to achieve policy objectives, the main reliance is placed on the monobank-monobudget system which was created in the early thirties and was a pioneering move by the first socialist country to provide an optimal financial structure for stimulating planned economic growth under conditions of reasonable monetary equilibrium. The various methods that have been used by the Soviet Union to achieve macro equilibrium can be classified into categories corresponding to those common in the noncommunist countries: monetary, fiscal, and income policies. The first includes credit planning and regulation of currency circulation. The second consists essentially of variations in planned budget surpluses and their use, government borrowing, and changes in tax rates (mostly the turnover tax on individual products). The third, income policy, involves, in the broadest sense, determination of the share of the national product earmarked for household consumption, with administrative changes in wage policy and allocation of resources and, if necessary, mid-stream adjustments in five-year plan targets.

The above classification of economic policies is subject to the qualification that many aspects of fiscal policy have, in fact, significant monetary aspects, while others, such as the manipulation of the turnover tax on individual products, are an important element in price formation and, therefore, in income policy. Policies pursued to cope with chronic shortages of consumer goods have included efforts to increase the flow of such goods above the quantities originally planned by "overfulfilling" the plan, to adjust the composition of industrial output between producers' and consumer goods, and to change the "assortment" of products available to households. Since the mid-fifties, measures to increase the supply of consumer goods to relieve inflationary pressures have also included limited encouragement of private production by members of *kolkhozes,* fuller use of by-products and industrial remnants in consumer goods production,[6] and allocating an increasing share of foreign exchange earnings for consumer goods imports (primarily from other socialist countries).

MONETARY POLICY

Even though in the Soviet economy money is reduced to the function of "numeraire" and isolated from influences of the balance of payments as well as from fluctuations in domestic gold production, it is nevertheless a necessary ingredient of a centrally controlled (or administrative) economy which is too complex for barter and direct distribution of goods to consumers via a voucher system. Soviet monetary policy encompasses basic arrangements

---

[6]Failure of the flow of consumer goods to match the increase in money income due to delays in completing new factories or to the accumulation of finished goods in factories may also involve bank action. However, prior to the Reform, the failure of financing for a specific project to reach the planned amount would normally lead to interruption of construction or allocations of additional funds from some reserve pool of investment funds (at the disposal of some ministries) rather than to credit financing.

(the separation of currency circuits, for example) and longer-range decisions (such as working capital norms and credit planning), rather than day-to-day activities designed to influence aggregate demand, as already discussed in Chapters 3 and 6. It is thus more appropriate to speak of monetary strategy than of monetary policy, and assign it the role of an organic component of the planning process rather than that of an independent tool for influencing current economic activity. Monetary policy in the Soviet Union is, in fact, limited to controlling the aggregate amount of currency (household money), the volume and structure of credit, and the level of enterprise balances. It plays hardly any role in setting investment priorities or in achieving increases in productivity and affecting the transfer of human and material resources between industries and regions.

Although one can identify at any one time the general objectives of the State Bank's credit and note-issue policies, it is difficult to tie these separate aspects into something that would add up to a "socialist monetary policy." Western views on Soviet monetary policy depend on a number of things: the period considered; the definition of what constitutes monetary policy (for instance, whether manipulation of the budget surplus constitutes monetary policy); whether price setting is considered a "monetary means," as Holzman proposes;[7] and whether one believes that price stability is an absolute priority, or, as Hodgman claims, that authorities are only concerned with achieving a degree of price stability consistent with a desired rate and pattern of output growth.[8] Montias holds that the role of the monetary and financial system is limited to assuring that material plans can be carried out without financial impediments.[9] Most Western economists agree with Powell that Soviet monetary policy has no quantitative objectives; at best, the Ministry of Finance and the State Bank can take post-factum actions to correct their collective mistakes.[10] Others believe with Pickersgill that "an economy in which goods and services are exchanged for money and in which

---

[7][131], p. 130, f. 1.

[8][122], p. 108.

[9]See Chapter 3, footnote 5. This is the conclusion of Montias with regard to Poland; see [118], p. 56.

[10][140], p. 1.2a.

workers are paid in units of generalized power" will have at least an implicit monetary policy.[11] Ames makes the additional point that "nonmonetary measures" may and, in fact, frequently are based on monetary analysis and aim at the preservation of monetary equilibrium, so that the fact that a remedy is "nonmonetary" does not mean that it has no "monetary" aspects.[12]

Neither the degree to which overall targets have been achieved nor shortcomings in certain areas of the economy and in individual industries can be traced directly to the financial system in general or its monetary aspects in particular. Yet the question has been raised whether monetary policy, although passive, might not have contributed to achieving the goals set by planners.[13]

Soviet monetary policy focuses on the flow of consumer purchasing power rather than on the total stock of money. With prices set administratively and the scope for fluctuations in currency turnover minimal, Soviet monetary policy operates, in fact, on the basis of what Hodgman has called "an inverted equation of exchange" by adjusting M to T.[14] One problem is to determine in which way control of money to absorb and sterilize excess purchasing power is shared between the State Bank and the budget.

Maintenance of equilibrium in the consumer market is greatly facilitated by the physical and operational separation of consumer money from enterprise money. The proper growth of currency in circulation is one of the "proportionalities" claimed to be a keystone of Soviet planning. This increase is determined within an implicit analytical framework that is not unfamiliar to Western economists. The rise in consumer disposable income projected from the planned growth targets for GNP at a planned (normally unchanged) price, after allowing for projected voluntary savings, yields an estimate of the required increase in currency in circulation, assuming stable velocity. If the flow of consumer goods and services cannot be increased correspondingly, inflationary pressures will develop as currency accumulates in the hands of consumers. If spendable income cannot be reduced sufficiently,

[11][138], p. 217.
[12]Ames [99], p. 172.
[13]See, for instance, Wiles [253].
[14]In Holzman [122], p. 123. Earlier, the Hungarian economist Varga made the same point in [252].

credit to the economy must be cut, if budget surpluses, deposits held by enterprises and collective farms, household savings, and such minor potential offsets as profits of the State Bank cannot absorb the excess currency. It is in this sense that the "planned" increase in circulation "determines" the volume of credit, a statement that is frequently found in Soviet literature and one that, to Western economists, appears to put things upside down. Constant official emphasis is on limiting credit and maintaining levels of circulating currency that neither push *kolkhoz* market prices far above official food prices nor produce persistent consumer goods shortages and queueing.

In addition to limiting currency in circulation, the basic objective of bank policy is to offset any changes in the velocity of household cash which may result from dishoarding, usually as a result of precautionary buying in anticipation of shortages.[15] When the level and distribution of spending do not conform to the underlying plans, only minor remedial action can be taken by the State Bank through administrative improvisation.

If excessive issuance of credit produces redundant balances in the accounts of the state-owned sector of the economy—in addition to or instead of an excessive flow of purchasing power to households—the problem is tackled by administrative intervention, either by transferring cash balances among individual enterprises (thus obviating the need to borrow by some of them), or by speeding up loan collection.

Holzman, who authored the most detailed study of the period from the start of the first Five-Year Plan in 1928 to 1957 credits improved direct bank controls over aggregate payroll expenditures rather than deflationary monetary and fiscal policy for the considerable easing of inflationary pressures after World War II.[16] Other Western students of the Soviet economy view the post-World War II decline and ultimate stabilization of prices, accompanied by a decline of free-market prices relative to official prices, as the result of a "fully-administered price decline" rather than a monetary deflation.

---

[15]Given the low level of financial savings until the middle sixties, surges in the velocity of currency due to dishoarding or withdrawals from savings accounts have never assumed large proportions. Concern with variations in velocity and attempts to study its determinants go back to the early thirties.

[16][240], p. 188.

FISCAL POLICY

Budget policy has been a key element in Soviet financial policy. The various aspects of this policy involve not only decisions about the level of the budget and the size of planned surpluses, but also such matters as the use of surpluses as a source of bank credit, the structure of taxation, virtually compulsory loans (see below), and the determination of the portion of budget revenue channeled into capital formation. In view of the central role of the budget in economic planning and the overall apportionment of resources between the socialized sector and the consumption sector, overall fiscal policy has been a more important financial regulator than monetary policy.[17] Budgetary policy has been used for basic decisions regarding longer-run periods (normally the duration of a five-year plan), rather than as an economic steering mechanism or for "fine tuning" when performance failures occur or miscalculations become apparent. Its chief characteristic has been a gradual restructuring of the revenue side. The precise point at which revenue for the financing of public investment, general administration, and provision of collective services is collected is largely a matter of convenience.

Since 1924, when the first steps toward overall financial planning were taken, the budget has shown a surplus, except for the war years. The interpretation of budgetary surpluses for individual years is complicated by a variety of factors, including the treatment before 1963 of the net increase in savings deposits as a regular source of revenue and the availability of bank credit to individual enterprises for discharging their liabilities toward the budget, including payment of the state's share of profits.

Budget surpluses have been an important source of increases in bank resources. Sterilized cumulative surpluses are more comparable to additions to bank capital than to banking claims.[18] In fact, a very large but unknown part of the liabilities of the State Bank consists of such Treasury deposits (perhaps 40 percent). Thus, by systematically building up its deposits at the State Bank the

[17]Powell, in Holzman [122], p. 576. He arrived at a similar conclusion for the pre-World War II years in [140].

[18]In contrast to China, the Soviet Union does not specifically neutralize such surpluses in a frozen Treasury account. See [123], pp. 138ff.

Ministry of Finance transfers to it command over a certain amount of real resources which, until recently, at least, the Bank has used mainly for making working-capital loans to enterprises.

Personal taxes have not played a significant part in the Soviet fiscal system since taxation of wage and salary earners was reduced to a nominal level in 1958.[19] In recent years, personal taxes have been applied mostly to the private income of state employees (such as income from the private practice of doctors and lawyers), to individuals producing goods or providing services outside the socialized sector, and to bachelors and small families.

The insignificance of the private sector has kept income taxation, in contrast to some other socialist countries, from becoming a potent means of syphoning off excess purchasing power. Nevertheless, due to the growth of nonwage taxation and the tax base itself, the share of revenue raised from this source rose from 5 percent in 1940 to over 8.2 percent in 1971. It must be kept in mind when interpreting this increase that, prior to 1957, compulsory loan subscriptions at the place of employment were equivalent to withheld payroll taxes. (In fact, government borrowing from the population during the twenties and thirties comprised a substantial element of overall financial policy.)

The relatively small reliance placed on personal taxes veils the basic fact that a much larger part of the social income than in the Western countries has been absorbed and disposed of by the budget. For instance, the total tax burden as a percentage of personal income, which Holzman computed to obtain an estimate of the *ex ante* inflationary gap, doubled between 1926 and 1936. According to Holzman's estimates, the average true rate of taxation oscillated between 51 and 60 percent in the 1932–1940 period, and rose further in the years immediately following World War II, reaching a peak of almost 69 percent in 1949.[20]

The two main sources of budgetary receipts, enterprise profits and turnover taxes, have already been discussed in Chapter 5. The overall amount of profits is determined by planning of economic performance, including the setting and attainment of profit

[19]See Burmistrov [19]. For the history of personal taxation, see Maryakhin [60]. See also Davies [109] and Zverev [95].

[20]Holzman [121], Table 53, col. I for the 1926–1936 comparison, and col. IIA for the average rate.

margins and the degree of plan fulfillment. The setting of the profit rates by industry and of turnover taxes on individual products are important means toward maintaining demand-supply equilibrium.

On balance, while the burden of taxation has remained heavy, decreasing emphasis has been placed on the turnover tax. Selective reductions in turnover tax rates for individual products and their abolition for all services in 1957 have been used to stabilize the cost of living by offsetting, when deemed desirable, production cost increases. The share of the turnover tax in total budgetary receipts declined gradually from 62.7 percent in 1940 to 31.6 percent in 1970 (see Table 8.1), but contrary to Professor Liberman's view, it is still far from "becoming more and more a dying, rudimentary form of taxation."[21]

The form of taxation, however, affects mainly the nominal rather than the real value of incomes. The type of tax will have only marginal effect on the distribution of the social product and the pattern of output.

Internal loans have been used from 1922 to 1956, as a means of absorbing excess purchasing power. Loan drives were conducted very much like political campaigns. Efforts to achieve subscription goals included attractive terms (including various kinds of real-value guarantees), appeals to the gambling instinct (by distributing interest in the form of lottery prizes), and to patriotism (by earmarking the proceeds of individual issues to the financing of specific major projects of national significance).

From 1927 to 1956, loans were issued annually, ostensibly to help finance voluntarily industrialization and the war effort, but, in fact, as a means of implementing a program of forced savings. Loans quotas were assigned to individual factories and other places of employment and subscriptions were collected over the year in installments by payroll deduction. Subscription was quasi-obligatory, although some allowance was made for the family responsibilities and other particular circumstances of each worker. The nonvoluntary character of subscriptions to government loans was openly recognized. The amount of such loans was gradually raised from 20 million (new) rubles for each of the three issues of 1927 to 320 million rubles for a single issue in 1956, the year in which their issuance was discontinued. The maturity of

---

[21]Liberman [54], p. 160.

TABLE 8.1

The Share of Turnover Taxes in Total Budgetary Receipts,
Selected Years
(billions of rubles)

	1940	1950	1960	1970
Total receipts[a]	16.9	39.2	76.2	156.2
Turnover taxes	10.6	23.6	31.3	49.4
Turnover tax as percentage of total	62.7	60.2	41.1	31.6

SOURCE: Computed from [86].

[a] Excludes receipts from Government loans, but not from savings deposits.

such "mass loans" was initially ten years, but was lengthened
to twenty in 1936. By the beginning of World War II, bonds for
a total of 5 billion rubles (roughly equivalent to about the same
amount of dollars) had been placed. It is estimated that about 15
percent of the costs of World War II were met by the issuance
of loans. Loans were frequently over-subscribed and issued for
amounts exceeding the target originally set.

At the time these forced loans were discontinued (when interest
payments on outstanding indebtedness rose close to amounts of
new money that could be raised in annual drives), subscriptions
through payroll deductions amounted to 6 to 7 percent of total
wage disbursements and 7.5 percent of total government revenue.

Holders of government bonds suffered losses in principal and
income, beginning in 1930, as a result of several conversions into
longer-term issues, exchange into a consolidated loan at an unfa-
vorable rate at the time of the 1947 ruble conversion, and successive lowering of the interest rate originally set. At the time forced
loans were discontinued, payment of interest on the bonds outstanding was discontinued altogether, transforming them into
interest-free loans. The date of the start of retirement operations,
originally set at 1977, was later advanced to 1974, and is to be
completed in 1990.[22]

---

[22]In addition to compulsory loans, "free" lottery loans with a higher yield (3 instead of 2
percent) have been available on tap since 1947. Since 1958, it is the only security sold. The
amount of such loans outstanding at the end of 1973 was 3.4 billion rubles. For a history of
government borrowing, see Zverev [94] and "Gosudarstwennye Zaimy" in [27].

INCOME POLICY

Income policy includes a number of activities: the control of wage rates and the aggregate wage bill, the entire area of state-*kolkhoz* relations, price setting for goods and services, and determining the range of free services to be offered.

Most, if not all, of the elements of income policy enter into the planning process itself. Thus, adjustments in wages and prices, including those achieved through varying the turnover tax, together with decisions on changes in production and foreign trade patterns, reflect basic decisions underlying the five-year plans. However, adjustments are also made in midstream. They are usually designed to compensate for deviations in actual results from plans or to achieve final goals different from original intentions (for instance, to increase the flow of goods to households at a faster pace than originally planned). Income policy may also involve, in individual years, increasing income selectively by raising hourly wages, providing incentive payments and bonuses, raising stipends and old-age pensions, and extending these to additional population groups. The most important instance of the latter was the granting of state pensions to members of collective farms in 1958.

Continuous efforts are made to keep the compensation of labor, by far the most important source of consumer purchasing power, within the limits specified in each enterprise's plan. This control of the "wages fund" is one of the most important tasks of the State Bank.[23] Failure to control payrolls effectively was the principal cause of pre-World War II inflation. The improved control of currency disbursements in the fifties has greatly reduced inflationary pressure and has made effective price stabilization possible. Since that time, the policy of the authorities to pass on the benefits of greater productivity through price cuts rather than by increasing nominal wages has reduced potential strains on monetary management.

During periods of increasing availability of consumer goods, real purchasing power of the population has been enlarged by

[23]See Galimon [28].

lowering the turnover tax levied on specific items, by cutting prices for various categories of consumer goods thus acknowledging the reductions in production costs of consumer durables, and by reducing, at times by substantial amounts, the cost of food items distributed through government and "cooperative" channels. Subsidies have also been quite widely used and manipulated when price changes to reflect higher costs appeared undesirable or when it seemed desirable to sell some food and other items below cost.

As a means of absorbing excess purchasing power in the household sector, the Soviet Union has resorted several times to general upward price adjustments. Price increases for consumer goods reduce the real value of cash balances in the hands of the population while increasing budgetary resources.

Since prices have no direct effects on production, the level of average factory prices at which output is sold to organizations in charge of distribution and exports can be set to facilitate administration of the economy. Average-cost pricing and average profit-margin targets are used for this purpose. Some prices are set to achieve noneconomic goals such as combating alcoholism or encouraging reading of official publications.

From Inflation to Price Stability

Since the initiation of central planning, the degree of inflationary pressures acting on the Soviet economy has depended to a large extent on the skill with which credit, fiscal, price, production, and inventory policies have been combined and applied to specific situations, and on how close the prognosis of future developments has been to actual performance. It is less than obvious what contribution monetary and credit policy have made to limiting inflationary pressures during the pre-World War II period. For the period following the war, an almost complete lack of relevant data precludes any attempt to quantify their influence.

Since the required monetary statistics, such as currency in circulation, are not available, the underlying developments must be inferred from fragmentary and indirect evidence. On the question of what indirect measures best reflect inflationary pressures, opinions among students of the Soviet economy differ. Some have used official price indexes[24] or those constructed by Western experts, while others have relied on evidence of changes in inventories or savings deposits. Another indirect measure of inflationary pressures is the relationship between budget surpluses and the expansion of short-term credit. The use of this indicator is, admittedly, beset by a number of difficulties; for instance, some of the resources available for lending are derived from current budgetary appropriations "for the reinforcement of the resources of the State Bank" rather than from past or current surpluses. Furthermore, it is not known what part of the increase in bank credit has resulted in a net increase in currency in circulation. While some broad assumptions and adjustments can be made, they do not yield a sufficiently complete and reliable picture, either for individual years or for selected periods.

PRICE DIFFERENCES IN PARALLEL MARKETS

Still another measure of inflationary pressure may be obtained by comparing price movements in the parallel markets which have operated in the Soviet Union. Prior to 1935, when a uniform price system was established for goods sold by state stores, several separate markets were operating in addition to the *kolkhoz* market, which has remained by far the most important free market.

Price levels and movements in these markets differed because of compartmentalization of supply and differentiated demand schedules, and because of shifts in these schedules in response to a variety of factors, including relevant price changes in competing but different markets.

During the pre-1935 period at least three categories of prices

---

[24]For a comprehensive review and critique of Soviet price data, see Jasny's pathbreaking study [124], and Bornstein, "Soviet Price Statistics," in [161], which has an extensive bibliography. See also Chapman [108], Chapters 2 to 6. A considerable amount of Soviet price data is summarized in tables and charts in Malafeev [57]. This monograph contains a detailed discussion of price history and a surprisingly candid discussion of inflationary pressures. It also includes a chronology of party and government decisions regarding prices between 1917 and 1963.

were relevant for households: (1) ration prices for goods to the urban population holding ration cards; (2) commercial prices for goods purchased predominantly by urban households (higher than ration prices); and (3) free *kolkhoz* market prices at which households could buy food. Prices in two special markets completed the price structure: (4) prices in "cooperative" country stores (the state network of retail stores in the villages), at which farmers could buy manufactured goods; and (5) prices (in gold rubles) in special stores for foreigners and the few Soviet citizens able to pay in foreign exchange.

The unification of prices and the abolition of rationing at the end of 1947 left only two price systems—official prices in state stores, now incorporating the network of cooperative stores, and the *kolkhoz* market.[25]

The failure to drain off excess purchasing power or to increase the availability of consumer goods and services can be traced by comparing price movements between these markets. The *kolkhoz* market is the only market in which prices are set by producers. It consists of thousands of stores and stands through which *kolkhozes* and, especially their individual members, sell that part of their output for which they have freedom of disposition. This market has been the most important—and visible—indicator of the intensity of inflationary pressures. When the urban population cannot satisfy its demand at the state retail stores and seeks to obtain additional food in the *kolkhoz* market, a redistribution of purchasing power takes place, and a restructuring of the demand for final products results. However, since the propensity of the *kolkhoz* farmers to save is apparently higher than that of the urban population, some reduction of repressed inflation takes place. On the theory that, for all practical purposes, the *kolkhoz* market has been the only, or at least by far the most important, outlet for such excess demand, the ratio of prices in that market to those in state stores has been used as a rough indicator of inflationary pressures (see Table 8.2).[26]

---

[25]Jasny [124].

[26]While special stores for sales against convertible foreign exchange have continued in existence in a modified form, they do not play the same role as before World War II and are, in fact, much more limited to serving tourist and some privileged groups of Soviet citizens.

PERIODS IN SOVIET MONETARY EXPERIENCE

The monetary experience of the Soviet Union can be divided into five periods:

1. The years of war communism and of the New Economic Policy prior to the currency reform of 1924.
2. The period between 1924 and the introduction of the credit reforms of 1930–1932.
3. The period from 1933 up to the Soviet Union's entry into World War II.
4. World War II and on to the currency conversion at the end of 1947.
5. From 1948 to the present, which subdivides into a period of deflation through 1954 and one of considerable price stability thereafter.

The first two periods have been analyzed by several writers and have already been dealt with briefly in Chapter 2.[27] Since our focus is on the monetary system that emerged after the 1930–1932 reforms, only the periods following them will be reviewed here. The available price data for the entire period 1928–1970 are summarized in Table 8.2.

1932–1940. The credit reforms of 1930–1932 created a financial system which would have made it possible to achieve an equilibrium between material and monetary flows. However, the actual

[27]See Arnold [100], Katzenellenbaum [126], Reddaway [142], and Yurovski [92]. Holzman has developed an indicator of repressed inflation based on an estimate of the effect of the spillover of the urban population's purchasing power into the *kolkhoz* market for food products. This index, which Holzman qualifies as partial, is the ratio of the difference between actual expenditures in the *kolkhoz* market and the same expenditures valued at official retail prices at state stores to the sum of total purchases from these two sources valued at state store prices. Such a comparison of fixed and free prices for food is, of course, only a rough indicator of the strength of inflationary pressures (see Table 8.4). The formula is given in [240], p. 170. Short-term fluctuations, and in some cases longer-run comparisons as well, are influenced by the changes in each market's share of total food sold and in fixed prices in the state stores. They are also affected by the construction of the price indexes being compared and by the limitation of the available estimates of the quantities sold and prices charged in the thousands of separate outlets operated by individual *kolkhozes,* in some cases at a considerable distance from the point of production. Also, some purchases from *kolkhozes* and of the private output of their members bypass officially recognized markets from which price data are collected. A more sophisticated version of this measure takes into account the share of food purchased in the free market as well as prices reported in this market.

TABLE 8.2

Indexes of Retail and Related Prices

	Retail Prices in State and Cooperative Stores (1937 = 100)		Kolkhoz Market[c] (1937 = 100)	Retail Prices[a] (1940 = 100)	Cost of Living[e]		Consumer Prices[f] (1950 = 100)
	Malafeev[a]	Moorstein-			1937 Weights (1937 = 100)	Current Year Weights (1937 = 100)	
1928	18.7				20.9	14.3	
—							
1931		19.7					
1932	47.6	36.4	430				
1933		54.5	250				
1934		64.3	200				
1935		83.2	170				
1936		94.2	100				
1937	100.0	100.0	100		100	100	
1938		100.0					
1939		102					
1940	118.8	126		100	142	136	
—							
1944		149					
1945	259.1	168					
1946		237					
1947	381.5	346			327	294	
1948		300					
1949		268					
1950	221.3	222		186			100.0
1951	202.1	206					

Year					(1960 = 100)			
1952	191.4	198			161			
1953	173.5	180	220	202				
1954	163.2	170						
1955	163.2	170	188	178				76.6
1956	163.4	171						
1957	163.2	171						
1958	166.8	175						
1959	166.2	174						
1960	164.0	173			139	100		76.3
1961	163.1							76.4
1962								77.9
1963					141			78.8
1964								79.1
1965					140		121	77.8
1966							121	76.9
1967							120	76.9
1968					139		128	77.0
1969					139			77.7
1970								77.9
1971								77.7
1972								78.5

[a] Malafeev [57].

[b] Moorstein-Powell, [134], Table P-3, pp. 635–636; for 1937, 1940, 1948–1955 from Bergson [103]; interpolated (straight line and free-hand interpolations) for other years as explained on pp. 574–576 and 637. For 1956–1960, official index, changed in 1955.

[c] Holzman [240].

[d] Official index from [86], 1969, p. 625. Not available on this or any other base prior to 1940.

[e] Chapman [108], Table 6. See Ch. VI for detailed description.

[f] David W. Bronson, private communication.

policies pursued through the successive five-year plans of accelerated industrialization did not bring about price stability. The credit reform hardly slowed the rise in consumer prices, and the flow of purchasing power to consumers continued to exceed the available supply of consumer goods at official prices by considerable amounts, so that a state of repressed inflation developed. Consumer prices rose sharply between 1933 and 1936 (from 54.5 to 94.2, according to the Moorestein-Powell Index), and more slowly (by about 10 percent for the entire three-year period) between 1936 and 1939. As Table 8.1 shows, they rose sharply again between 1939 and 1940.

The inflation was the joint consequence of a systematic underallocation of resources to consumer goods production and of a wage drift which was an almost unavoidable by-product of the industrialization policy pursued. The supply situation in this period was worsened still further by a reduction of food supplies resulting from the forced collectivization and related farm policies. The vigor of the inflationary pressures is evident (or can be derived) from official statistics, despite their shortcomings, gaps, and inconsistencies.[28]

Control over payrolls was introduced soon after the credit reform early in 1933, in the form of monthly and quarterly "standard certificates for wages," issued to individual enterprises. To allow for the increase in average skills and to attract workers into the rapidly growing industrial area authorities *planned* average wage increases of up to 9 percent in some years. *Actual* annual increases, however, were considerably larger, ranging up to 25 percent or more a year. Thus, the "wage drift" alone was typically in excess of the projected overall rate of increase.[29]

Moreover, according to Pickersgill's estimates, the income velocity of currency circulation rose from 5.9 in 1933 to 14.9 in 1937.[30] At the same time, neutralization through budget surpluses

---

[28]Atlas [163], p. 88, claims, apparently on the basis of unpublished data, that in the five years immediately preceding World War II (1935–1940) currency circulation was permitted to increase only in proportion to the availability of consumer goods through trade channels. He gives a coefficient of correlation of .96 for this period between these two magnitudes.

[29]See Holzman [121], p. 39, 309–310; and [240], p. 177.

[30][138], Table III, p. 55.

of monetary expansion resulting from issuance of short-term credit was quite moderate.[31]

Powell found that for 1935–1937 available evidence scarcely suggests any systematic coordination of credit and budgetary policy, while for the thirties as a whole, the money stock and budgetary surpluses were *negatively* correlated. If the authorities did, in fact, pursue a policy of using surpluses to offset undesirable movements in the money stock, its effects must have involved lags of an undetermined nature.[32] Powell concluded that while excess monetary demand in the period between the credit reform and World War II possibly served to assure a maximization of output, "monetary policy has more frustrated than facilitated the attainment of those ultimate objectives which the system was meant to serve,"[33] namely, price stability, orderly distribution of the social product, and growth. It may be added that the burden of a widening and tightening of financial controls must be counted among the "real consequences" of the failure of the monetary and banking system prior to World War II to effectively deal with excess monetary demand.

The pre-World War II inflation cannot be considered a planned policy of financing forced industrialization through inflation. Indeed, the successive plans projected a decline in the price level designed to pass on to consumers a large part of the benefits of rising productivity. The first plan (1928–1932) also provided for a growth of currency circulation (62 percent) slower than that of the increased availability of consumer goods (80–90 percent); no doubt, however, a considerable monetary overhang existed at the start of this period.

Clearly, before World War II there were enough leakages in the control system and enough weaknesses and uncertainties in the underlying plans to result in an almost continuous rise in the price level (though some diminution of inflationary pressures is reflected in the sharp drop of Holzman's indicator from 17.3 in 1933 to 7.7 in 1940). Actual spending could rise above the

---

[31][121], pp. 53 and 229.
[32][140], pp. 267, 296–298.
[33][140], p. 337.

amounts planned *ex ante* primarily because enterprises exceeded the planned amounts of payrolls, and, to a limited extent, because consumers activated currency hoards. As a result, a significant disequilibrium between monetary demand and the available supply at fixed prices characterized the years between the credit reform and the Soviet Union's entry into World War II in 1941.

1941–1947. The financing of the Soviet war effort involved neither large-scale issuance of currency nor borrowing from the State Bank.[34] Prices rose rapidly, particularly during the first three war years (1941–1943). In July 1943, prices for the main categories of farm products in the *kolkhoz* market were 18.7 times their July 1941 level (having reached a peak in April 1943); the *kolkhoz* market's share of food sales rose between 1940 and 1945 from 20 to 51 percent, and of all retail sales, from 14 to 46 percent. According to Malafeev's calculations, the weighted index of prices of goods sold in the state and *kolkhoz* market in 1945 was still 325 percent of the 1940 level, while the index of prices in state and cooperative stores alone was nearly 2.2 times higher.[35]

During World War II, the State Bank continued its usual activities, which were disrupted in large areas of the national territory for several years by military operations and by the German occupation. As in other countries engaged in war, it serviced the currency needs of the army. Its normal credit activities were complicated not only by the temporary loss of territory to the occupying armies of Germany and its allies, but also by the large-scale evacuation of factories to Siberia, Central Asia, and other areas removed from the theatre of operations. It is remarkable that neither the use of Soviet currency by the invading armies (along with occupation currency issued by them), nor the dislocation of normal economic activity and administrative structure in occupied areas, nor the subsequent incorporation into the Soviet Union of large territories on its Western border resulted in monetary chaos.

The war-generated overhang of liquidity consisted essentially of currency in the hands of consumers, especially the farmers,

---

[34]Deficits in the earlier war years amounting to a total of 32 billion rubles were followed by small surpluses in the last two years (1944 and 1945).

[35][63], pp. 234, 235, and 407.

who had been unable to spend their income during the war years because of the shortage of goods. It was removed by the currency conversion of 1947 (see Chapter 3).

1948–1972. Following the currency conversion of 1947, which abolished wartime rationing, the trend in prices was almost continuously downward until 1954; since then, average consumer prices have remained about level. The share of the *kolkhoz* market in total retail sales (valued in prices actually paid in both markets) declined from 12.0 percent in 1950 to 4.5 percent in 1960 and 2.8 percent in 1969.[36] In the postwar period, the State Bank has been clearly more effective than before in controlling disbursements from enterprise balances, and spending for unauthorized purposes, particularly for wages, has been significantly reduced. For instance, any overspending on payrolls is required to be offset by compensating reductions in aggregate wage payments by the offending enterprise in the following three to five months.

The degree to which fiscal policy has contributed to maintaining a relatively high degree of price stability is not clear. Yet the contrast between the period before World War II and that following the currency conversion of 1947 is striking. In the eleven years beginning January 1, 1930, the cumulative budget surplus of 26.4 billion rubles (most of which was sterilized in the treasury account of the State Bank) was little more than half as great as the 50.6 billion ruble increase in short-term loans outstanding. By contrast, in the years 1951 through 1956, budget surpluses exceeded increments in bank loans.[37] However, as Holzman points out, judging from price changes in individual years, over short-run periods the budget surplus-loan expansion offset mechanism was no more effective in the fifties than it had been in the thirties.

Fluctuations of consumer goods prices in state stores, in the *kolkhoz* market, and in the ratio of the two price indexes since the end of World War II must be viewed from the perspective of a huge increase in money income during this period. With the sum of taxes and other deductions (mainly state loan subscriptions)

---

[36][92], 1969, p. 600. Valued in state store prices, the decline was from 11.4 to 3.0 and to 1.8 percent, respectively.

[37]Powell in Holzman [122], p. 4. It must be kept in mind that in Soviet budgets the sale of government bonds is considered a regular source of receipts.

rising at a more moderate rate than monetary income, total disposable income in 1970 was more than three times as large as in 1950, according to official data. In spite of a rapid rise in population, real 1970 per capita income deflated by official retail prices was more than four times as large as twenty years earlier (Table 8.3, last line), since these prices on balance show a decline over the period. During the same time, the proportion of food purchased in the *kolkhoz* market, which is not reflected in the official price index, declined, particularly after 1958, while the percentage of income saved increased sharply.

The main components of monetary income and their disposal are summarized in Table 8.3. Gross earnings of wage and salary workers constitute the bulk of money income. Wage payments to the members of *kolkhozes* and various types of transfer payments (mainly pensions), accounting for more than one-fifth of the total in 1970 (against 12 percent in 1950), rose even more rapidly. Net income from the sale of farm products by the *kolkhozes* and their individual members in 1970 was slightly more than double the 1950 level and a much larger part of income generated in the *kolkhoz* sector was distributed in money wages. "Other income," of which military pay is the largest component, declined gradually in the two decades.

A detailed examination of the Soviet price indexes cannot be undertaken here. Most Western scholars have considerable reservations on many accounts, but are inclined to accept them as rough approximations reflecting the basic changes over time. According to the official retail price index[38] (Table 8.2, column 4), the consumer prices remained virtually unchanged during the sixties, following a sharp decline during the fifties.

The fact that since the end of World War II prices in the *kolkhoz* market have continued to exceed food prices at state stores suggests that available supplies, choice, and quality of food carried by state stores continue to be deficient. The ratio of the two price indexes rose sharply between the fourth quarter of 1950 and 1955 (see Table 8.4), and Holzman's indicator of suppressed

---

[38]The size of the bias in the available official price indexes is unknown. Thus, during 1969–1970, ceilings were placed on the supposedly free collective farm market prices. At the same time, there has been increased evidence in recent years of surreptitious price increases for various consumer goods. See Bush, "Soviet Inflation," in Laulan [127].

TABLE 8.3

Disposable Money Income, Selected Years, 1950–1970
(in billions of rubles)

	1950	1955	1960	1965	1970	1972
Gross earnings of wage and salary workers	31.1	43.3	60.0	89.1	132.0	148.9
Collective farm wage payments	1.1	3.1	5.1	9.1	13.5	14.7
Net income from the sale of farm products	4.5	4.5	6.0	7.2	9.6 }	15.8
Other[a]	5.4	5.8	3.9	3.4	3.5 }	
Transfer payments	4.8	6.9	11.3	15.7	24.4	27.1
Total money income	47.0	63.5	86.2	124.4	183.0	206.5
Direct taxes	3.6	4.8	5.6	7.7	12.7 }	15.1
Other deductions[b]	2.9	3.3	0.4	0.4	0.7 }	
Total disposable income	40.5	55.4	80.2	116.3	169.5	191.8
Per capita disposable income (rubles)	224.8	282.4	274.4	503.7	698.2	
Index of real per capita disposable income[c]	100.0	164.0	218.3	288.0	400.8	

Source: Bronson and Severin in [152 and 153]; for 1972 preliminary estimates (communication from M. Bronson).

Note: Totals may not add up due to rounding.

[a] Mostly military pay.

[b] 1950 and 1965 include 2.7 and 3.1 billion rubles of government loan subscriptions, respectively.

[c] Deflated by the official consumer price index (1950 = 100).

TABLE 8.4

Indicators of Inflationary Pressures, Selected
Years, 1940–1971

I. Ratio of Collective Farm Market to State Retail Prices for Food

1940 Annual average	1.78	1955 Four quarters	1.74
1945 Annual average	5.33	1955 Annual average	1.75
1947 Four quarters	2.98	1960 Annual average	1.35
1950 Four quarters	1.25	1964 Annual average	1.63

II. Holzman's Indicator[a]

1932	17.1[b]	1950	2.5	1954	4.2
1933	17.3	1951	3.4	1955	4.1
1940	7.7	1952	4.8	1956	2.8
		1953	3.5		

III. Partial Indicator of Suppressed Inflation
(1955 = 100)

1950	39	1960	30	1966	24
1955	100	1961	38	1967	24
1956	59	1962	37	1968	22
1957	40	1963	36	1969	25
1958	41	1964	39	1970	22
1959	32	1965	28	1971	23

Sources: For I, 1940–1955, see Holzman [240], pp. 168–170; for 1955–1964, see Bronson and Severin in [153], p. 514, revised and updated by the authors. For II, including formula for the indicator, see Holzman [240], pp. 168–170. For III, see Bronson and Severin, as above.

[a] 1950–1956: fourth quarter only.

[b] Probably understated; see [133], p. 258.

inflation rose from 2.5 to 4.1. Bronson and Severin,[39] who have recomputed Holzman's indicator of suppressed inflation on the basis of more recent data and carried it forward to 1971, found an even greater rise between 1950 and 1955 (based on annual averages). The decline in the overall price level prior to 1955 is explainable largely by a reduction in state store prices, while the subsequent decline through 1960 was due to a decline in the share of the higher-priced *kolkhoz* market in total food sales. The index of repressed inflation rose again moderately and irregularly between 1960 and 1964, reflecting rising *kolkhoz* market prices, with disposable money income up by nearly 30 percent at the end

[39]David W. Bronson and B. Severin, "Recent Trends in Consumption and Disposable Income in the USSR," in [153], p. 500. I am indebted to D. Bronson for supplying the revised and extended data, shown in Table 11.

of the four-year period,[40] but it declined through 1966 and fluctuated little thereafter.

The much improved post-World War II price experience, during the sixties in particular, was due, at least in part, to a more skillful coordination of fiscal and bank policy which made it possible to achieve a declining and eventually stable price level. Since a considerable part of the typical worker's budget during the war had been spent on food purchased at free market prices, an initial upward adjustment of food prices at state stores was required in the first postwar years to reduce the spread between official and free market ("commercial") prices in order to make abolition of food rationing feasible. This, however, did not bring a complete unification of the price system. The real income of wage and salary earners was fairly rapidly reestablished by subsequent price reductions, mainly for manufactured products.

Factors Contributing to Price Stability

The Soviet Union has managed to avoid the inflationary crises that have created considerable difficulties in many of the other socialist countries[41] and, in the sixties, was able to widen options available to consumers. While it is difficult to assess the relative contributions of the main financial tools in achieving the impressive degree of price stability prevailing in the sixties, the following have clearly been the most important contributing factors. 1. Closer adherence to financial plans (improved "financial discipline") by enterprises. 2. A more successful balancing of currency flows going to the population vis-á-vis the increased availability of consumer goods. Since the discontinuance after 1957 of the forced placement of government bonds, the authorities' ability to attract a large volume of voluntary deposits into savings banks also helped to keep the growth of effective demand within desirable limits. 3. Greater efficiency and promptness in absorbing excessive amounts of currency paid out, mainly by manipulation

[40]Unpublished estimates by D. Bronson.
[41]See, for instance, Podolski [139] and the articles on Poland by Brzeski and by Montias in Grossman [118]. On China, see Hsiao [123].

of administered prices and of turnover taxes. 4. The more efficient control of wages, and more importantly, greater success of the State Bank in controlling actual withdrawals of currency for payrolls.

Many unanswered questions remain, however. Did the system offer much more scope for monetary and credit policy beyond the role it actually played? No doubt from the thirties to the mid-sixties the system by and large fitted the requirements of the centrally directed economy. But was there room, without undermining its principal characteristics, for developing a market sector or para-market mechanisms through which production and distribution of certain consumer goods and services would be guided by monetary demand and prices would reflect the play of supply and demand? Could a wider application of monetary tools and processes have achieved more efficient resource use within the framework of planners' intentions? Could the operational aspects of the monobank have been improved significantly without undermining the basic premises of a banking system whose main function was to make real flows meet plan objectives, not to influence them? Could credit financing of investment, even along the modest lines of the 1965 Reform, have contributed to reducing completion delays and thus diminish the volume of real resources not contributing to current output? These questions with regard to the past have assumed added significance since the launching of the Reform.

9

The Reform Ten Years Later

ALMOST ten years after it was initiated, evidence as to the contribution the Reform has made so far to increasing the efficiency of the Soviet economy and the rate of growth of GNP is still inconclusive; this is particularly true of the financial aspects of the Reform, which alone concern us here. In assessing the economic growth of the Soviet economy since 1965 in its various significant aspects (such as the relatively more rapid improvement in consumer well-being), it is well-nigh impossible to disentangle the influence of measures considered part of the Reform from those that are, in essence, the continuation of policies initiated several years earlier, many of which are associated with the name of Khrushchev. These include the monetization of *kolkhoz* operations, greater emphasis on progressive technology, a minimum income for farmers and higher minimum wages for workers, greater emphasis on housing and managerial training, and greater mobility of the labor force.

The direct effects of the Reform on labor productivity, unit costs, profitability, and the distribution of the social product are obscured by changes in the computation and presentation of official basic data, and by lack of information as to which of the new rules and policies are actually being implemented. There is evidence that outward compliance has not been accompanied by significant changes in old ways, and that postponement or suspension of the new system has resulted in considerable differences among industries. In many cases, the general principles of the Reform have been modified and adapted to the conditions and

183

requirements of individual industries, product lines, and economic administrations and regions.

By the time the twenty-fourth Communist Party Congress was held in March 1971, the term "economic reform" had nearly vanished from the scene.[1] Subsequently, certain measures were taken that actually represent a back-sliding from the Reform: additional targets ("directive indicators") were reintroduced (such as labor productivity targets at the enterprise level and experimental targets for wage cost per unit of output, authorized by individual ministries and republic authorities), and the progressivity of payment schedules for bonuses was reduced. Some important measures, initially announced as an integral part of the Reform, were never put into effect, while others were introduced only partially. Alongside all this, however, some measures are being passed from time to time that are designed to implement various aspects of the original reforms. Instead of simplifying the workings of the economy, the Reform, by superimposing new rules on a system that retained its basic structure, merely added to its complexity. Fear of the consequences of departures from familiar routine and uncertainty about the effects of the new arrangements on output, productivity, availability of inputs, and disposal of outputs—as well as concern about their authority and relationship with supervisory bodies—caused many enterprise directors to take a wait-and-see attitude and to actually resist change, covertly and even openly.

It is abundantly clear that resistance and downright sabotage by bureaucrats, believing themselves threatened by the changes and the complexity of the changes introduced in the financial mechanism, has caused considerable confusion. By and large, these changes were inadequately prepared for. Where room was left for interpretation and adaptation, the Reform resulted in a variety of combinations of the old and the new. Additional rules, norms, and techniques were frequently added to, rather than substituted for, what existed before. Ever since the inception of the Reform, the best ways of introducing the new financial techniques and of adapting them to specific conditions in individual industries have

[1]See Grossman in Dodge [112] and [238] and Schroeder [249] and [251]. See also J.E.C. [154], Prybylola [246].

been the subject of discussion in meetings, conferences, newspapers, and journals.

The fact that money flows, credit, and interest rates now play a more important role than before the Reform in oiling the wheels of the economic machine to increase its efficiency does not in itself represent a significant change. Nor does the new emphasis on financial incentives necessarily reduce interference from the central authorities. "Financial levers" can be manipulated no less than "norms" or other physical ratios, constraints, and targets— with the same potential for misallocating resources and offering inadequate incentives.

Greater availability of retained funds and bank credit is an essential condition of, but no guarantee for, decentralizing investment decisions. The main problem of socialist economies is not to raise enough investment financing but to optimize its use. So far there is no evidence that enterprises have been able to exert greater influence on the patterns of investment and to reduce the time lag between the inception and the completion of a project.

The Reform has failed in its central objective—to provide financial incentives powerful enough to maximize enterprise efforts to introduce advanced technology. This is important, for it has been identified by proponents of the Reform[2] as essential for improving the performance of the Soviet economy, together with decentralization of research and development and heightened interest by ministries and other supervisory authorities in the introduction of new technological processes and more advanced machinery.

Failure to come to grips with the central problem of the role of prices as a resource allocator has limited the significance of the various changes introduced under the Reform. The postulate of marginal pricing and clearing the market may not be adequate for steering the economy in a direction that would conform with the intentions of the responsible political authorities. However, while producers need not be guided by prices alone, planners

[2]See, for instance, V. Trapenznikov's important article in *Pravda* in August 1964 and his critical comments on the failings of the Reform in *Sotsialisticheskaya Promychlenost'* (Socialist Industry), December 3, 1970.
    On the introduction in July 1971 of specific sales targets for technologically advanced items in individual enterprises see earlier discussion.

must be ready to accept existing price relationships as sufficiently realistic to provide a basis for rational decisions. Adjustments in the price structure stemming from the Reform have attempted to make demand enter the process of price formation, but have nevertheless been made bureaucratically.

There is little evidence to suggest that the new "financial levers" operate as market allocators rather than merely as substitutes for orders from the planning center. An interest-free loan (or loan proffered at a preferential rate) may be a sugar-coated order; can the director afford not to take it without having to face up to "public criticism"? A considerable number of arrangements under the new system provide opportunities for continuing administrative interference, such as setting differentiated capital charge and depreciation rates. Actual experience so far suggests that survival of administrative controls has interferred with the play of "financial levers," which in many cases operate merely as auxiliary mechanisms of the command economy.[3]

The use of some indicator of profitability as a guide for structuring output and making investment decisions is important, whether such decisions are made by the central authorities or by the enterprise. But a significant improvement in enterprise efficiency is likely to require greater enterprise autonomy in the disposition of profits than has been in evidence. Only to the extent that the profit level significantly and directly benefits them will the individual enterprise and its staff have sufficient incentive to maximize profits as contrasted with meeting profit targets.

There is little evidence that this has been a significant result of the modest restructuring of financial flows. The enterprise director is still far from being a quasi entrepreneur, although he has somewhat more latitude than before in planning as well as in day-by-day operations. By restructuring production in favor of sellable items with the largest profit margin, he can attempt to increase profits beyond what they would be solely on the basis of productivity gains and enlarged volume, provided he is not exceeding the limits imposed from the outside. He is not free to set prices for his output, or to choose among substitutable inputs. The much-

---

[3]It is significant that in explaining the benefits of the new system, authorities emphasize that it will help to "disclose" hidden reserves, which apparently escape detection through the existent systems of financial and other controls.

emphasized contractual relationships he is free to establish with his suppliers are, in fact, limited to a spelling out of such details as delivery dates, since sources of supply, quantities, and general specifications of inputs are determined by outside agencies. Few of the intended changes in supply arrangements for raw materials, intermediate products, and capital goods, designed to introduce some degree of flexibility, have been implemented.

Administrative economic agencies (such as *glavks*) are still not operated on a business accounting basis. In spite of the emphasis on the managerial aspects of the Reform, most of the main problems of optimal industrial organization remain unresolved. The most important single change since the Reform was the creation of large horizontal or vertical groupings of enterprises *(ob'edineniye)*. It is uncertain whether such larger groupings (an organizational form that has become important in several of the smaller socialist countries) retaining the enterprise as the basic operating unit will be more than administrative substitutes for the present subdivisions of industrial ministries. Only modest progress toward the creation of such larger operating units has been made so far.

The emphasis on money and the role of credit in achieving a less wasteful use of resources on the microeconomic level must be viewed in the light of past failures to achieve satisfactory results in this area. As long as interest rates remain rigid and unresponsive to either demand or supply, their role in achieving an optimal allocation of resources is likely to remain essentially that of another administratively determined variable.

Is something identifiable as a "socialist monetary policy," rather than merely an improved use of credit and rechanneling of financial flows, about to emerge as a result of the Reform? Even though an answer still cannot be hazarded, it appears that the new developments are more likely to enhance the role of the State Bank as a financial intermediary than to endow it with the attributes of a central bank in the Western sense, or give it a greater role in managing aggregate demand. At best they will make access to credit increasingly dependent on the individual enterprise's profitability, its balance sheet, and, indirectly at least, the quality of its management. But even if the monobanker is ultimately permitted considerably more flexibility than in the initial stage of the Reform in dealing with microeconomic problems, thereby becoming a more efficient commercial and investment banker, this would not necessarily entail a basic change in the role of banking and the credit system.

So far the "new system of economic steering" has gone little beyond giving formal recognition to money as an agent of economic activity. It has not assigned to money any precise new functions. Hardly anything has been done beyond legitimatizing the role of money as a result of a tedious discussion on the "goods-money relationship." The role assigned to money may change if the relative weights attached to the plan and to the market in the new scheme of things shift in favor of the second, even if market processes and feedbacks are still limited to the consumption sector.

Is there room in the reformed economy for a specific socialist monetary and financial policy, as distinguished from monetary planning? What is the precise role of money in the new system of economic guidance? To what extent are money flows to guide rather than merely to reflect real flows? And how is the shift from the control function to an allocative and incentive function to be accomplished? Will the role of money be enlarged from microfinancial controls to a macroeconomic tool?

In order to acquire a market function, money must become a true "bearer of options" in the production as well as in the household sector. The transformation of passive into active money hinges on a number of factors. A price system balancing demand and supply and reflecting relative scarcities and substitution options is the *sine qua non* of such a system; without it, maximization of profits cannot serve as a guide to enterprise behavior, and domestic prices cannot guide foreign trade. Money must acquire a bigger role in emitting directional signals to production. This requires a unification of money in domestic uses.

To sum up: ten years after it was launched, it still is uncertain to what extent Reform has improved the functioning and effectiveness of the Soviet economy. The problem of optimizing the use of resources, tackled even before the Reform by Soviet policy makers from various angles (for the economy as a whole, for individual branches like power and transportation, and for individual industries like coal), remains unsolved. The contribution of the

Reform to this problem has been minor, since one of its primary objectives is increasing the efficiency of existing investment rather than optimization of new investment.

Because of its limited scope (compared, for example, to the 1968 measures in Hungary), the immediate impact of the Reform was modest as is evident from comparisons made in the transitional years between enterprises that shifted to the new system and those that continued under the old rules. The same conclusion emerges when considering the overall achievements of the eighth Five-Year Plan (1966–1970) and of the ninth Plan, which is drawing to its end, although bad weather and the resultant decline in agricultural production, still basic to the Soviet economy, were significant contributing factors.

It would lead us beyond the scope of this study to probe into the reasons why the Soviet Reform was begun so half-heartedly by cautious politicians and was later almost stopped in its tracks by bureaucrats who felt threatened by the changes. The reasons are complex and—like everything else in the Soviet Union—by no means related primarily to economic considerations.

Appendix A

The Organization and Operations of the State Bank

THE key element in the internal structure of the State Bank is the Board *(upravleniye),* consisting of a chairman, several vice chairmen, and other members (typically, heads of the principal departments of the head office).

In the Western countries, central banks (and sometimes also commercial banks) are frequently headed by forceful personalities who leave their imprint on the policies of their respective institutions, where they frequently remain for extended periods of time. In the Soviet Union, the heads of the State Bank have come from a variety of backgrounds, ranging from the inner circle of old Bolsheviks to career employees who reached the top after a succession of promotions. Few have remained very long in the position of Chairman of the Board, and none can be identified with any particular policy of the State Bank.[1]

At the end of 1970 the Bank's staff numbered over 133,000, excluding employees of savings bank offices. Women, who represent the bulk of the personnel, frequently occupy top level positions, such as managers of local branches or deputy managers of

---

[1]In some cases, individuals with no particular credentials in the field of finance, such as Marshal Bulganin, have headed the State Bank. For posterity, former heads of the State Bank are "nonpersons." The two historical monographs published by the Bank (with Chairmen Korovushkin [49] and Poskonov [70], respectively, listed as editors) do not mention the name of one single individual associated with the Bank. Similarly, attempts to trace views expressed by its successive chairmen produce little beyond a series of speeches and articles in the Bank's monthly review, endorsing whatever happened to be the current economic policies of the Party and pledging support of them.

regional offices. By contrast, in pre-revolutionary Russia, women were not eligible for bank employment until just a few years prior to the outbreak of World War I, even for the most routine jobs.

To perform its clearing control functions, the State Bank employs a large number of bookkeepers, accountants, and inspectors, in addition to the employees engaged in routine banking operations (such as cash, fiscal, and deposit transfer operations).[2] On the local level, the staff includes a large proportion of professional employees designated as economists, who specialize in analyzing operations of specific enterprises and industries.[3]

The highly centralized character of the State Bank's structure leaves little latitude for initiative of lower-echelon officials. In particular, managers (directors) of local branches have little scope for independent action.[4] One of their principal responsibilities is to attract deposits of organizations such as *kolkhozes* and of various public organizations that are not required to bank all their funds, and to request higher level offices for aid if they find that local needs require credit or currency allocations in excess of quotas initially assigned to them. Officials of branches are expected, however, to take the initiative in areas not directly

---

[2]It may be significant for the way in which the State Bank regards the relative importance of its various activities that when it instituted a system of premium payments for its staff following the Reform, the amount of currency received and counted was chosen as the single criterion for measuring the performance of each branch. According to another source, the percentage of overdue loans serves as a second criterion for determining performance.

[3]A good picture of the role of economic analysis in the State Bank can be obtained from Bogdanova [15] and the article by Barkovskiy, the head of the Planning and Economic Department ("Economic Work in the Offices of the State Bank") as well as from other contributions to a collection of essays edited by Bunich [18]. The following opening sentence of an article on "The analysis of the economics of collective farms" by M. Nesmiy is typical for what is conceived to be the main task of economic analysis: "The large changes in the economy of collective farms as a result of more intensive techniques require a strengthening of the control by the ruble on the part of the bank and of the financial administration" (p. 236).

On the training of bank employees, see Khalturina [180] and Matveev and Khalturina [191].

The foreign exchange and planning department is concerned primarily with planning and operations rather than research. Creation of a research institute within the State Bank that would be concerned with problems of monetary circulation has been advocated in recent years by several Soviet economists, among them Levchuk (a member of the Bank's staff) [53], p. 213.

[4]The following statement by the manager of the largest regional office made almost five years after the launching of the Reform is significant: "Our main attention is concentrated on controlling the execution of orders and circulars of the higher-echelon authorities of the Bank."

related to banking; this includes measures for improving the flow of consumer goods and services, an activity that usually goes under the name of "mobilizing local resources" and largely consists of finding use for by-products and remnants of local industries, and means for improving personal services available to the population.

Local branches, being mainly operating offices, basically comprise three divisions—loans, cash, and settlements. They normally service all enterprises, collective farms, and at least the larger government units located in their territory, which generally coincides with one or several lower administrative units of a republic.[5] In most cases the number of accounts serviced by a local office is small enough for bank officials to have intimate knowledge about each enterprise or collective farm whose account it holds. Local State Bank offices are subject to pressures by local authorities that may be strong when local payrolls or pride are involved.

The Bank's work load is determined by outside rule makers. Costs depend essentially on the operating efficiency of its staff and the kind of office equipment allocated to it.[6] They are related not only to the volume of deposit transfers or loans, but also to the amount of detailed financial auditing and physical on-the-spot verification which in turn depend on the standard procedures applying to a given enterprise according to its location and administrative affiliation.

A good deal of the workload of the State Bank offices consists of verifying and auditing balance sheets, operating statements, and sales and inventory records of individual enterprises to determine the exact amount of obligatory transfers from the enterprise's general account to the Treasury, to the Investment Bank, and to various special accounts (such as the various "funds" constituted from retained earnings).

Deposit transfers absorb a large part of the staff's work. Their volume has risen much more rapidly than GNP, partly reflecting

[5]To meet the credit needs of large enterprises with plants or other establishments in various parts of the country, one local or regional branch of the Bank is designated as the principal servicing office of each.

[6]Since the interest rates and the volume of credit which it can dispense is centrally determined, a State Bank office has practically no control over its income.

the growing complexity of the production process and partly the changes in industrial organizations, financial flows, and banking techniques. The remonetization of the relationship between the state and collective farms also played a significant role in this process. The total volume of payments grew more than fifteenfold between 1940 and 1970, from 95 billion to 1,480 billion rubles (excluding repayments of loans), almost twice as rapidly as GNP.[7]

Some of the control responsibilities bear only a remote relationship to banking, such as the responsibility for reporting on the execution of production and labor utilization plans of individual enterprises. An official history of the State Bank comments that "the organizational structure of the credit and monetary system gradually evolved in the direction of transforming the State Bank into an all-state apparatus of accounting and control."[8]

In spite of continuous surveillance and petty tutelage, control by the ruble is passive; its objective is formal compliance with norms and plans, not optimum deployment of resources; to discover deviations from set limits, not independent assessment of the efficiency with which an enterprise uses cash balances and loans. Even the effectiveness of routine and formal controls has been questioned by various Soviet economists, who suggest that they should be replaced, or at least supplemented, by adequate economic analysis. Therefore, much of that has been limited to

---

[7]Close to three-fourths of all payments are for goods and services, the remainder representing mainly the various financial flows discussed in Chapter 5. The number of payments is inflated by the control functions of the State Bank and the Soviet cost accounting methods. For example, each individual purchase by a summer camp of medicines from a drug store must be paid for separately (while in Western countries monthly billing would be the most common). Shortages of materials also result in additional payments not customary in Western countries: a retail food organization, in addition to requiring very frequent, and sometimes daily settlement of all deliveries, would also bill all its outlets for reusable containers (such as milk bottles) and make offsetting payments upon their return.

[8]Poskonov [70], p. 86. In some respects, the State Bank has taken over the control function exercised in the first post-revolutionary years by the "Workers' and Peasants' Inspection."

de Maegd, in the most detailed investigation of this subject undertaken by a Western observer, comments: "As a body for business control the State Bank is part of a controlling system which also comprises administrative organs as well as social and political organs and financial institutions other than the State Bank. The financial organs are less involved than the other bodies of control in the appreciation of business activities. Moreover, the State Bank is different from all other bodies of control in that it exercises its control as part of its usual financial transactions." [131], p. 470.

providing background data for the establishment of plans, norms, and prices, and to comparing the performance of groups of enterprises within the same industry or operating under similar circumstances, with the main goal of obtaining empirical data for the revision of norms and other standard ratios.

Branch and regional officials of the Bank are also expected to assist local political authorities in developing specific policies to close potential inflationary gaps *(razryv)* identified during the preparation of the Cash Plan (see Chapter 3). It is, indeed, difficult to determine any clearcut limits to the staff's participation in activities related to the improvement of economic performance. Bank officials on all levels are brought face to face with various economic problems and into close contact with party authorities and government officials. Thus, lower-echelon Bank officials report at meetings of city, rural, and regional soviets and of the corresponding Communist Party organization on such matters as the fulfillment of the Cash Plan, and discuss steps that might be taken to increase production and lower unit costs, and to achieve a more intensive use of local resources to increase the flow of consumer goods.

The State Bank plays a very significant role as a source of statistical information for planners on the national and, even more important, the territorial level. As a rule, such internal data are not available in published form.

The State Bank publishes a minimum of statistical information on its current activities. It does not publish an annual report. Two of its monographs, one published on the occasion of its fortieth anniversary and the other on the fiftieth anniversary of the October Revolution, contain statistical appendices with some historical data. The statistical yearbook of the Central Statistical Office, *Narodnoye Khoziaistvo SSSR,* contains a section on finances which includes statistics for all banking institutions combined on an annual basis, the latest data being about two years old by the time they are published. The statistical data released by the State Bank either directly (usually in its monthly bulletin *Den'gi i Kredit*) or in the several monographs reviewing its activities over time ([75] and [76]; also [41] and [55]) deal mostly with the structure of its deposit liabilities and lending. While their analytical value is limited, the most important of these statistics are summarized in the tables below and commented upon in the balance of the appendix.[9]

All data are published on an annual basis which does not permit evaluation of the significance of seasonal swings in credit granted or outstanding. Also, since all data are *ex post,* it is not possible to compare analysis of actual lending with projections. Even the published data cannot easily be fitted together, correlated, or made consistent over time. Frequently, no absolute base is given, but only percentage distributions or percentage changes from year to year, and even these must be culled from occasional articles or reports. In spite of the uniformity in the underlying accounting records, published figures are frequently inconsistent from year to year, or show revisions for a number of past periods, some of which, no doubt, are due in large part to unexplained administrative reclassifications.

While at the start of 1971 the number of state-owned enterprises and other economic organizations with accounts at the State Bank (the sum of the first two lines in Table A.1) was virtually the same as immediately before the outbreak of World War II, the proportion of borrowers among them has increased significantly. Nevertheless, nearly 40 percent of enterprises still made no use of credit. The sharp decline of collective farm accounts primarily reflects the shrinkage in their number through consolidations and, perhaps, also the shifting of accounts by some small units in remote locations to savings banks. The latter factor presumably also explains the decline of the number of accounts of trade unions and other voluntary and similar public organizations.

The four thousand offices of the State Bank carry over four million separate accounts (Table A.2). For many clients, several separate accounts are maintained, so that the number of accounts

---

[9]A member of the State Bank's board recently pointed out that despite the enormous quantity of data generated by the State Bank, it is far from being in a position to develop into a central social accounting center. See Barkovskiy [168]. One reason is that 50–60 percent of all payments are made via clearing arrangements and no data are available on the industry of the payer and the payee.

According to another official of the State Bank, "The information system which has been in existence until the present does not correspond fully to the increased requirements and existing challenges. Indicators of enterprise performance do not provide the basis for drawing conclusions concerning its efficiency, labor productivity, use of capacity and of invested capital, as well as with regard to the way in which various elements of costs affect profitability and the rate of growth of output, sales and profits." Sminov [203].

TABLE A.1

Number of Clients of the State Bank
(in thousands, beginning of the year)

	1941	1951	1961	1971	1973
Enterprises and economic organizations					
receiving loans	120	138	131	164	159
Other	147	123	105	102	122
Collective farms *(kolkhozes)*	236	129	46	33	32
Nonprofit and similar organizations	341	420	330	268	285
Total	844	810	612	568	598

SOURCE: Through 1971: *D.K.*, September 1971, p. 50.
NOTE: Government units not included.

considerably exceeds the number of clients. Thus, in addition to the basic current (clearing) account, an enterprise may have one or several special accounts for funds earmarked for major maintenance and repair expenditures[10] and for various local or nationwide clearing arrangements. It also may have one or several loan accounts for borrowings that differ by purpose or maturity.[11]

Changes in the number of loan accounts may merely reflect changes in procedure. The trend toward granting accommodations for more broadly defined purposes and the shifting to loans on turnover resulted in a declining number of special loan accounts. Recently, there has been a tendency to merge separate loan accounts into one single loan account. A further step toward simplification in certain industries has been a move toward merging the clearing and loan accounts of an enterprise.

More than 800,000 separate accounts are maintained to fulfill the Bank's function as the fiscal agent of all levels of government.

[10]Only depreciation reserves available for current maintenance and repair are kept at the State Bank. The remainder, as well as all other enterprise funds to be used for financing fixed investment, must be kept on deposit with the Investment Bank; unspent balances in such accounts are included with "accounts of other credit institutions" shown in statistics published by the State Bank.

[11]Trade establishments, which typically carry a large part of their inventories on credit, must pay all sales proceeds into the loan account; alternatively, they must transfer to it a specified part of all sales proceeds from the clearing account. This procedure has some similarity to the revolving credit in the United States. A collective farm would have a current account and a number of loan accounts for working capital and investment purposes. Public organizations may have several separate special-purpose accounts.

TABLE A.2

Number of Accounts at the State Bank, by Category
(in thousands, beginning of the year)

	1941	1961	1967	1971	1973
Clearing accounts of enterprises[a]	296	316	310	307	341
Capital maintenance and repair accounts	73	79	117	n.a.	n.a.
Current account of collective farms	246	125	93	49	49
Short-term loan accounts	260	561 ⎫	1,281	572	553
Long-term loan accounts[b]	1,290	804 ⎭		559	546
Accounts of other credit institutions	272	75	98	n.a.	n.a.
Treasury (budget) accounts	847	897	847	n.a.	n.a.
All other accounts[c]	324	1,361	1,697	n.a.	n.a.
Total	3,608	4,218	4,443	4,175	4,096

SOURCE: Through 1971: *D.K.*, Sept. 1971.

n.a. = Not available.

[a] Includes accounts in connection with decentralized clearing.

[b] Includes accounts for the financing of investments. The bulk of loan accounts is for long-term credits to collective farms.

[c] Current accounts of nonprofit units, as well as various special accounts of enterprises, such as for acceptances executed.

In addition to the accounts of the central government, this figure includes the accounts and sub-accounts of various territorial and functional units of government and various transfer accounts related to the accumulation and disbursement of resources for investment in the state-owned sector of the economy.

Published data on deposits (Table A.3) relate to only four selected categories of accounts. In particular, they do not include those of the government investment and those related to foreign trade, credit, and aid. Table A.3 below shows, for selected years, deposit liabilities of the State and Investment banks to the main segments of the economy. In recent years, the share of the State Bank accounted for about 90 percent of the total.[12]

[12]The complexity of Soviet accounting as applied to the banking system is an area that must remain outside the bounds of the present monograph. See, in addition to Campbell [106], Ryausov and Tertus [72] and Khlynov [45] and [181].

Appendix A

TABLE A.3

Bank Balances by Category of Depositor
(in billions of rubles, beginning of the year)

	1941	1951	1961	1967	1973
State enterprises and economic organizations	1.5	2.7	5.5	10.0	19.0
Cooperative enterprises and organizations	0.1	0.1	0.1	0.5	0.8
Collective farms	0.4	0.7	0.9	5.2	4.6
Trade union and other membership organizations	0.2	0.3	0.6	1.2	6.0
Total—all banks	2.1	3.8	7.1	17.0	30.4
State Bank only	1.9	3.3	6.5	15.1	26.4

Source: [65], 1972.

Note: Budgetary accounts not included. Details may not add up to total because of rounding.

Appendix B

Availability of Monetary Data

MOST of the significant data generated within the monetary system are not published. Clearly, most of the statistical data required for the analysis of Soviet monetary performance are available to the management of the State Bank, and some have occasionally been made available on a confidential basis to a few Soviet writers who are either members of the Bank's staff, or members of official research or teaching institutions. Published data, on the other hand, particularly for the period after World War II, are meager indeed. In contrast to many other areas of economic statistics, data in the monetary and credit fields have hardly improved since the end of the "statistical blackout" that began in the late thirties.

We owe to Raymond P. Powell a systematic, thorough and up-to-date critical exploration of Soviet monetary statistics for the entire period following the hyperinflation of the early 1920's.[1] Edward Ames has attempted a partial reconstruction for selected years of the balance sheet of the soviet banking system and of the State Bank, respectively.

Selected data on the liabilities of the State Bank on a consistent basis for selected years from its founding to World War II have been published only recently and are given in Table B.1. No similar data are available for the assets side of the balance sheet, except for loans.

Reconstructing the balance sheet of the State Bank for the years since 1937 can be attempted in two ways. The broader

[1]In [149]; for earlier explorations in this field, see his doctoral dissertation [140] which covers 1928–1940.

TABLE B.1

Liabilities of the State Bank, Selected Years, 1923–1938
(millions of rubles)

	October 1 1923	October 1 1925	October 1 1929	January 1 1933	January 1 1938
Capital and retained earnings	3	19	62	125	266
Treasury deposits	2	68	108	203	1,718
Deposits of enterprises	3	46	103	845	1,522
Deposits of other credit institutions		*a*	27	274	406
Interoffice clearings	*a*		1		360
Currency	1*b*	98	244	805	1,518
Other	2	7	11	158	40
Totals	12	239	557	2,411	5,830

SOURCE: Melkov [61], tables on pp. 65, 73, 83 and 88.

NOTE: Components may not add to totals due to rounding. Data for 1938 corrected for misprint.

a Less than 1.

b The bulk of currency consisted of Treasury issues.

approach is to aim at something similar to a consolidated statement of the U.S. monetary system, including currency liabilities and gold and related monetary reserves. The alternative approach is to add to the current deposit liabilities an estimate of the Treasury balance accumulated from cumulative budget surpluses and currency in circulation. In his 1972 study, Powell reviews in detail the sources, nature, and limitations (including unexplainable inconsistencies) of data on the main components of the assets and liabilities of the State Bank as well as of the other banks, including savings banks, that have been active in the period since 1928.

Powell's two tables,[2] Table 1, *Balance Sheets of the State Bank,* and Table 9, *Distribution of Monetary Assets by Holders* in [146] which present the most relevant data, are for selected years only (1928, 1933, 1937, 1940, 1946, 1951, 1956, 1961, and 1967). They include figures from various official Soviet and secondary

[2]Powell's data in [149], Table 172 for "all banks" as published by the Central Statistical Office (TSU) apparently do not include the Bank of Foreign Trade, since they are identical to the total for the State and the Investment Banks alone.

sources, as well as some of Powell's own estimates. Powell makes rough currency estimates for 1940 through 1956; he also includes some guesses for a number of other items for some years subsequent to 1956. For example, Treasury deposits for 1956 are estimated on the basis of one writer's (Sitnin's) statement that this account "doubled" between 1956 and 1961, although a State Bank publication carries the information that it "more than doubled." Powell also notes that an author close to the State Bank (Allakhverdian) states that budgetary resources account for "over 50 percent" of bank loans and for "over 40 percent" in two successive editions of his book (see footnotes to Powell's Table 1, row 14). To cite another example, Powell's currency estimates for the selected post-World War years are anchored in an estimate by Konnik for the single year 1958 described by the latter as obtained "by approximate calculation."[3]

Ames[4] presents *A Partial Statement of the Balance Sheet of the Soviet Banking System* for seven selected years between 1940 and 1961. On the assets side, he lists only the major categories of credit, and on the liabilities side, only deposits, including those of the savings and of the investment banks, but excluding those of the Treasury. For four years, a residual labeled "other State Bank liabilities" (and a "wild guess" for a fifth year) is given which is the arithmetic difference between total credit and the specified categories of deposits. It includes, in addition to note circulation, cumulative budget surpluses and some other unspecified liabilities.

Ames also estimates "Apparent Changes in Soviet Deposits and Notes, 1956–61" by subtracting from annual changes in total credit (without, however, allowing for cancellations) funds pro-

---

[3]Moreover, one should always keep in mind that not all books in the monetary field published in the Soviet Union are available abroad, so that the inconsistencies among statements and inference from percentage changes (absolute data are practically never given) discussed by Powell might even increase if sources not used by him are combed for possible clues to changes in currency circulation and other relevant data. Thus, Melkov's data (Table B.1) were apparently not known to Powell.

According to Usoskin, the share of budget surpluses in total liabilities in 1958 was about 40 percent. This is three times the share at the beginning of 1941. Melkov [61] believes this entirely consistent with a cumulative budget surplus for 1941–1958, which amounts to 25.4 billion (old) rubles, since part of this surplus was used to pay subsidies to lower consumer prices (which did not appear in the budget!) and for other purposes.

[4][99], Tables 10-8 and 10-9, pp. 167–168.

vided by budget surpluses (adjusted for those reflecting changes in savings accounts, which are shown separately). Changes in deposit accounts are then used to derive from the residual (credit *not* financed by budget surpluses or finding a counterpart in savings deposits) the "apparent increase in note issue." Changes in coin circulation are left out of consideration, as are, apparently, notes issued by the Treasury, unless they are assumed by Ames to be a State Bank liability.

I have considerable reservations regarding attempts to construct a combined or consolidated statement of the Soviet banking system, not only because no information is available on the magnitudes and changes of some of the principal liability items but also because of the character of the banks whose balance sheet would be combined with that of the State Bank. Any implication that a consolidated statement may be comparable to similar statements available for many nonsocialist countries would be highly misleading.

A fairly complete picture of changes in the main assets and liabilities of the State Bank can be obtained from Melkov's monograph published in 1969. The capital and reserves of the State Bank amounted at the beginning of 1967 to 3 billion rubles, against only 0.8 billion on January 1, 1959 [61], p. 115, and only 160 million rubles on January 1, 1941 (p. 108).

From 1959 to 1966 (the period of the Seven-Year Plan), cumulative Treasury surpluses deposited with the State Bank amounted to 15.5 billion rubles, following a cumulative excess of budgetary receipts over expenditures, 1941–1958 (including the war years) of 25.4 billion rubles, but in 1963 the Treasury balance was reduced by the amount of the deposit liabilities of the savings bank system, when it was transferred to the State Bank and channeling of net increases in savings deposits into the budget was discontinued. The accounting adjustment made in 1963, which merely substituted the State Bank for the Ministry of Finance as the recipient of household savings, had no direct effect on the credit policy of the Bank. At the beginning of 1967, savings deposits were equivalent to almost one-third of all the credit extended by the State Bank [61], p. 114. Currency in circulation has become a smaller part of total liabilities, since Government deposits rose more than credit extended; savings deposits became a liability of the State Bank and the relative importance of all other liabilities remained about the same [61], p. 108.

In the case of the Investment Bank, partial substitution of loan for grant financing since 1965 does not justify considering budgetary funds held pending disbursement in a different light than before—they certainly still are not liabilities to the Treasury in the ordinary sense.[5]

A consolidation of the Savings Bank's statement with that of the State Bank presents the problem that prior to 1963, except for occasional small purchases of state loans, its assets were redeposited with the Treasury (and treated as ordinary budget receipts).

The Bank for Foreign Trade also holds some Treasury funds pending their disbursement (such as loans and grants to foreign nonsocialist—typically, underdeveloped—countries) which cannot be considered as a liability to the Treasury in the usual sense.

[5]In addition to the Treasury's working balances and accumulated surpluses of previous years, the State Bank also held funds representing transfers to serve as a source of funds for specific lending programs, mainly for long-term loans to *kolkhozes*.

Bibliography

Books—Russian[1]

1. Aizenberg, I. P., *Osnovy Ustoichivosti Deneg Pri Sotsializma* (Foundations of the Stability of Money under Socialism), 1964.
2. Aleksandrov, A. M., *Finansy Sotsializma* (Finances of Socialism), 1965.
3. ———. ed., *Gosudarstvennyi Byudget SSR* (The State Budget of the USSR), 1965.
4. ———. ed., *Khozyaistvennaya Reforma i Finansy* (The Economic Reform and Finances), 1967. (A collection of articles by the staff of the Leningrad Financial Institute.)
5. Altshuler, A. B., ed., *Valyutnye Otnosheniya vo Vneshney Torgovle SSSR* (Foreign Exchange Relations in the Foreign Trade of the USSR), 1968.

[1]The subject matter dealt with in this study is normally covered in Soviet monographs and textbooks under two separate headings: "money and credit" and "budget and finances." Two official monthly publications, *Den'gi i Kredit* (Money and Credit, quoted below as *D.K.*), published by the State Bank, and *Finansy* (Finances), published by the Ministry of Finance, are primary sources of current information on these two areas; neither carries regular statistical tables. The former publishes each month a synopsis of deliberations of and decisions taken by the Board of the State Bank, while the second carries similar accounts on the activity of the "Collegium" (committee of sub-cabinet and other senior officers) of the Ministry of Finance and of the Board of the Investment Bank. Relevant books and articles published in the Soviet Union between 1946 and 1966 can be found, grouped under 14 subject headings, in *Finansy, Den'gi i Kredit, Bibliograficheskiy Ukazatel', 1946–1966* (Finances, Money and Credit, Bibliographical Guide), 1967.

6. Atlas, M., *Razvitie Gosudarstvennogo Banka SSSR* (The Development of the State Bank of the USSR), 1958.
7. ———. *Razvitie Bankovskikh Sistem Stran Sotsializma* (The Development of Banking System in the Socialist Countries), 1967.
8. Bachurin, A. B., *Sovershenstvovanie Planirovaniya i Uluchshenie Ekonomicheskoi Raboty v Narodnom Khozyaistve* (Perfection of Planning and Improvement of the Economic Work in the National Economy: Proceedings of a Unionwide Conference), 1969.
9. Barkovskiy, N. D., and Kartashova, K. S., *Kreditnoe Planirovanie v SSSR* (Credit Planning in the USSR), 1966.
10. Baskin, A. I., Smirnov, V. I., and Smirnov, P. V., *Finansy i Khozyaistvennyi Raschet v Snabzhensko—Sbytovych Organizatsiyakh* (Finances and Economic Accounting in Supply and Marketing Organizations), 1969.
11. Batyrev, V. M., Kaganov, G., and Yagodin, I., *Organizatsiya i Planirovanie Denezhnogo Obrashcheniya v SSSR* (Organization and Planning of Monetary Circulation in the USSR), 1959.
12. Belkin, V. D., *Ekonomicheskie Izmereniya i Planirovanie* (Economic Measurements and Planning), 1972.
13. Belkin, V. D., and Ivanter, V. V., *Ekonomicheskoe Upravlenie i Bank* (The Management of the Economy and the Bank), 1969.
14. Bogachevskiy, M. B., *Finansy i Kredit SSSR* (Finances and Credit of the USSR), 1964.
15. Bogdanova, E., *Ekonomicheskaya Rabota v Uchrezhdeniyakh Gosudarstvennogo Banka* (Economic Work in the Offices of the State Bank). 1970.
16. Boguslavskiy, M., Greben', Ya., and Proselkov, A., *Bankovskiy Uchet i Operatsionnaya Tekhnika* (Bank Accounting Procedures and Operational Techniques), 1960.
17. Borovoy, S. Ya., *Kredit i Banki Rossii, Seredina XVII Veka—1861* (Credit and Banks of Russia, mid-17th Century to 1861), 1958.
18. Bunich, P., ed., *Ekonomicheskaya Rabota v Finansovo-Kreditnoi Sisteme* (Economic Work in the Financial-Credit System), 1965.
19. Burmistrov, D. V., *Nalogi i Sbory s Naseleniya v SSSR* (Taxes and Levies on the Population in the USSR), 1968.
20. Bychkov, P. S., *Oborotnye Sredstva Sotsialisticheskikh Promyshlennykh Predpriyatiy* (Working Capital of Socialist Industrial Enterprises), 1966.
21. Chachulin, F. G., *Katalog Bon i Denznakov* (Catalogue of Tokens and Money Surrogates), 1927.
22. Chernyshova, T., *Kreditirovanie Promyshlennosti po Oborotu* (Extending Credit on Turnover to Industry), 1969.

23. Darkov, G. D., and Maksimov, G. K., *Finansovaya Statistika* (Financial Statistics), 1969.
24. D'yachko, A., Makhov, B., and Freiman, T., *Vyplaty i Vozmeshcheniya Khozorganan Sredstv iz Byudzheta* (Payments and Compensation Paid to Economic Units from the Budget), 1970.
25. Dzhavadov, G. A., *Reforma i Upravlenie Promyshlenost'yu* (The Reform and the Management of Industry), 1970.
26. Eremeeva, G., *Razvitie Sberegatel'nogo Del v SSSR* (The Development of Savings Banking in the USSR), 1958.
27. *Finansovo-Kreditnyi Slovar'* (Financial-Credit Dictionary), 2 vol., 1961 and 1964.
28. Galimon, L. S., ed., *Kontrol' za Raskhodovaniem Fondov Zarobotnoi Platy* (Control of Payroll Funds), 1962.
29. Gerashchenko, V. S., *Kredit i Ekonomicheskoe Stimulirovanie Promyschlennogo Proizvodstva* (Credit and the Stimulation of Industrial Production), 1966.
30. ———. ed., *Denezhnoye Obrashchenie i Kredit SSSR* (Monetary Circulation and Credit in the USSR), 1966.
31. Gindin, A., *Kak Bolsheviki Natsionalizirovali Chastnye Banki* (How the Bolsheviks Have Nationalized the Privately Owned Banks), 1962.
32. Gindin, I. F., *Banki i Promyshlenost' v Rossii* (Banks and Industry in Russia), 1927.
33. ———. *Russkie Kommercheskie Banki* (The Russian Commercial Banks), 1948.
34. ———. *Gosudarstvennyi Bank i Ekonomicheskaya Politika Tsarskogo Pravitel'stva* (The State Bank and the Economic Policy of the Tsarist Government), 1960.
35. ———. *Kak Bolsheviki Ovladeli Gosudarstvennym Bankom* (How the Bolsheviks Seized the State Bank), 1961.
36. Golev, Ya. I., *Sel'skokhozyaistvennyi Kredit v SSSR* (Farm Credit in the USSR), 1958.
37. *Gosudarstvennyi Bank SSSR k XXII S'ezdu KPSS* (The State Bank of the USSR: Report to the 22nd Congress of the C.P. of the USSR), 1961.
38. Gryzanov, Yu. P., *Novyi Poryadok Planirovaniya i Ekonomicheskogo Stimulirovaniya v Torgovle* (The New Procedures for Planning and Economic Stimulation in Trade), 1970.
39. Illinich, A. Ya., and Tkachenko, G., *Sberegatel'noe Delo* (Savings Banking), 1969.
40. Ikonnikov, V., ed., *Denezhnoe Obrashchenie i Kredit SSSR* (Monetary Circulation and Credit in the USSR), 1962.

41. Ipatov, P. F., *Finansovo-Kreditnaya Sistema SSSR* (The Financial-Credit System of the USSR), 1968.
42. Isaev, B. L., *Integrirovanie Balansovoy Sistemy v Analize i Planirovanii Ekonomiki* (Integration of Balances in the Analysis and Planning of the Economy), 1969.
43. Kartashova, K. S., *Finansy, Kredit i Raschety v Kolkhozakh* (Finances, Credit and Accounting in Kolkhozes), 1970.
44. Katsenelenbaum, Z. S., *Krugooborot Sredstv v Sotsialisticheskom Sel'skom Khoziaistve* (The Circular Flow of Funds in Socialist Agriculture), 1959.
45. Khlynov, N., *Operatsii po Beznalichnym Raschetam* (Non-cash Settlements), 1965.
46. Komissarov, V. P., and Popov, A. N., *Mezhdunarodnye Valyutnye i Kreditnye Otnosheniya* (International Foreign Exchange and Credit Relations), 1965.
47. Konnik, I. I., *Den'gi v Sotsialisticheskom Ob'shchestve* (Money in the Socialist Society), 1962.
48. ———. *Den'gi v Period Stroitel'stva Kommunisticheskogo Obshchestva* (Money in the Period of the Building of Communist Society), 1966.
49. Korovushkin, A. K., *Kreditnaya Sistema v Semiletke* (The Credit System in the Seven-Year Plan), 1960.
50. Kronrod, Ya., *Den'gi v Sotsialisticheskom Obshchestve* (Money in the Socialist Society), Second rev. ed., 1960.
51. Lavrushin, O., *Kredit i Promychlenost'* (Credit and Industry), 1967.
52. ———., *Kredit v Sisteme Ekonomicheskikh Stimulov* (Credit in the System of Economic Stimulants), 1970.
53. Levchuk, I. V., *Ssudnyi Fond i Kredit* (The Loan Fund and Credit), 1971.
54. Liberman, Ya. G., *Gosudarstvennyi Byudget i Sotsialisticheskoe Vosproizvodstvo* (The State Budget and Socialist Production), 1966.
55. Lushin, S. I., *Edinstvo Materialnykh i Finansovykh Proportsii v Narodnom Khozyaistve* (The Identity of Real and Financial Proportions in the National Economy), 1970.
56. Lyando, A., *Voprosy Finansovogo Balansa Narodnogo Khozyaistva (Ocherki Istorii i Metodologii Sostavleniya)* (Problems of the Financial Balance of the National Economy; Essays on Its History and Methodology), 1963.
57. Malafeev, A. N., *Istoriya Tsenoobrazovaniya v SSSR* (1917–1973) (The History of Price Formation in the USSR), 1964.

58. Malein, N. S., *Kreditno-Raschetnye Pravootnosheniya i Finan-sovyi Kontrol'* (Legal Relations Concerning Credit and Settlements and Financial Control), 1964.
59. Margolin, N. S., *Planirovanie Finansov* (The Planning of Finances), 1960.
60. Maryakhin, G. L., *Ocherki Istorii Nalogov s Naseleniya v SSSR* (Essays on the History of Personal Taxation in the USSR), 1964.
61. Melkov, A. E., *Kreditnye Resursy Gosudarstvennogo Banka SSSR* (Credit Resources of the State Bank of the USSR), 1969.
62. Migulin, P. P., *Nasha Bankovskaya Politika* (1729–1903) (Our Banking Policy), 1903.
63. Orlov, K. Ya., and Shimanskiy, V., *Reforma i Torgovlya* (The Reform and Trade), 1970.
64. Parchodko, A. P., Milirud, B. T., and Obushinskiy, E. I., *Kredity Gosbanka i ikh Ispol'zovanie v Pishchevoi Promyshlenosti* (The Credit of the State Bank and Its Use in the Food Industry), 1964.
65. Pessel', M. A., *Kreditirovanie po Oborotu* (Extension of Credit on Turnover), 1965.
66. ———., *Efektivnost' Kreditirovaniya Promyshlenosti* (Effectiveness of Credit Financing of Industry), 1970.
67. Piletskiy, A., *Beznalichnye Raschety i Khozyaistvennaya Reforma* (Cashless Settlements and the Reform of the Economy), 1969.
68. Plotnikov, K. N., ed., *Finansy i Kredit v SSSR* (Finances and Credit in the USSR), 1967.
69. Popov, V. F., ed., *Gosudarstvennyi Bank SSSR, 1917–1957* (The State Bank of the USSR), 1957.
70. Poskonov, A. A., ed., *Kreditno-Denezhnaya Sistema SSSR* (The Credit and Monetary System of the USSR), 1967.
71. Rumyantsev, A. M., and Banich, P. G., eds., *Ekonomicheskaya Reforma, Ee Primeneniye i Problemy* (The Economic Reform: Its Realization and Problems), 1969.
72. Ryauzov, N. N., and Tertus, A. F., *Bankovskaya Statistika* (Banking Statistics), second edition, 1961.
73. Sharapov, S., *Bumazhnyi Rubel* (The Paper Ruble), St. Petersburg, 1895.
74. Shenger, Yu. E., *Ocherki Sovetskogo Kredita* (Essays on Soviet Credit), 1961.
75. Shermenev, M. K., *Finansovye Rezervy v Raschirenom Vosproiz-vodstve* (Financial Reserves in the Enlarged Reproduction), 1973.
76. Shevelev, V. A., *Banovskiy Kontrol' v Promyshlenosti* (Banking Control in Industry), 1962.

77. Shvarts, G., *Beznalichnyi Oborot i Kredit v SSSR* (Deposit Transfers and Credit in the USSR), 1963.
78. Sitnin, V., *Den'gi i Denezhnoe Obrashchenie v SSSR* (Money and Monetary Circulation in the USSR), 1957.
79. Slavnyi, I. D., *Ocherki Planirovaniya Denezhnogo Obrashcheniya* (Essays on the Planning of Monetary Circulation), 1961.
80. ———., *Denezhnoe Obrashchenie i Ekonomicheskaya Reforma* (Monetary Circulation and the Economic Reform), 1966.
81. Smirnov, A., *Ekonomicheskoe Soderzhanie Naloga s Oborota* (The Economic Meaning of the Turnover Tax), 1963.
82. Solntsev, V. F., and Fisenko, M. K., eds., *Finansy Sel'skogo Khozyaistva* (Finances of Agriculture), 1970.
83. Taflya, I., *Pryamye Raschety v Narodnom Khozyaistve* (Direct Settlements in the Economy), 1965.
84. Tatur, S. K., *Khoziaistvenyi Raschet v Promyshlenosti* (Business Accounting in Industry), 1970.
85. Tsagolov, N. A., ed., *Problemy Sovershenstvovaniya Organizatsii i Upravleniya Sotsialisticheskogo Proizvodstva* (Problems of Perfecting the Organization and Management of the Socialist Production), 1969.
86. *TsSU, Narodnoye Khozyaistvo SSSR v 1972 Godu* (Central Statistical Administration, The National Economy of the USSR in 1972), 1973 [and earlier years].
87. Trubenkov, V., *Valyutno-Obmennye Operatsii v SSSR* (Foreign Exchange Operations in the USSR), 1963.
88. Tulebaev, T., *Byudzhetnoye Planirovanie v Soyuznoi Respublike* (Budget Planning in a Soviet Republic), 1969.
89. Usoskin, M. M., *Organizatsiya i Planirovanie Kredita* (The Organization and Planning of Credit), 1961.
90. Vlasenko, V. E., *Teoriya Deneg v Rossii* (The Theory of Money in Russia), 1963.
91. Yunik, I. B., and Miseyuk, K. A., *Finansirovanie i Kreditirovanie Kapital' nykh Vlozheniy v Selskom Khozyaistve* (Financing and Extension of Credit for Investment in Agriculture), 1965.
92. Yurovskiy, L. N., *Denezhnaya Politika Sovetskoy Vlasti, 1917–1927* (The Monetary Policy of the Soviet Government), 1928.
93. Zverev, A. G., *Finansy SSSR za XXX Let* (Thirty Years of Finances of the USSR), 1947.
94. ———., *Gosudarstvennye Zaimy i Vklady v Sberegatelnye Kassy* (Government Loans and Deposits in Savings Banks), 1957.
95. ———., *Natsional'nyi Dokhod i Finansy SSSR* (National Income and Finances of the USSR), 1961.

96. ———., *Problemy Tsenoobrazovaniya i Finansy* (Problems of Price Formation and Finances), 1966.

English and Other Languages—Books

97. Aghad, E., *Grossbanken und Weltmarkt,* Berlin, 1914.
98. Allakhverdyan, D. A., ed., *Soviet Financial System* (Translated from the Russian) Moscow, 1966.
99. Ames, Edward, *Soviet Economic Processes,* Richard D. Irwin, Homewood, Ill., 1965.
100. Arnold, Arthur Z., *Banks, Credit and Money in Soviet Russia,* Columbia University Press, 1937.
101. Becker, Abraham S., *Soviet National Income, 1958–1964,* National Accounts of the USSR in the Seven Year Plan Period, University of California Press, 1969.
102. Beckhart, B. H., ed., *Banking Systems,* Columbia University Press, New York, 1954.
103. Bergson, Abraham, *Economics of Soviet Planning,* Yale University Press, 1964.
104. Bornstein, M. and Fusfeld, D. R., eds., *The Soviet Economy: A Book of Readings,* fourth ed., Richard D. Irwin, Homewood, Ill., 1974.
105. Cameron, Rondo, ed., *Banking in the Early Stages of Industrialization,* Oxford University Press, London, 1967.
106. Campbell, Robert W., *Accounting in Soviet Planning and Management,* Harvard University Press, 1963.
107. Carr, E. H., *The Bolshevik Revolution, 1917–1923,* Penguin Books, New York.
108. Chapman, Janet G., *Real Wages in the Soviet Union Since 1928,* Harvard University Press, 1963.
109. Davies, R. W., *The Development of the Soviet Budgetary System,* London, 1958.
110. Degras, Jane, ed., *Soviet Planning: Essays in Honor of Naum Jasny* (with an introduction by Alec Nove), Basil Blackwell, Oxford, 1946.
111. Denis, H., and Lavigne, Marie L., *Le Problème des Prix en Union Soviétique* Cujas, Paris, 1965.
112. Dodge, Norton T., ed., *Analysis of the USSR's 24th Party Congress and 9th Five-Year Plan,* Cremona Foundation, Mechanicville, Md., 1971.

113. Eörsi, G., and Harmathy, A., eds., *Law and Economic Reform in Socialist Countries,* Akadémiai Kiadó, Budapest, 1971.
114. Epstein, E., *Les Banques Commerciales Russes,* Giard, Paris, 1925.
115. Feiwel, George E., ed., *New Currents in Soviet-Type Economies,* International Textbook Company, Scranton, Pa., 1968.
116. Gallik, Daniel, Jesina, Cestimir, and Rapawy, Stephen, *The Soviet Financial System: Structure, Operation and Statistics,* U.S. Census Bureau, Washington, D.C., 1968.
117. Garvy, George, *Money, Banking and Credit in Eastern Europe,* Federal Reserve Bank of New York, 1966.
118. Grossman, Gregory, ed., *Money and Plan,* University of California Press, Berkeley, 1968.
119. Hahn, Gerhard, *Investitionslenkung im Sowjetischen Wirtschaftssystem,* Fischer, Stuttgart, 1967.
120. Hirsch, Hans, *Quantity Planning and Price Planning in the Soviet Union* (translated from the German), University of Pennsylvania Press, 1961.
121. Holzman, Franklyn D., *Soviet Taxation,* Harvard University Press, 1955.
122. Holzman, Franklyn D., ed., *Readings on the Soviet Economy,* Chicago, 1962.
123. Hsiao, Katherine H., *Money and Banking Policy in Communist China,* Columbia University Press, 1971.
124. Jasny, Naum, *The Soviet Price System,* Stanford University Press, 1951.
125. Karcz, J. F., and Timoschenko, V. P., *Soviet Agricultural Policy, 1953–1963,* Food Research Institute Studies, Stanford, 1964.
126. Katzenellenbaum, S. S., *Russian Currency and Banking 1914–24,* London, 1926.
127. Laulan, Yves, ed., *Money, Banking and Credit in Eastern Europe,* Brussels, NATO, 1973.
128. Lavigne, Marie-L., *Le Capital dans l'Economie Soviétique,* SEDES, Paris, 1961.
129. Lenin, Vladimir, *Collected Works,* Moscow, 1960.
130. Leptin, Gert, *Methode und Effizienz der Investitionsfinanzierung durch Abschreibungen in der Sowjetwirtschaft,* Duncker & Humblot, Berlin, 1961.
131. Maegd, Hugo De, *De Kontrole van de Staatsbank op de Economische en Financiale Bedrijvigheid van de Nijverheids—ondernemingen in de Soviet-Unie* (The Control of the State Bank over

Economic and Financial Activities of Industrial Enterprises in the Soviet Union), Ghent, 1969. (Privately printed in Flemish, with an English summary).

132. Menz, Gertraud, *Das Sowjetische Bankensystem,* Duncker & Humblot, West Berlin, 1963.

133. Meznerics, Iván, *Banking Business in Socialist Economy,* Akadémiai Kiadó, Budapest, 1968.

134. Moorstein, Richard H., and Powell, Raymond P., *The Soviet Capital Stock, 1928–62,* Irwin, Homewood, Ill., 1966.

135. Neuberger, Egon, ed., *International Trade and Central Planning,* University of California Press, 1968.

136. Normano, J. F., *The Spirit of Russian Economics,* Day, New York, 1945.

137. Nove, Alec, *The Soviet Economy,* McGraw-Hill, 2nd ed., New York, 1966.

138. Pickersgill, Joyce, *Soviet Monetary Policy, 1914 to 1937* (unpublished PhD. dissertation), University of Washington, 1966.

139. Podolski, T. M., *Socialist Banking and Monetary Control,* University Press, Cambridge, England, 1972.

140. Powell, Raymond P., *Soviet Monetary Policy* (unpublished PhD. dissertation), University of California, Berkeley, 1952.

141. Pryor, Frederic L., *The Communist Foreign Trade System,* The MIT Press, 1963.

142. Reddaway, W. B., *The Russian Financial System,* Macmillan, London, 1935.

143. Rosovsky, H., ed., *Industrialization in Two Systems,* John Wiley, New York, 1966.

144. Seidenstecher, Gertraud, *Preis-, Kredit- und Finanzpolitische Aspekte der Wirtschaftsreformen in Osteuropa,* Berichte des Bundesinstituts für Ostwissenschaftliche und Internationale Studien, Cologne, 1967 (processed).

145. Spulber, Nicolas, *The Soviet Economy,* rev. ed., Norton, New York, 1969.

146. State Bank of the USSR, *Banking in the USSR.* Lectures delivered at the 15th International Banking Summer School, State Bank of the USSR, Moscow, 1962.

147. Strauss, Erich, *Soviet Agriculture in Perspective,* New York and London, 1969.

148. Studenski, Paul, *The Income of Nations,* New York University Press, New York, 1958.

149. Treml, Vladimir G., and Hardt, John P., eds., *Soviet Economic Statistics,* Duke University Press, 1972.

150. Turgeon, Lynn, *The Contrasting Economies,* New York, 1969.
151. United Nations, *Report of the United Nations Seminar on Planning Techniques,* September 1964, 8–22, Moscow, 1965.
152. U.S. Congress, Joint Economic Committee, *Comparison of the United States and Soviet Economies,* Washington, D.C., 1959.
153. ———. *New Directions in the Soviet Economy,* Washington, D.C., 1966.
154. Hardt, J. P., ed., *Soviet Economic Prospects for the Seventies,* Washington, D.C., 1973.
155. Volin, Lazar, *A Century of Russian Agriculture: From Alexander II to Khrushchev,* Harvard University Press, 1970.
156. Wilczynski, Jozef, *The Economics and Politics of East-West Trade,* Praeger, New York, 1969.
157. Zaleski, Eugene, *Planning Reforms in the Soviet Union, 1962–66,* University of North Carolina Press, 1967.
158. Zotschew, Theodor D., *Die Aussenwirtschaftlichen Verflechtungen der Sowjetunion,* Kieler Studien No. 97, Paul Sieback, Tübingen, 1969.
159. Zwass, Adam, *Monetary Cooperation Between East and West,* International Arts and Science Press, White Plains, 1975.

Articles—Russian

160. Agraponov, B., "Internal Financial Resources of Enterprises," *D.K.,* December 1971.
161. Allachverdyan, D., "Financial Planning and its Perfection in the Current Period," *Finansy,* November 1970.
162. Atlas, Z., "The Socialist Monetary System," *D. K.,* August 1965.
163. ———., "The Role of the Credit and Monetary System in the Socialist Industrialization of the USSR," Paper given at the Vth International Congress of Economic History, and summarized in *D.K.,* April 1971.
164. ———., "V. I. Lenin on Monetary Policy and the Role of Money in the Erection of Socialism," *D.K.,* December 1969.
165. ———., "Regarding the History of the Creation of a Single Monetary and Credit System in the USSR," *D.K.,* May 1972.
166. ———., "The First Bank Note of the New Socialist Type." On the Occasion of the 50th Anniversary of the Chervonets, *D.K.,* November 1972.
167. Barkovskiy, N., "Credit Planning Under the New Conditions," *D.K.,* June 1957.

168. ———., "Credit and the Role of the State Bank Under the New Conditions," *D.K.,* February 1970.
169. Belobzhetskiy, I., "The Use of the Funds for Economic Stimulation and Their Financial Control," *Finansy,* July 1970.
170. Brazovskaya, T., "The Problem of the Charge for Funds," *Finansy,* January 1971.
171. Chebanova, N., "Cashless Settlements in the Light of Lenin's Teachings," *D.K.,* February 1970.
172. Chetverikov, P., "V. I. Lenin on the Socio-Economic Role of Savings and the Practical Aspects of the Work of Savings Banks," *D.K.,* December 1969.
173. Churkina, Z., "An Important Advance in the Work of Savings Banks," *D.K.,* January 1974.
174. ———., "The Pawnshop as a Consumer Service Establishment," *D.K.,* July 1972.
175. Fain, L., "The Nationalization of the Moscow Narodny Bank," *D.K.,* March 1970.
176. Garber, I. I., and Doinikova, I. A., "Credit Agreements," *D.K.,* May 1974.
177. Gerashchenko, V., "V. I. Lenin on Economic Accounting," *D. K.,* February 1970.
178. Gindin, M., "The Structure of Cashless Settlements," *D.K.,* June 1967.
179. Kartasheva, L., "Working Capital of Enterprises and Bank Credit," *Finansy,* January 1971.
180. Khalturina, O., "Economic Education in the Gosbank of the USSR," *D.K.,* January 1973.
181. Khlynov, N., "Development of Bank Accounting," *D.K.,* August 1967.
182. Kochkarev, V., and Glinskiy, V., "Capital Funds of Kolkhozes and State Bank Credit," *D.K.,* January 1970.
183. Komin, A., "Some Questions on Perfecting Planned Price Formation," *D.K.,* January 1970.
184. Kondrashev, D., "The Methodological Basis for the Revision of Wholesale Prices," *D.K.,* May 1966.
185. Konstantinova, Yu., "The Intensification of the National Economy and Finance," *Finansy,* December 1970.
186. Levchuk, I., "Long-term Farm Credit in the USSR," *D.K.,* July 1967.
187. Levchuk, I., and Melkov, A., "Concerning the Propriety of Credit," *D.K.,* April 1970.
188. Lisitsian, N., "Concerning the Importance of Money in Working Capital and Its Rational Use," *D.K.,* November 1970.

189. ———., "Internal Financial Resources of Enterprises and Bank Credit," *Voprosy Ekonomiki,* March 1969.
190. Mamonova, I., "The Interest Rate on Loans and Its Differentiation," *D.K.,* March 1972.
191. Matveev, G., and Khalturina, O., "The Preparation of Bank Specialists," *D.K.,* May 1971.
192. Miloserdova, A., "Concerning the Effectiveness of Short-term Loans," *D.K.,* October 1971.
193. Mitel'man, E. L., "Profit, Rentability and the Interest Cost of Credit," *D.K.,* February 1967.
194. ———., "Payments Offsets and Their Development," *D.K.,* January 1968.
195. ———., "The Development of Direct Crediting by the Bank," *D.K.,* May 1970.
196. Novoselov, P., and Blyukova, N., "Analysis of Credit Sales," *D.K.,* February 1970.
197. Petrakov, N., "The Steering of the Economy and Economic Interest," *Novyi Mir,* August 1970.
198. Petrov, V. D., "Some Questions Concerning the Differentiation of Rates on Loans," *D.K.,* December 1973.
199. Polyakov, M., "International Payments of the USSR Over 50 Years," *D.K.,* May 1970.
200. Seidenvarg, V., "General Principles in Considering the Optimal Relationship Between Own and Borrowed Working Capital of an Enterprise," *Finansy,* December 1970.
201. Shirkevich, N., "The Creation of the Budgetary System of the SSR," *Finansy,* January 1970.
202. Slavnyi, I., "Monetary Circulation and Questions of Economic Planning," *D.K.,* June 1970.
203. Smirnov, N., "Concerning the Information on the Management of Credit and Money," *D.K.,* April 1971.
204. Sotnikov, A., "Trade in the New Five-Year Plan and the State Bank," *D.K.,* February 1972.
205. Sotnikov, A., and Mezhiborskaya, S., "The Development of Credit Relations between the Gosbank and Trade," *D.K.,* January 1973.
206. Stundyuk, A., "Production Associations; Extensions of Credit and Settlement of Payments," *D.K.,* April 1972.
207. Taflya, I. D., "Once Again Concerning Decentralized Clearings," *D.K.,* November 1973.
208. Tarasov, L., and Utkin, V., "The Formation of Funds of Economic Stimulation in Enterprises with Planned Losses," *Finansy,* January 1970.

209. Vinokur, R., "The State Budget of the USSR and Its Role in the Enlarged Socialist Reproduction," *Finansy,* September 1970.
210. Zakharov, V., "Some Questions Concerning the Development of Credit Relations," *D.K.,* May 1971.
211. Zavalishchin, M., and Shor, A., "Concerning the Refinement of Depreciation Rates Now in Force," *Planovoye Khozyaistvo,* February 1970.
212. Zotov, M., "On Increasing the Role of Money and Credit in the Development of Agriculture," *D.K.,* December 1970.
213. ———., "Data on the Development of the State Bank of the USSR," *D.K.,* September 1971.

English and Other Languages

214. Altman, Oscar L., "Russian Gold and the Ruble," *IMF Staff Papers,* April 1960.
215. Ames, Edward, "Soviet Bloc Conversions," *AER,* June 1954.
216. Baran, Paul A., "Currency Reform in the USSR," *Harvard Business Review,* March 1948.
217. Berliner, Joseph S., "Monetary Planning in the USSR," *American Slavic and East European Review,* December 1950.
218. Birman, A., "Reform in a Nutshell," *Soviet Life,* February 1970.
219. Borisov, V., "The Growth of Savings in the USSR," *Problems of Economics,* September 1967.
220. Bornstein, Morris, "The Reform and Revaluation of the Ruble," *AER,* March 1961.
221. ———., "The Soviet Price Reform Discussion," *QJE,* February 1964.
222. Brzeski, Andrzej, "Finance and Inflation under Central Planning," *Osteuropa Wirtschaft,* September and December 1967.
223. Bush, Keith, "Soviet Gold Production and Reserves Reconsidered," *Soviet Studies,* April 1966.
224. Campbell, R. W., "Marx, Kantorovich and Novozhilov: Stoimost' versus Reality," *Slavic Review,* October 1961.
225. ———., "Economic Reform in the USSR," *AER,* May 1968.
226. Clarke, Roger A., "Soviet Agricultural Reforms Since Khrushchev," *Soviet Studies,* October 1968.
227. Decaillot, M., "La Charge sur les Fonds Productifs en URSS," *Revue de l'Est,* Vol. II, No. 4, October 1971.
228. Davis, R. W., "Soviet Planning Process for Rapid Industrializa-

tion," *Economic Planning,* Vol. 6, No. 1, 1966. (Reprinted in Bornstein and Fusfeld.)

229. Familton, R. J., "East-West Trade and Payments Relations," *IMF Staff Papers,* March 1970.

230. Francuz, Henryk, "The International Bank for Economic Cooperation," *IMF Staff Papers,* November 1969.

231. Garvy, George, "Banking and Credit in the Framework of New Economic Policies in∙ Eastern Europe," *Banca Nazionale de Lavoro Quarterly Review,* September 1966.

232. ———., "The Origins of Lenin's Views on the Role of Banks in the Socialist Transformation of Society," *Journal of Political Economy,* Spring 1972.

233. ———., "Banking Under the Tsars and the Soviets," *The Journal of Economic History,* December 1972.

234. ———., "Post-Reform Changes in Banking in Eastern Europe," *Banca Nazionale de Lavoro Quarterly Review,* December 1975.

235. Gekker, Paul, "The Soviet Bank for Foreign Trade and Soviet Banks Abroad: A Note," *Economics of Planning,* Vol. 7, No. 2, 1967.

236. Goldman, Marshall I., "The Reluctant Consumer," *Journal of Political Economy,* August 1965.

237. Grossman, Gregory, "The Reforms and Money," *L'Est* (CESES), Vol. 1, 1972.

238. ———., "Economic Reforms: A Balance Sheet," *Problems of Communism,* November–December 1966.

239. Holzman, Franklyn D., "Soviet Inflationary Pressures, 1928–1957: Causes and Cures," *QJE,* LXXIV, May 1960. (Reprinted in Holzman [132].)

240. Il'in, V., and Koryagin, B., "The Sale of Goods to the Public on Credit," *Problems of Economics,* February 1969.

241. Kaser, Michael, "The Ruble and Soviet Gold," *International Currency Review,* March–April 1971.

242. ———., "The Soviet Balance of Payments," *International Currency Review,* May–June 1974.

243. Leeman, Wayne A., "Bonus Formulae and Soviet Managerial Performance," *Southern Economic Journal,* April 1970.

244. Liberman, I., "Payment for Funds: Their Budgetary and Cost Accounting Functions," *Problems of Economics,* October 1962.

245. Montias, J. M., "Planning with Material Balances," *AER,* December 1959.

246. Prybyla, Jan S., "Soviet Economic Reforms in Industry," *Weltwirtschaftliches Archiv,* Vol. 107 (2), 1971.

247. ———., "Soviet Economic Reforms in Agriculture," *Weltwirtschaftliches Archiv,* Vol. 109 (4), 1973.
248. Roussel, Suzanne, "Les Catégories de la Valeur et la Monnaie dans l'Economie Soviétique," *Revue de l'Est,* Paris, July 1972.
249. Schroeder, Gertrude E., "Soviet Economic Reforms: A Study in Contradictions," *Soviet Studies,* July 1968.
250. ———., "Soviet Economic Reform at an Impasse," *Problems of Communism,* July–August 1971.
251. ———., "The Reform of the Supply System in the Soviet Industry," *Soviet Studies,* July 1972.
252. Varga, Stefan, "Das Geld im Sozialismus," *Weltwirtschaftliches Archiv,* Vol. 89 (2), 1957.
253. Wiles, Peter, "Soviet-Type Inflation," Paper given at the CESES International Seminar on *The Price System in Eastern Europe,* Florence, Italy, September 1966 (processed).
254. ———., "The Political and Social Prerequisites for a Soviet-Type Economy," *Economica,* February 1967.
255. Wyczalkowski, Marcin R., "Communist Economies and Currency Convertibility," *IMF Staff Papers,* July 1966.
256. Zauberman, A., "Gold in Soviet Economic Theory," *AER,* December 1954.
257. *Moscow Narodny Bank Quarterly Review,* "The International Bank for Economic Co-operation," Winter 1964.

Index

Allakhverdian, D.A., 201
All-Union Bank for Financing Capital
  Investment (Stroybank), 69
American Review of Soviet and East-
  ern European Foreign Trade, 141n
Ames, Edward, 161, 199-201
Atlas, Z., 24n

"Balance of Money Income and
  Expenditures of the Population,"
  44
Bank for Foreign Trade, 29, 52, 200n,
  203; and Credit Reform of 1930-
  1931, 31,; and Soviet foreign trade
  and payments, 139, 152-55
Bank for International Settlements
  (BIS), and Soviet Union, 151
Banque Commerciale pour l'Europe du
  Nord (Paris), 154-55
Banque de France, 23
Bolshevik Revolution. See October
  Revolution
Bretton Woods conference (1944),
  151
Bronson, David W., and B. Severin,
  and inflation index, 180
Brzeski, Andrzej, and money in the
  Soviet Union, 42
Bulganin, Marshal, 190n

"Cash Plan," and financial planning,
  44, 194
Central Intelligence Agency (CIA),

and Soviet gold production, 145,
  148
Central Statistical Office (TsSu), 200n
  investigation of enterprise funds,
  102; yearbook of, 194
Chapman, Janet G., on price indexes,
  28n
China: and money supply data, 7n-8n;
  and Soviet foreign trade, 137; and
  Soviet-owned banks, 154; vs. Soviet
  Union, and budget policy, 163n;
  and techniques to deal with excess
  liquidity, 157n
Chlenov, B., 54
COMECON: and Soviet foreign trade
  and payments, 137-41 *passim*, 141-
  43; trade, and IIB, 151
Commissariat, and capital use tax, 94-
  95; *See also* Ministry of Finance
Communist Party: and banking, 60-61,
  190n, 194; and demise of People's
  Bank, 26; membership dues, and
  Savings Banks, 68
Communist Party Congress (1971),
  and Reforms of 1965, 184
"Complex Program,"137
"Construction Bank," 69n
Council of Ministers: and financial
  changes, 82; and money and credit,
  53; and premium schemes, 104
Credit Administration, department of,
  15, 43-44
Credit Plan, and financial planning,

219

/